D0915897

When work has become impossible to bear because you work in a job that has no meaning to you and provides no challenges, or you don't feel valued and are not fulfilled, or when you are bullied or mobbed, with this book you will find the courage to move forward—Barrie Jaeger shows you the way. The author has created an important and practical tool for self-analysis and for helping creative and sensitive people to change their lives: live up to your calling and all else will fall into place.

—Noa Davenport, Ph.D., coauthor of *Mobbing, Emotional Abuse in the American Workplace*

Making Work Work for the Highly Sensitive Person

Making Work Work
for the Highly
Sensitive Person

Barrie Jaeger

McGRAW-HILL

New York Chicago San Francisco Lisbon
London Madrid Mexico City Milan New Delhi
San Juan Seoul Singapore Sydney Toronto

The *McGraw·Hill* Companies

1 2 3 4 5 6 7 8 9 0   AGM/AGM   0 9 8 7 6 5 4 3

ISBN 0-07-140810-X

McGraw-Hill books are available at special discounts to use as premiums and sales promotions, or for use in corporate training programs. For more information, please write to the Director of Special Sales, Professional Publishing, McGraw-Hill, Two Penn Plaza, New York, NY 10121-2298. Or contact your local bookstore.

 This book is printed on recycled, acid-free paper containing a minimum of 50% recycled de-inked paper.

Library of Congress Cataloging-in-Publication Data

Jaeger, Barrie.
  Making work work for the highly sensitive person / Barrie Jaeger.
      p. cm.
Includes bibliographical references and index.
  ISBN 0-07-140810-X (hardcover : alk. paper)
  1. Vocational guidance. 2. Sensitivity (Personality trait) I. Title.

HF5381.J425 2004
158.1—dc22
                                    2003018138

Contents

Acknowledgments

This book would not have made it into your hands without the wonderful contributions of many many HSPs who so willingly shared their stories, their struggles, and their unrelenting desire to find a better way.

Thank you, Catherine Post, for your in-depth understanding of the HSP and keen reading of various versions of this book. Judith Munson for providing excellent feedback. Dr. Stephanie Machell, for your knowledge of psychotherapy and healing modalities and your reading of several chapters. Jacquelyn Strickland, for explaining the MBTI in relationship to the HSP, which unfortunately didn't get into the book. Thomas Eldridge and the readers of your Sensitive Newsletter. Therapist Gary Linker, for your wonderful and compassionate understanding of the HSP temperament. Also the talented medical intuitives, Varena and Martha, for your excellent insights into the HSP from your vantage point.

Thanks to my editor, Nancy Hancock and her associate editor, Margaret Leder, for your encouragement and support. My patient friends, for putting up with me as I did vanishing acts to write and later popped up again. My cats, for their willingness to be second fiddle to a computer. My mother and "aunt" Ruthie, my dear aunt and uncle, Marie and Jim, for your tremendous moral support and encouragement through good and hard times.

And thanks to Elaine Aron, for pointing us all in a new direction.

Foreword

For years those who identify themselves as highly sensitive have been asking for help about their career challenges. Having inherited a trait possessed by only about 20 percent of the population, they are bound to feel different, have different vocational goals, and need different treatment at work. Highly sensitive people (HSPs) are so fortunate that Barrie Jaeger has written this book for them.

Indeed, nonsensitive types will gain a tremendous amount from this book, too, because Dr. Jaeger, in typical HSP fashion, has gone far beyond what would have been more than adequately helpful. Yes, she has creatively discussed how to develop good boundaries, manage stress, ask for what you need, and know when to move on and what to seek in the next job. But she has also penetrated to the heart of the matter of work for all of us, HSPs or not, through her highly original yet simple concepts of Drudgery, Craft, and Calling. As a psychotherapist, I use these terms often to clarify work problems for my patients and what to consider when making career changes. But I was a slow convert.

Barrie and I became colleagues through discussing her work on self-employment. She was studying it, and when she heard of my work, she put the two together, realizing that a high percentage of the self-employed were HSPs. We both instantly saw why, being self-employed ourselves. We could work at our own pace, doing less but actually accomplishing more. We knew that the quality of our ideas increases with more hours away from our desk, not with more hours at it. Our creativity increases with kindness and encouragement from others, not with hassles and criticism. But how many employers would dare to give HSPs "special treatment" and put those truths into practice? No, no matter how quiet the office or how pleasant the lighting, we knew from personal experience that an HSP was not likely to be really happy and productive while working for others.

Still, I knew that self-employment can be stressful and risky. And combining it with finding one's Calling–that seemed awfully romantic and unrealistic. "You have to provide what others will pay for"—that's what my stiff-necked grandfather told me.

However, I knew Barrie's conclusion from her interviews of HSPs was right the moment I heard her say it: We HSPs *must* have meaningful work. Humans are the only species we know of that will commit suicide if they feel that their life has no meaning, and those who feel that desperate about their work are probably mostly HSPs! Urging them to find meaningful work is not unrealistic—it's the purest realism. Being so conscientious, they will keep working where they are needed, long after Craft has become Drudgery. They are so good for their job. But is their job good for them? For that to happen, it must be their Calling. Again, it sounds romantic, but it is simply the truth.

I, however, did not know how to translate that truth into good advice. Barrie Jaeger did. Although I was often asked to write a book on HSPs and work, it was this very issue, of meaningful work, that stopped me. I *love* my work. And I am able to be self-employed—I doubt I could survive six months at a "regular job," even as a professor at a university or a therapist in a clinic. The demands, constrictions, and "office politics" would wear me down. But mainly, I have to be on my own to be able to do the work I feel I *must* do. So I felt I would be a hypocrite providing glib advice about how to get along with a nasty boss or in a noisy office when I myself did not have to deal with any of that. And as for advising them to take off and find their Calling, I feared that too many just would not be able to make a change or would feel they could not. They had to support others, or they had no money to pay for new training, or their past history had damaged their personalities so much that they lacked confidence and hope, which caused them to doubt that any good change could happen to them.

Further, what encouragement could I offer about something better being out there? Most corporate cultures are such that no HSP could ever be happy. It's money first, ethics and quality second. It's getting ahead first, taking care of each other as a team second. And frankly, I even doubt that HSPs can work 40 hours a week without suffering, but look at the hours most of them must work? In short, I felt I had nothing encouraging to say and no right to say it from my safe spot above the fray. No, I was happy to have someone else write a book on HSPs and work.

All I can say is, thank goodness it was Dr. Jaeger who did it. This woman really knows her stuff. And, even knowing all about the workplace, she can give encouragement! Indeed, I would say this book mainly provides reasons for courage and ways to have courage. I am so happy that someone can give that encouragement and that I can pass it on to others.

Courage. As minorities who are often painfully aware of things that others do not notice (including being more sensitive to pain itself), HSPs need and have a lot of courage. Yet they rarely recognize when they are showing it. As one of Dr. Jaeger's interviewers said, "I wish I had more courage. I left my job because I was so desperate, so afraid. I had been getting up and going everyday to a job that I hated, full of people with whom I had so little in common. It sapped all my energy, trying to pretend that I was interested. But I had to get out of there. It would be worse to stay in that situation and wake up one day to find that I had lost my dreams through a need for so-called 'safety' and 'security' through that job."

To me, leaving that job took courage.]There is no courage if we feel no fear. If plunging ahead into the unknown to try to find one's true work is not courage, I do not know what is. And Barrie Jaeger is giving that courage. Reading this book for the first time, I felt real hope for us all in this area and for our world. It is at work that HSPs are able or are forced to interface with the often troubled and troubling non-HSP world. Here is where hope and support are most needed. Financial and social support would be nice, but Barrie provides what counts—emotional support. Soul support.

Yes, some HSPs will have serious emotional issues or obstacles to finding their Calling, but Dr. Jaeger goes ahead and plows into working on what they need to do. By providing through her interviews the experiences of HSPs who have succeeded along with those on the way and those stuck, the HSPs who are ahead are lending a hand. In this book, readers are not just people with problems reading about others who are successful. Everybody's an HSP, everybody's dealing with the same issues. If some can solve them, they can teach others. We're all in it together. That's encouragement.

Readers are going to like Barrie's style, too. She's friendly, funny, and she makes you feel her HSP interviewees are right there with you. She also adds new insights and angles on being an HSP–for example, her thorough discussion of "being intense" and how it affects both us and others, and why HSPs are often the targets of bullies. And she often uses her own dilemmas as an example. She's no superior work guru teaching us lowly folks how to think more like the CEO that she is. She's known Drudgery firsthand.

Ah, that concept of Drudgery. It's so useful. It helps me reassure clients that their bad feelings about "good jobs" are perfectly understandable. It even helps with marital problems—equality is not only about how many hours each works, but how much Drudgery each must endure. If one person works long hours at work he or she loves, and the other "can stay home all day," but the only work there is Drudgery, who works harder? Dr. Jaeger tells us.

Above all, she's firm: If you're an HSP especially, you can't go on in a Drudgery job. Satisfying work is probably life's greatest blessing for anyone. But it is a necessity for HSPs. We *can't* do Drudgery. Not for long. Like a horse that won't leave a burning barn, Barrie Jaeger goes in there and firmly takes you by the halter and gets you moving. "*You can't stay here.*" Horses die in fires and HSPs are equally certain to die emotionally (and probably physically too) in certain jobs. This death just takes a little longer. It takes courage to say that to readers. But it's the truth.

It is a great pleasure to recommend this book to you. I think it will change your life.

—Elaine Aron

Making Work Work for the Highly Sensitive Person

The Journey Begins

It's very hard to be overqualified like this. By nature, I require a lot of independence at work. I can't take it when too many people come through here in a day; much less when they are difficult or rude to me. I feel like I've been on this road a long time. I just want to do something that makes me happy! Satisfaction would be so much more important to me than high pay. Will it ever change?

—ANONYMOUS HSP

A week after getting my Ph.D., I was driving home from northern California, wondering what am I going to do now. I'd given up a successful freelance career to finish the degree program I'd neglected, and so I hadn't worked in a few years.

My doctorate was on the meaning of work and the work ethic. I've never settled comfortably into any traditional job, and why some people love what they do while others hate it has always fascinated me. But now that I'd finished my dissertation and gotten my degree, I was in the midst of problems concerning work that I'd been thinking and writing about. A few blocks from home I saw a huge Help Wanted sign at a Chinese fast-food store, and, curious, I thought, *Why not?* So it was that I found myself delivering food that weekend. After the second weekend, I told my boss that I was quitting. He begged me to stay, and feeling sorry for him, I continued to work there. I was yelled at by customers for being late, got lost, forgot credit card machines, couldn't read the maps in the dark without a magnifying glass and a flashlight, and, being 40-something years old, felt out of place surrounded by 18-year-olds.

When I left for good two weeks later, I was not only back to my original problem of what was I going to do, but now I wondered why I'd even taken the job. And why did I cave in and stay two more weeks at a job I didn't like? Considering my educational background, why hadn't I looked into working for a corporation? Was I afraid? What was an expensive Ph.D. worth to me if I wasn't going to use it?

I felt like a failure then, not just because I wasn't good at what I did—though at times I actually was good at it—but because I wasn't happy. All my life, no matter what intellectual challenge any professional job offered, it was never enough to satisfy me. At most, I lasted two years. And if I took lowly work, I found I couldn't be satisfied just filing, doing data entry, or schlepping food, with only my innate belief in the work ethic to sustain me. I kept dreaming of finding something more attuned to who I was, but I couldn't quite put my finger on what that would be. In fact, the closer I'd get to sorting it out, the more frightened I became. My dreams just didn't seem possible. Maybe I was a wimp and not cut out to work in the "real world"?

Yet all along, I can see now, my confidence in myself had been improving, sometimes gradually and sometimes very fast. Though I resisted my intuition, it was nudging me in the right direction. My Calling, whatever it was, seemed to tease me. At times it lured me one way, and once there, it changed direction entirely. Looking back, every step taken out of an intuitive sense of rightness turned out to be a natural evolution in personal growth and a necessary step toward where I am today.

We work so hard at finding just the right job. The real job is finding ourselves, and letting our Calling do the work of finding us. I believe that even if all you do in life is grow as a human being, you can't help but find your Calling. I always thought the *job* was the Calling—but it's not. As long as I was focused on the job, I got nowhere fast. But when I focused on my own personal growth, my real work seemed to smile and wiggle closer to me. It was as if the work was drawn to me, not the other way around.

Why Work Doesn't Work

This book is *not* about how to interview and land a job. There are no lists of the best 100 companies for the sensitive person. This book is a detector. It teaches us how to detect jobs that are not right for us and tells us why the needle goes haywire for us in some jobs. The detector is inside of us and has been sending us signals for years. But if we're in too many jobs that don't work, then our detector hasn't been working. We'll spend some time learning what it is we're detecting and how to translate its signals.

Being Sensitive Can Affect Your Career

How well prepared you are for your job, how much you know, or your preference for the job are not the heart of what will make work *work* for you.

Consider the example of two highly sensitive men, both leaders, who were inexperienced when they began their jobs. Neither had a similar position before, and both faced tremendous problems, including wars, people working against them even within their own governments, and tragedies in their personal lives. Both men became more religious as they aged. Both could be warm and interactive with people, but also melancholy, stubborn, even enigmatic. Both were fatalists who believed their destinies were controlled by a divine power.

The two men were Abraham Lincoln, the U.S. president, and Nicholas II, the last czar of Russia. The difference between them was the way they grew as sensitive human beings.

While Abe Lincoln initially had no experience in government, he had a keen political instinct and a willingness to learn and grow. Instinctively, he knew how to use his sensitivity to improve his relationship with life and with people. For example, he used his intuitive abilities to look at the long-term consequences of the Civil War on a future generation of Americans, and he thought about plans for national healing.

Czar Nicholas, on the other hand, did not want to lead, and did not use his intuition wisely when he confronted difficulties. Instead, he shut down emotionally, becoming insular as the intense stress and problems of World War I and his collapsing government overwhelmed him.

This comparison between the two men is not meant to sum up the good and bad when it comes to being sensitive. Rather, I'm pointing out certain ways in which they used their sensitivity—for one, it brought out strengths; for the other, weaknesses. And my point is that our sensitivities can make work worse or better for us, depending on how we use them.

I've talked to sensitive people who were in senior management, entrepreneurs who built million-dollar companies, maids, lawyers, artists, the self-employed, and the unemployed—you name it. While our temperament does not make or break our chances at whatever success we wish to have in life, it can be a boost or a drag. One of my own challenges was to ascertain what that boost and drag amounted to, and having put it down on paper, you can decide if my discoveries help you improve your edge.

But the true key is in your own self. Grow as a person, and your Calling will grow toward you.

How This Book Began

Making Work Work for the Highly Sensitive Person is the product of over four years of conversations, surveys, and interviews with nearly 200 highly sensitive people—often referred to throughout this book as "HSPs."

Elaine Aron supported my dream of writing this book almost five years ago. She gave me suggestions and encouragement, and now she graces *Making Work Work for the Highly Sensitive Person* with her foreword. Her own book, *The Highly Sensitive Person,* is a must read. It's our "owner's manual," as one interviewee said to me.

In this book, I will discuss the nature of the HSP sensitivity, but my focus will be on workplace conditions. A large portion of the interviewees have read *The Highly Sensitive Person*[1] and have spent several years integrating the information and adapting their perceptions, behaviors, and attitudes about themselves as HSPs in the world. It takes time to integrate what it is to be an HSP into one's life. In terms of workplace issues, however, there were no differences in the hopes and dreams or the issues faced between those who knew they were highly sensitive people and those who didn't realize it. Men tended to be more comfortable with confrontation, and women frequently mentioned that emotions brought on tears.

Many individuals, in all walks of life and from around the world, were interviewed. Everyone took the HSP self-test—the seven-point scale used in clinical research by Dr. Elaine Aron and Dr. Arthur Aron—and a Keirsey Temperament Sorter. The majority scored very high on the HSP self-test. Many people mentioned here are under a pseudonym.

Frequently, the HSPs I interviewed were gifted, multitalented, with strong imaginations, intense emotional awareness and range of emotional expression, and restless minds eager to learn and consume knowledge in huge gulps. Emotionally, they were frequently indignant with and frustrated by the roughness of the business world, and with the frenetic pace or with the verbal or social behavior that resulted in hurts to others or to themselves. Some felt helpless and/or lacked the confidence to complain or make changes; others fought the system or quit in protest.

Their wide-ranging interests and active imaginations indicated the depth and richness of their potential, abilities they usually couldn't channel into the workplace. They often expressed the feeling of not belonging, of being out of step with their office or not fitting in. Even those whose careers were rising and were promising stars in senior management positions felt out of place in the modern world of work. Often, the stresses and demands of the workplace took a considerable toll on their physical and emotional health.

It seems that HSPs do gravitate to the big picture and are deeply concerned about the larger issue of work and the attitudes, values, and behaviors in the workplace. They are frequently concerned about the lack of appreciation an employee is shown, as well as corporate greed, with its focus on the quantitative rather than qualitative aspects of work. About half the people I interviewed were self-employed and typically happier than their employed counterparts.

In a survey given to 150 highly sensitive people, the general consensus was that work is unsatisfying. Corporate America was seen as cold and unresponsive to, or unfeeling of, the needs of its employees. Asked to give a grade to their workplace conditions, HSP employees typically gave lower grades (B to F) to working conditions, people at work, and the actual work they did than were given by other employees. HSPs who were self-employed gave more As across the board, even though their income was less satisfying. But work/life balance was a challenge for both employed and self-employed HSPs.

While it's fruitful for HSPs to look at what they can contribute to the big picture, it's even more important to stay focused on personal goals. Every time you clearly define your boundaries, every time you take care of yourself when under stress, you're doing as much to advance the global needs of HSPs, and of all workers, as you would if you were involved in large-scale corporate transformations.

There is a glimmer of hope in all of them, a desire to find work that will inspire them. As the self-confidence and self-acceptance of interviewees strengthened, I could see more Craft work happening, with inklings of Calling whispering in the wind. While we all love being in a Calling, it takes work to sustain ourselves there. We must never stop growing, because personal growth is what attracts our Calling to us.

Three Working States

Long before I began this book, I'd been exploring work in terms of three states: Drudgery, Craft, and Calling. Over the years, I've likened them to three "faces," drawing upon body language, which conveys so much about whether you love your work, hate it, or merely consider it "just a job." When creating the material for the chapters describing each of these states, I developed a composite picture, as a forensic scientist would put together a face based on snippets of information from this person and that. As I listened to the stories people told me, I asked myself lots of questions, like what they all had in common when they experienced the conditions they described. The result is the material you'll find in each chapter.

The problem with writing about Calling is that once you step into the topic, it's hard not to get pulled up into its vastness; the visionary qualities are powerful, like strong winds that take you soaring into the sky. While Drudgery implodes you, Calling expands you. Both, when cultivated, start to grow like tiny seedlings and become either a dark shadow or warm sunshine that envelops you and permeates your world. Within these worlds, changes can happen suddenly or slowly.

The core of this book revolves around examining the three states of work: Drudgery, Craft, and Calling. These words evoke feelings, thoughts, and images, and are accurate barometers of what work is for each of us. The chapters follow a natural progression of what we experience and need as we struggle in Drudgery, emerge from this existence into the light, and move toward work that satisfies us emotionally and mentally. When you're through with this book, you'll be able to review your own history, know which jobs were Drudgery, and better understand some of the reasons why. You'll know what Craft work is and recognize the signals of your Calling and the hazards of this wonderful energy.

Drudgery is very old. It goes back thousands of years, to the beginning of human existence. For a long time work was hard and painful. You can see this even in the origins of the word "work" in the Romance languages.

Craft began to appear with civilization and the development of fine skills. But a Calling is very new and has many qualities that can only be found when one is self-actualized. This doesn't mean that everyone who loves their job is always happy or in a Calling, but the energy of a Calling speaks of the heart and joy of an individual. And since happiness itself is a relatively new experience for human nature, finding a Calling is elusive until happiness becomes a more pronounced part of life. But it's a place where someone has the ideal environment to hold his passion. Sometimes that will require you to be original, and HSPs have a hard time sustaining originality, because it means being truly self-aware, having clear and steady boundaries, and being willing to be seen.

In many ways, this book is like cultivating a garden, and you are both the garden and the gardener. As such, you must know the importance of boundaries or limits. That's one of the numerous definitions of the word *limit*: a boundary. In your "garden," there are *limits* to what you can do; there are *limits* that need to be established with others; there are *limits* you didn't realize you need; and there are other self-imposed *limits* you can release. We will explore all kinds of limits and ways to cultivate your sensitivities so that they're nurtured in the workplace.

My Personal Wish

So many times, as I've talked with HSPs, I can see exactly where they came from and where they're going. Especially to those in Drudgery, I have something to say.

So often, HSPs stay in Drudgery far too long. When they leave, they're exhausted, emotionally and perhaps financially. The pain lingers a long time. Some suffer burnout and chronic fatigue syndrome and need years to regain their full strength. And in that interim, they must still earn a living. So I urge you to listen to the stories about Drudgery, in the hope that you'll realize that no matter how convinced you are that it's impossible to get out, it's not impossible. It just seems that way.

Drudgery will deceive you; it will slowly boil you to death, just as the frog in the pan is slowly killed by the water's slowly rising temperature. This sounds gruesome, but it is indeed what happens to HSPs who stay in Drudgery too long. How long is too long? Don't wait until you feel emotional pain, major stress, and depression. I would dearly love to see the time spent in Drudgery cut in half or more, and I hope, if you realize that you're in this working state, the information in this book will help you know what's happening to you and what you can do about it. The practical speaks with such a loud voice in Drudgery. And the practical paints a very high wall, almost impossible to scale. But it's not. It's the fear and worry in you that is speaking. It's what's called "learned helplessness."

How to Use this Book

Making Work Work for the Highly Sensitive Person has several tasks. First, to give a comprehensive profile of the HSP in the workplace and the types of challenges and successes we can have. And second, to show how HSPs have resolved various problems. Much of this information will come from those who know about their HSP temperament and have used that information to develop a creative work style.

The chapters follow a natural progression for getting yourself from Drudgery to Calling. Every chapter is carefully designed to walk you through all the steps necessary to improving the way you think and live as an HSP. The next several chapters, for instance, explore self-confidence, the importance of good boundaries, accepting yourself and trusting your feelings, new skills for stress management, and letting your HSP nature be more visible. These skills are necessary if one is to advance to Craft or Self-employment. Finally, difficult people, and finding a Calling, round out the book.

Of course, since the book is designed to be read from beginning to end, the chapters should be read consecutively. You may want to take breaks, to digest the information, but keep in mind that each chapter builds on the previous one, and provides essential information necessary to take forward into the subsequent chapters. As we progress, each chapter will give you another piece of the puzzle you need to gain greater control of your work, and greater self-awareness of your sensitive traits and how they impact your sense of vocation and career direction.

When you are in Drudgery or are overstimulated, work doesn't work under any circumstances. Chapter 3, "Time Out for Healing," helps the HSP discover ways to relax, recharge, and take control of one's life.

As we noted above, we'll go into Drudgery, the lowest level we can reach in jobs that are "just a job," as well as examining Calling, the highest and most desired state of bliss in work. In fact, the two states, different as they are, complement each other in many ways. Both generate intense feelings in HSPs, of loathing in one and joy in the other. They mirror each other: What's missing in one is found in the other. Find what's missing, and you'll have the other. I'll show you how to find the missing pieces, so you can stay out of Drudgery and spend most of your time in Calling or Craft.

To stay out of Drudgery, the reader will learn that one needs good stress management, a willingness to let others know what you need, and good personal boundaries. Many end up in Drudgery because they failed to take care of these issues. Chapters on stress management, Craft, being visible, and dealing with difficult people follow.

We will of course discuss self-employment, because it's part of the evolution of work, and it's a route that for some HSPs provides a natural and comfortable place. HSPs have many attributes that would make them good candidates for self-employment, but they fear this route. I'll try to make it less frightening and more meaningful, should you wish to explore this option.

1

What Is a Highly Sensitive Person?

I wish I had more courage. I left my job because I was so desperate, so afraid. I had been getting up and going everyday to a job that I hated, full of people with whom I had so little in common. It sapped all of my energy, trying to pretend that I was interested. But I had to get out of there. It would be worse to stay in that situation, and wake up one day to find that I had lost my dreams, through a need for so-called 'safety' and 'security' through that job.

—ANONYMOUS HSP

When Work Doesn't Work

How many people feel trapped in a job they don't love and without a clue as to how to unravel the mystery of getting where they wanted to go? Certainly I have been in this predicament. Many of us stayed too long in these depressing jobs and left drained and in need of healing. Some continued to cycle back into other equally depressing situations, and others eventually found their way to work that was rewarding and that "worked" for them.

Highly sensitive people have a hard time with work because they're exquisitely sensitive in a variety of different ways. This can be intense emotions, acute sensory awareness—the subtle feel of fabrics, the faintest odors easily detected, sounds heard that are barely perceptible to others—restless minds eager for new information, vivid imaginations. Our sensitivity to our environment can well result in overstimulation, leaving us without any residual energy to carry us over into the evening or the next day. The stress of being mismatched with a job can take more out of us than just the chores of the day. It can reach a point that our lives diminish and grow dim, depression can set in, and health problems can arise.

And yet, many HSPs—people like us—do get out, do find their way to work that they love. It happens all the time. You'll meet them in this book. Some are young, some middle age; men and women, educated and not. But we all have in common the reality that we're highly sensitive people.

Dr. Elaine Aron, author of *The Highly Sensitive Person*,[1] says our sensitivity is hardwired into our nervous system and is probably inherited. It's found in 20 percent of the population.

While this greater level of sensitivity or intensity can vary from person to person, the heightened awareness implicit in HSPs means that more information is coming to them than is coming to the other 80 percent of the population. The HSP is like a gallon bucket holding two gallons of water. Sometimes we can feel overwhelmed, as if we're drowning while others around us are calmly swimming to shore. Conversations and events, for example, don't "roll off" our backs as easily as they do for others.

I've spent several years talking with HSPs all over the country, hearing their stories, their successes and failures, in order to understand them and seeking to know why some have made it and some haven't—at least not yet. In fact, this book is not about finding the right job, or how to job-hunt or interview. Society focuses on the job, and says, "Define the job, look at what you'd like to do, and then do it." But I don't believe this is the right approach for highly sensitive people who have a problem at work or with certain kinds of work. I said it in the introduction, and you'll read it in this book again, often:

> **Grow yourself, and your real work will grow toward you. This is what the sensitive person needs to do.**

Workplace Sensitivity Test

This test covers many areas where we are most likely to be highly sensitive at work. As you look at the items, work experiences may come to mind, or not. The scoring is visual, so you do not have to give yourself an absolute number. Try to take it at a time when you can have some quiet and reflection. You may wish to use this to compare your own changes over time at different jobs. There is no perfect answer. This is an opportunity to get to know yourself and look at the bigger picture of how you experience work as a Sensitive Person, the amount of overstimulation or rest experienced at any one time.

LOW	MEDIUM	HIGH
0	5	10

_____ I often accommodate the needs of others at the expense of my own.

_____ I am often tempted to withdraw, or actually do withdraw, rather than deal with conflict.

_____ I have been told that I can be overwhelming to others.

_____ I feel out-of-synch with the prevailing cultural norms.

_____ I have been made uncomfortable or even unwell by environmental conditions that don't seem to affect others.

_____ I have been told I'm too intense.

_____ I have been told I'm too serious.

_____ I continue to process experiences long after they're over.

_____ At times I take on more than I can realistically do because everything sounds so interesting.

_____ I need more sleep than most people.

_____ Having a busy schedule for too many days overwhelms me, even if I enjoy all that I am doing and want to do it.

_____ I can see all sides of an issue, not just the one I prefer/agree with.

_____ I notice small changes in others and my environment.

_____ I become readily absorbed in what I am doing.

_____ If you asked me for 50 different uses for a brick, I could give 75.

_____ I find it hard to walk away from things.

_____ I have strong attachments to people, places, things.

_____ My mind goes blank when I'm put on the spot.

_____ I am deeply disturbed by others' insensitivities.

_____ I find it hard to do things that don't interest me.

_____ I cry when I'm angry/overwhelmed/more easily than others.

_____ I need time alone.

_____ Sometimes I feel like a raw exposed nerve.

_____ I'm afraid of infringing on others' rights if I ask for mine.

_____ I am excessively aware of others' feelings.

_____ I need work congruent with my values.

_____ I have a bizarre sense of humor.

_____ I am good at calming and reassuring others.

_____ I pick up the feelings others don't acknowledge having.

_____ Others' moods—and even their presence—affects me.

_____ I sometimes feel irritable/overwhelmed around others without knowing why.

*Developed by Stephanie T. Machell, Psy. D., Barrie Jaeger, Ph.D., Catherine Post, MSW

Intensity and the Highly Sensitive

The concept of the highly sensitive person is relatively new, at least in its current format. That is, although it overlaps with the categories of giftedness, shyness, introversion, and possibly the Myers-Briggs type indicator, certain aspects of HSP temperament have not been well understood, and so the more we can know of ourselves, the more power we have to grow from that knowing.

It does take time to understand what it is to be an HSP, and I'd like to shorten your learning curve. To start, "sensitivity" means not only the tendency or ability to pick up more subtle details, information, and stimulation than other people, but that the HSP experiences greater *intensity*. I liken this intensity to that of a stress machine and will merely note for now that internal states—our thoughts and feelings—can cause stress.

The Bucket and the Thimble: The Paradoxical Nature of HSP Intensity

An HSP once said to me: "I feel like I'm the one with a bucket, and everyone else has a thimble; I'm always overwhelming others."

Indeed, this intensity we bring to everything can be a problem for us and for others. There is a difference between being aware of where we are (and being centered and calm in that awareness), and the perceptions of others (and our being centered and calm, listening to their perceptions). And we bring our intensity to both situations.

While we can get used to this level of intensity, we're often unaware not only of how much it can take out of us, but how powerfully it can affect our perceptions of what we're capable of doing. And this translates into a belief in our ability to succeed. So it's important to examine what this intensity is like, how we use it, and how it impacts our perceptions of ourselves.

Like you, I would guess, at times I've been told that I take things too personally, that I worry too much or give importance to the slightest change in language or gesture. For example, when I'm getting into one of my more creative spaces, I begin to imagine all sorts of projects, and then I take on a lot more than I can handle. Emotionally, I want to do it all, even if the reality is that I can't, given my lifestyle and the current projects on my plate. So my perception of myself, slightly altered by my enthusiasm, gives me the momentary feeling that I can do a lot more and that I can be "out" more than I can handle. And if I'm not careful, I'll berate myself for overdoing and taking on too much.

The same thing can happen with pulling back and hiding out when the world overwhelms us. Only in that case, I find I'm retreating a long way from where I was a moment ago, to a point where I'm now nearly invisible. HSPs are aware of being invisible, or seeming to be, and others have commented on this too. Thus it is that our intensity can take us farther out (on a metaphorical limb) or deeper in, than may be truly necessary for the occasion.

It's possible that intensity can alter our perceptions enough that the HSP takes five steps further one way than necessary, and has to retrace his or her steps (which adds to stress) to return to where they were before. It follows that the more we understand our intensity, the better we can compensate for this tendency. Remember to give yourself credit for being aware of this intensity and realizing that, "Wait a minute, I don't have to let it take me extra paces than I need to go." In contrast, the non-HSP, who has less intensity and thus less skewed perceptions, will not have the same degree of difficulty. Nor will non-HSPs then berate themselves as much.

Not that intensity is wrong, or that where intensity takes us is wrong. "Majority rules" applies to voting, not to personal development. You may be perfectly satisfied to be five steps away from where you were before. But now you know *how* you got there; and it wasn't by magic. You got there because the intensity got you processing, thinking, perhaps worrying, and as a result, you followed your thoughts and feelings into new directions. If you're happy with where it takes you, fine. But again, when it comes to self-realization, the point is that you know *how* you got there.

Also, it's important to know that intensity itself is *stress*. We live in a fast-paced business world, and that pace probably accelerates our processes so that without realizing it, we're stressing ourselves more than we need to. Just by the process of our own intensity picking up speed and moving us out into the world or deep within, farther than we need to be, we intensify stress. So we should observe our intensity so that we can at least take baby steps toward stress management. Observing how intensity carries you forward, it might be an interesting experiment to go only two steps, stop, and see what happens from that vantage point. The terrain might just be different enough to provide a rewarding discovery.

Observing Ourselves

We do need to find a happy medium between our perceptions of ourselves and the perceptions others have of themselves and us. Ideally, of course, it would help if we could remain centered and balanced as we and others express our perceptions. No doubt you've noticed that the perceptions of others can be stressful for us. Again, not because there's anything wrong with HSPs' perceptions, but because of our intensity, we're "covering more ground." If non-HSPs could do this too, they also would find themselves moving five steps away from where they were before, when they only meant to go two steps.

If you answered many of the above Sensitivity Test questions with "High" you can consider yourself intensely sensitive. But a lot of the same issues I'll discuss will also apply to those who score moderately, though not to the same acute degree. And furthermore, as I said earlier, you might be intense about some things and not about others. One can be intense mentally, but not emotionally or in the realm of the senses. Some HSPs say that they don't take things personally, yet they are acutely sensitive in other ways. Or they mention being acutely sensitive emotionally and mentally, but not physically. Experiences will vary, so pick and choose what makes the most sense to you.

In my research with HSPs, and especially with those interviewed for this book, I have found that highly sensitive people frequently have a higher level of intensity across the board in the area of emotions and imagination; that they have eager, restless minds in addition to an ability to acutely feel the sensory aspects of their world. And because we feel deeply, our responses will reflect our intensity.

The intense side of ourselves is the substance we take with us to work every day and drag home, limp and exhausted when we overdo, though nurturing and cherishing it so we can give even more. HSPs can sustain higher peaks of emotions longer, like joy, anger, or depression. Think of intensity as the far end of a range, with the other end being a very light, casual attention to something. For example, two people walking see some flowers. Person A pauses and says, "Oh, a flower," but quickly moves on. Person B stops and stares, fascinated, and says, "Oh, a flower!" and then slowly moves away, pausing to look back.

We compare ourselves to others and expect ourselves to be able to keep the pace and stimulation level that those around us can do. So we often don't pay close attention to the signals that all but overwhelm us. Comparing stories, understanding what overwhelming intensity and sensitivity is like for ourselves and others, refines our ability to assess the depth and breadth of this intensity.

What does this intensity look like in our lives? Here are some examples of how it is manifested in a variety of human conditions:

> Being able to retain a passionate interest, lasting months to years, in one subject.

> Connecting previously unconnected "dots" and to develop an in-depth picture of the long-term implications.

> Becoming a professional athlete.

> Sitting in front of a painting for hours, absorbed and entranced with it.

> Prone to being imprinted by a traumatic experience that remains for a long time.

> Being a master worrier, fixing upon worst-case scenarios.

> Having an incredible ability to ruminate.

> Having the ability to tap into one's value system and explore numerous deeply held values very early in life and retaining this ability throughout life.

We don't have to be intense 24 hours of every day. We can control our intensity level with rest, meditation, physical exercise, spontaneous play, and other relaxation techniques, which we'll go into in the chapters on healing and stress management.

More on Intensity and Stress

As we said above, intensity is a form of stress, and it also leads to stress. Jon Kabat-Zinn, in his wonderful book *Full Catastrophe Living,* says stress is everywhere. Some of it we can't control (like gravity), but we can do something to minimize the impact of most stress to ourselves. He says that "a stressor can be an internal as well as an external occurrence or event. For instance, a thought or a feeling can cause stress and therefore can be a stressor."[2]

You have the power to affect the balance point between your internal resources for coping with stress and the stressors that are an unavoidable part of living. By exercising this capacity consciously and intelligently, you can control the degree of stress you experience ... you can develop a way of dealing with change in general, with problems in general, with pressures in general. The first step, of course, is recognizing that you are under stress.[3]

Indeed, understanding our HSP nature and improving our chances for greater happiness and well-being in our work—*without succumbing* to the high stress and feelings of being overwhelmed we have often felt in our work—is what this book is about. We'll go into stress in great detail in Chapter 4, "Stress Management the HSP Way," but it's important to touch on it here.

There are four kinds of generally recognized stress. Each of them is increasingly more disruptive to a person:[4]

➤ Acute stress (short term)

➤ Episodic acute stress

➤ Chronic stress

➤ Traumatic stress and post-traumatic stress disorder (PSTD)

Everyone has frequent experiences that fall into the category of acute stress. Remember, stress doesn't always feel bad. *Acute stress* is associated with wide-ranging positive and negative events like sports, an argument, or a disappointment when discovering that your favorite restaurant is being torn down for a shopping mall. Stress every day, in a perfect world, would surface and fade, and our system would return to an unstressed state. HSPs, however, because of our acute sensitivity to subtle details, are more likely to be distressed by experiences that do not normally affect the rest of the population. So there are greater opportunities for acute stress.

If our intensity rises high enough, it creates anxiety—whether we're conscious of it or not—and takes us to the next level of *episodic acute stress*. HSPs can get into episodic acute stress rapidly, and the resulting overstimulation and anxiety.

> "One day, as the boss was talking to me ... I started to cry. I could not stop. Damn it, I thought. I tried to stop. Damn it, I thought, and still I couldn't stop."—Claire

Once we get anxious, our intensity often takes us to a more out-of-control place, and we may start ruminating: Why is this happening? What am I going to do? What are my options? Which option will work under rainy or snowy conditions? And so on. Or we may exhibit excessive worrying behavior: The boss hasn't smiled at me in two days, maybe he's mad at me about something. I must have goofed somehow, but I don't know what went wrong. I feel awful. I'm afraid I won't get that promotion. And this is when we become "famous" for our sensitivity and elicit comments about our being "too sensitive" or that we "take things too personally."

Later in this chapter, I'll discuss a technique for catching yourself just before you get into the ruminating or excessive worrying phase. It will take practice, but becoming aware that you are doing this is a very important step toward greater personal empowerment.

Like long-term financial problems, being a single parent, encountering a new boss who has an entirely different, and unpleasant, management style than your previous boss, with whom you got along, the depth and breath of *chronic stress* is longer lasting and more distressing than episodic acute stress. And it will happen a lot in the work situation I call Drudgery. Episodic *acute stress* can also occur here too, but chronic stress will certainly befall you if you stay in Drudgery too long. Events that get HSPs into these more intense moments can cause us more emotional and mental distress; worry, anxiety, fear, and the rest.

Traumatic stress, the most severe type of stress, can be brought about by any kind of major trauma, such as being in an auto accident and confronting surgery—possibly accompanied by fear as to the outcome. Or it can come about by being accosted by a stranger in sudden or unexpected circumstances. And trauma—as well as its offspring, post-traumatic stress disorder—has long-term repercussions on us and our work.

HSPs who've had traumatic experiences in their childhood are more likely to have longer spells in Drudgery because the emotional issues they experience are packaged with their earlier traumas. Those issues include shame, fear, serious self-doubts about one's abilities, and learned helplessness, and these could very likely impede career development. Previous experience with traumatic stress may act as a "ghost" out of your past, triggered by workplace events. For example, HSPs who report having a parent who screamed a lot when they were children have problems with screamers at work and find such behavior extremely stressful.

When it concerns the HSP, intensity ups the ante when it comes to stress. An HSP is more likely to experience a variety of mild to severe forms of stress, including everyday acute stress, which the other 80 percent of the population may not experience so intensely. It also increases the odds that problems at work will cause more serious forms of episodic or even chronic stress. When you stay in a job that is extremely painful for you (Drudgery), you could very well be giving yourself a "gift" of post-traumatic stress disorder when you leave.

> I get really stressed out, and I find ways to hide and protect myself. Either I space out at my desk or I take a break hiding in the restroom or my car—Anonymous HSP

What this means is that we HSPs have to work to be mindful and diligent about taking care of ourselves and developing strong personal and interpersonal boundaries, well-deserved self-esteem, and good stress management.

How Our Intensity Affects Others

As the bucket-holding HSP said, she's always overwhelming others. Our intensity can do this. We are the type who will ruminate and worry about something for a *long* time, but not everyone wants to hear about it. We're so used to being intense that we may forget when we're in the midst of this intensity and may be unaware of how it affects others. As one HSP said, it's like a superglue that gets poured into our brains, and we get stuck in a rut.

Work is one of those places where it doesn't pay to get stuck. Our intensity may be a bit much to others, or it may even be frightening. This imposes a responsibility on HSPs. At work, there isn't always the time to appreciate intensity. Work is a give and take, after all. Our intensity is not something everyone experiences, and it isn't reasonable or fair to expect others to understand this.

There will be times when our intensity will drive others away. Have you ever known someone who complained about the same problem over and over, at every break time, for days on end? They don't realize that they're alienating others around them. Nor is it to be expected that even an HSP's friends will always be willing to listen and experience the intensity either. Sometimes, being alone is the only thing we can do when we're in that intense place. And again, we need to be sensitive to others too.

Some people may be telling us to lighten up for loving reasons, and some not. Regardless, the admonition to lighten up is not a bad idea. True, it probably drives most HSPs nuts when others seemingly brush off their problems with the remark, "Don't take it so personally," or, "Let it roll off your back," or even, "Get out of the house." But there's a grain of truth in these and other statements. People are trying to tell us something.

Watch yourself as you get absorbed, and understand the courage it takes for others to tell you that you're intense or that you should take a break or lighten up. At work, people aren't going to tell you more than one or two times. Remember: The non-HSPs aren't our guardians, after all, or our keepers. Nor are they necessarily saying what they do because they're insensitive or unfeeling.

Managing Intensity

All this intensity can take its toll on us, physically, emotionally, and/or mentally. And while we may rail at how much we can do in comparison to others and thus may be compelled to limit ourselves, it's important to realize that, qualitatively, we're doing more than we think we are.

Our intensity gives us an edge. How to manage it, how to take care of ourselves so we don't overdo it, and crafting manageable ways of expressing this intensity without overwhelming ourselves or others—that's the challenge. (We'll explore this in detail in Chapter 4, "Stress Management the HSP Way.")

When I get involved with something, my breathing becomes shallow, my eyes are fixed in a stare, and I can feel my muscles tightening. I feel wrung out. This makes it impossible for me to get enough sleep, and I wind up adding more stress. It's really hard on me.—Anonymous HSP

Sensation Seeking

Sensation seeking, as Dr. Aron describes it,[5] has to do with the part of our brain that is drawn to new things. To survive, we need to simultaneously be ready to avoid or embrace change. Knowing whether a new thing is good or bad for us is part of the intelligent creature's learning curve. Some people are drawn to new things (high sensation seekers), while others are slower to be enticed (low sensation seekers).

HSPs can be sensation seekers in a variety of different ways, and learning how to manage them is their challenge. Some are high sensation seekers (HSSs) when it comes to adventures out into the world of sports or other physical activities. But it's not just about bungee jumping. Sensation seeking can be intellectual or emotional too. Some HSPs need lots of stimuli, lots of variety and new things to do, see, think about, or imagine. Some of us need to be involved in many things at once—from taking continuing education courses to constantly tweaking our filing system. One HSP I spoke to, for example, had been at the same job for over 20 years, yet had a wide variety of general interests he's maintained for years. But when our intellectual and creative needs must come from our work, then we have another set of challenges. We can often spot high sensation seekers who have an acute excitement or surge of enthusiasm for some newly discovered idea, thing, or event. I remember when I got my first computer. I became a sponge and didn't try to just soak up everything about it gradually, over time; no, it had to be done *right now.*

Many HSPs who are HSSs can easily overstress themselves. Therefore, moderating one's enthusiasm is important, so we don't overload ourselves and become overly stressed and exhausted. *Recognizing the difference between our intensity and our need for variety,* and the way we up the ante when things get too quiet for us, takes time and reflection.

I go from being all jazzed about something, and getting into it, and then adding more and more cool stuff, until I feel overwhelmed, helpless over my own schedule, choices, decisions. When that happens, I feel "squeezed," just by life. And I tend not to enjoy anything and lose my sense of humor. So I slow down, and I get all relaxed and peaceful. I have a nice doable schedule. And then what happens? I miss the excitement. So what do I do? I pack in the schedule, do all sorts of things that are a bit of an extreme *reach* for me … and before you know it, I'm back again into the land of acute overwhelm.—Juliana, Web illustrator

---

Our very enthusiasm for different things, it should be noted, can put us at risk of not carrying through on any one thing, or what can be characterized as a fear of success. So often, as one HSP told me, she will start down a path with an interest in learning something exciting, thinking, "This is it, my ticket to a satisfying and rewarding job," only to find herself off in another direction. What happened? Each idea was great, a natural for her. But her therapist said she had a fear of success. Was it that, or was she reinventing for herself, over and over, the thrill of the initial discovery? What do you think?

As Elaine Aron pointed out, we love learning new things but don't always want to do what we learn, which requires a different set of skills and putting ourselves in situations that we can't control as well as we can a learning environment. Sensation seeking can become a habit. And that suggests a way out, since habits can be modified in order to moderate our enthusiasm, so we don't become overloaded and exhausted.

I didn't get the hang of it [an HSP trait] right away. Most of the time went into understanding what it meant to be an HSP …and how it impacted my interpersonal relationship… what it meant to function in the world or to maximize comfort in the world, I guess I would have to say. Because I'm not only an HSP, I'm a high sensation seeker. —Sharon, medical lab technologist

Learned Optimism and Helplessness

To succeed in life, to achieve our dream of making work *work*, creating work we love, means we need optimism. Every leader, every successful person, everyone who has followed and found their dream says the same thing: You have to believe in yourself, and you have to believe you can do it. Optimism is learned.

My basic bottom-line premise is that finding your true work is not about finding the right job, it's about finding yourself, growing as a human being, and being happy with who you are.

So, what does this mean for you?

Because our level of sensitivity is found in only 20 percent of the population, most of the world doesn't see things through our eyes, and we're often labeled as different or wrong. Some HSPs are fortunate to grow up in loving homes where their sensitivity is not seen as a problem to be berated. Yet the imprint of rebuke on tender feelings can stay with the sensitive child well into adulthood, a cause of shame when we can't seem to do things just like everyone else. HSPs may grow up feeling different, out of sync, perhaps feeling that something was "wrong" with them. In fact, many of us learned to see ourselves as not fitting in and came to believe that we couldn't cut it in the world like everyone else.

Overcoming that initial shame—the negative belief that we're different—is important. As long as the feeling of shame is there, HSPs have a tendency toward "learned helplessness." This is why we may sometimes behave in a way that is not truly part of who we are.

There's no reason anymore to try to be "good enough" or prove my worth to everyone else like most people do, because, frankly, the normal, mediocre, mainstream way of doing things isn't good enough for me.... I think this is why my life up until now has been such a struggle—I've been trying to fit into the same peg as everyone else, and it doesn't work because I'm a different peg with different strengths, needs, and things to offer, which can only be accessed by following my inner guidance and spiritual guidance that inspires me.—Catherine, in career transition

---

Work is an environment where certain behaviors, emotions, and thoughts are expected, sometimes even required. And one of those emotional thoughts is "optimism." Businesses like to be upbeat, positive, with a "can do" attitude. Optimism is attractive. It makes us feel that the gas station will be filled with gas tomorrow, the bank will keep our money safe, and the office will pay our salary.

Rumination and Negative Cycles

As I mentioned earlier, HSPs are prone to applying their intensity to worrying or ruminating, when they're distressed. This is something we learn to do. This is the dark side of our lives, as opposed to the light, joyous side of life, where our enthusiasm to learn and explore gives us such delight. Both sides can be drawn out, sustained, and contained within us for long periods of time. And since our intensity creates stress, when the darker side of our nature predominates, we fall into the habit of learned helplessness, with its worry and anxiety.

> I know I should stop being so intense, but it's those times when I know I need to disconnect and walk away that I'm simply unable to do so.—Anonymous HSP

There's an old wives' tale which says that breaking the cycle of negative emotions and thoughts, even for a little while, is healthy. It's true. Modern psychology now backs it up. Rest for the body and spirit and renewed creativity happen when we break the prolonged spells of intensity. Fresh new endorphs can bubble up, and the cortisol that gets generated when we're stressed slows down.

To break the cycle of habit, to develop learned optimism over learned helplessness, you need to recognize your patterns. The expectation of helplessness, for instance, may arise only rarely or may arise all the time. The more you're inclined to ruminate, the more it arises. The more it arises, the more depressed you'll be. Martin Seligman, the father of the new positive psychology, points out in *Learned Optimism* that ruminating on a problem can exacerbate it.

Brooding, thinking about how bad things are, starts the sequence and begins the pattern. Ruminators get this chain going all the time. Any reminder of the original threat causes them to run off the whole pessimistic-rumination chain, right through the expectation of failure and on into depression.[6]

Does this sound familiar? It could easily describe an HSP running at full gallop into an intense emotional experience. Imagine you're out in the country, watching a rabbit in a field, grazing, enjoying the nice day. Suddenly the rabbit takes off and begins to race, upset at something that startled it. If you could go back in time a few minutes and *slow down this scene* and see what startled the rabbit, see the rabbit pick up on the thing that scared it, that caused it to leap into action, you'd be recognizing the beginning of the pattern.

In that rumination or worry, in that black hole we go into, our entire system consumes the energy of our body, emotions, mind, imagination, and spirit, just like when we're so jazzed on a new passion. This masterful phantasmagoria of our thoughts and emotions is whirling around us, and we get lost in our creations. It's like the rabbit that dashes off when something startles it. It's likely, in our version of a full gallop of emotions or thoughts, that we don't even notice what startled us.

It takes work to break the pattern, but if we can "capture the cycle" by recognizing when we begin the transition into this intense phase, we can consciously shift the pattern. This will help us control our stress and also give us better awareness of what triggers our reactions.

There are other advantages as well. Prolonged intensity is stressful on the poor body we've got, and we do ourselves a favor if we can shorten this cycle, break it so we can have some rest and let the unconscious mind work on the problem awhile. You could say that we HSPs are "control freaks" who are reluctant to allow our unconscious mind some "quality time" to deal with our problems. We give all the work to our conscious mind. To that I'd say: Just because you can't see or know what your unconscious mind is doing with a problem doesn't mean it's going to make a mess of it! In fact, the unconscious does a fabulous job of helping us—when we give it the opportunity.

Catching Yourself

To help us capture the initial point when we go into rumination, I'd like you to do an experiment with me. Capturing that crucial moment, before rumination and learned helplessness take over, is very valuable. The goal is to practice controlling our intensity and our ability to ruminate, so we can have more control over our experiences.

Be patient with yourself as you do this. Give yourself permission to experiment, to try tackling various experiences and seeing what you learn. The more you attempt this, the better you'll get at soothing yourself into a less intense phase. I find that I may not always get all the words or emotions at exactly the initial point, but that by going through this process, over time, I intuit more regularly what's happening, and that as a result, the intense phases seem to shorten just by consciously telling myself that I'm taking a break.

Have you ever had a terrific project you loved doing? You were jazzed; mentally, emotionally, and physically energized. All sorts of ideas were flowing; the creative juices were cooking. You were revved up and ready to blast off. You'll recognize, I trust, that there's a groove, like on a record, that your system develops when you encounter this experience over time. As you take this journey, you find yourself at a wonderful place where light, sound, and action all happen. The best in you is working. Positive thoughts flow, ideas percolate. It's an intense, neat place to be, because it feels enriching and satisfying. Can you recall such a moment? Stay with the memory, if you will. Cultivate it for a moment....

Do you recall what it felt like just before you transitioned into this groove and became immersed in the thrilling adventure? Noticing this transition point is very important. It might help if you would jot down a few thoughts or feelings.

Now let's try this on a worn pathway that some HSPs have as a result of painful experiences: our own personal Calcutta, where all the negative self-images are pinned on the walls; old fears, sharp words from the past that you're no good, etc. If you are too close to such an experience right now, you may be struggling even as you read this, but you're not there just yet. Just as we did before with a positive experience, can you see yourself starting down this path? *Can you feel your mind, still detached and observing, while your feelings begin to get in touch with fears?* Stay with this as you read. Sit with this memory for just a moment.

Noticing these transitional points is witnessing ourselves, being aware of our own process, which is being charged with energy and readying us to dive deeply into the experience. In psychology, being able to see ourselves at the point of taking this path is called "observing ego"—the ability of the self to step out of its patterns and stand as a separate being. It's easy for us to get so immersed in our thinking or emotional processes that we forget to be aware of the moment when our thoughts and emotions made this turn. And with so much stimuli coming at us all the time, retaining our sense of self, our boundaries, is very important.

Let's go back to the rabbit in the field and the idea of slowing down or playing back the scene to see what bothered it. Consider the rabbit as our emotions, which we just walked through an exercise to slow things down. As you visualize the rabbit now, imagine you and it are connected, that it knows what you think and feel. As it starts to get upset about something it picked up, you, as the human, can reassure the rabbit—the emotional part of you—that everything is calm and all is well. So your "rabbit" becomes calmer too.

Highly sensitive people are good at processing, thinking, ruminating, and being overly hard on themselves, due to their perfectionist and conscientious tendencies. And if there are body chemistries, or lifelong tendencies, to move them into depression it can create an additional difficulty.

All of this can work against us when we're under stress from severe problems. Because we're intense and can sustain deep thinking or emotional moods for long periods of time, we can do this when we're both in a good or bad place. The introverted HSP will want to hole up and be left alone, because he or she gets the best healing energy from solitude. But whether you're introverted or extroverted, if not caught quickly, all of these factors can result in long, intense spells of ruminating. The trick is to realize the value of short-circuiting any tendency you have that will lead you to dive into your usual style of self-analysis when you're dealing with a distressing and stressful condition.

Boundaries and Self-Awareness

The exercise I gave you earlier could be called a "boundary," since it sets limits around the intensity. Being unaware of the risks of too much stimulation, creating a "crash and burn" experience, with its attendant exhaustion and frustration, is not good. We need better self-awareness.

Every HSP I've talked to says they keep striving for better boundaries. This will be a lifelong challenge, but not an impossible one. Understand that because we are so sensitive, so aware at so many levels, we'll need to continually refortify our boundaries as waves of stimuli and information come into our bodies, emotions, and mind. All that information is pouring into our world regularly, and we're processing at several levels simultaneously.

Naturally, it's hard to know where our boundaries are, since it seems that stimulation is always shifting the space around us, depending on our existing level of rest or activity. So we're always going to be challenged at a basic, sometimes visceral level to maintain a thoughtful awareness of ourselves as separate, distinct individuals with our own ideas, feelings, and needs. Our boundaries are meant to keep sacrosanct the integrity and honesty of who we are. We have to know when to give in to the wishes of others, when to ask for what we need, and when to moderate our behavior so we can regroup and do self-care.

The HSP at Work

Imagine a sensitive person like yourself, at work in a modern, streamlined workplace where there are slots and niches to be filled. In such a place, creativity, while nice, is not often accepted or appreciated.

Some HSPs go through lots of jobs. Our curiosity and quick mastery of a job, our need for challenges that capture our imagination and passions, and/or the discomfort of depressing and boring jobs, make turnover among us high. For some, this feels like a failure, not only the inability to stay steadfast for a long period of time (long enough to get promoted to some cushy spot, with all those inner talents we've got), but in being unable to handle the job. "It's just a job, why can't you stick it out?" Does that sound familiar?

HSPs have a tremendous need to do meaningful work, the sort of work that will generate what I call "psychic income." This can consist of appreciation, or doing something with a direct cause and effect benefit to someone or some thing. Without this psychic income, the job is an albatross, tying us to a prison. We think we can do "just a job," and will try, over and over again, hoping the next one will last a little longer, be a little better than the one before. But let's face it, folks, doing "just a job" is a killer.

I do see a lot of HSPs not knowing what their work is. And I know one of the things I feel very much is going on is they're not being original enough. They are probably being too hemmed in by conventional jobs. They need a more original path, something that fits who they are, rather than trying to pour themselves into a conventional type of job. They provide more thoughtfulness. I think that's a very valuable role to have in the work-place.—Patty, Administrator for Senate Committee

---

I'll never forget temping as a typist in an insurance company when I was an undergraduate. I heard a fellow typist say she'd been at this same job for over 20 years, typing names and addresses on insurance forms. But it got more interesting, she said, when she worked on another form, where the information was *reversed.* You can imagine what I thought and felt at that moment. It doesn't matter what jazzes other people about their jobs, it's what jazzes you. Trust me, you can't tolerate "just a job," even if you pigeonholed it into a neat tidy corner in your life. Of course, there are some HSPs who must do this, because of family or other intense responsibilities. But our souls will suffer a loss of some kind.

So it's not unusual that HSPs grow out of jobs like a young child grows out of clothes—and many times feel badly about it, believing they have somehow failed because they can't find a job worth doing for 20 years. In contrast, other family members and friends have long-term established careers with socially acceptable status and other perks. This sense of failure bothers us, and we feel as if we're getting further and further behind. Middle-age HSPs say we're the proverbial late bloomers.

By the time I find something that works for me, I'm afraid I'll be too old to do it or to enjoy it.—Anonymous HSP

We're just as eager, just as competitive, as the next person. We want to do our best, and we enjoy the challenge. And we can compete, but we need to plan carefully when and how we orchestrate events in our lives. There are two parts to being overwhelmed: knowing what and how much something overwhelms us, and how much rest time we need to refresh ourselves. Hands down, people problems are rated the highest stressors by HSPs, well over things like the commute, the cold office, or the fluorescent lights. It's people problems that most affect our nervous system and our emotional well-being, and that necessitates additional rest and care for ourselves.

Consider a sine wave, an undulating curve. Rising stimulation would be depicted by the rising part of the curve, and the down part of the curve would be the fatigue and need for rest from the overstimulation, before the curve can rise again. Knowing our tolerance level, we can manage numerous little waves of stimulation from a variety of daily activities. Increased self-care comes when bigger stressors, people, come into the picture.

Values vs. Bottom-Line

"The biz world really knows how to extract its "pound of flesh"—and it usually *is* from the general vicinity of the heart!"

"Corporate America has forgotten the true value of life."

"It's a necessary evil. For me, I don't want any part of the greed, power, or head games."

These opinions express a view I find common among HSPs. Generally, HSPs are value oriented; we crave and seek meaning for everything in life. And the absence of meaning that connects at the heart—in a way that is "life affirming," as Tom, an economics professor, calls it—is extremely distressing.

There are two basic views of business, value and bottom-line, or economics. The last decades of the twentieth century saw a rise in bottom-line philosophy, including a growing perception of employees as inventory, to be shuffled about and disposed of in order to keep the profit-and-loss statements pleasing to those above them. Of course, corporations aren't always that black and white about people, but the pressures on many industries to keep up with bottom-line changes certainly added fuel to these attitudes.

Because HSPs by temperament are value based, we will consistently have an aversion to any philosophy that is not like our own. Certainly, the highly sensitive person will have an aversion to being considered a pawn.

And we're not alone, for many businesses do have value-based operations. I've talked with HSPs who eventually found employment in places where others were as sensitive and respectful as they themselves were.

Being in the right job is a combination of several things for the HSP, including knowing more about your own temperament and how it affects your work and choices, and managing your own overstimulation. You may be in a job that you believe is right for you, but if you're so overstimulated that you can't function in the right manner, then it's not the right job—until you can manage your own overstimulation. There are interesting tendencies in HSPs that affect how we experience work, which we'll go into later.

Roy, whom you'll meet again later, describes the HSP's role in a work situation where he or she can make a contribution and be recognized for it:

It becomes a balancing act because you have to be true to yourself, you've got to be able to protect yourself, and you've got to try to prevent [yourself from] falling into those situations that become overwhelming and either drive you over the edge, or drive you out, or simply make you sick.... The one word that sums up what most HSPs seem to be or could be ... is "facilitator." That word does more to describe what I do on a day-to-day basis.

... In some of the conversations I've had with people, even though they don't understand an HSP, in most cases they do recognize that we do make a difference, we make a contribution, and if we were not there, situations, events, would not go off nearly as well as they might have otherwise.

Growing Yourself and Your Career

Early in the chapter I said that to find work you loved, you have to grow. Before we go further, I encourage you to look at yourself in this light. Can you see your intensity? Do you have a glimmer of how it impacts on your relationship to life?

The following factors, which we have discussed in this chapter, apply to highly sensitive people:

➤ The need to protect ourselves from the overstimulation caused by the intense inner work we do (emotional, mental, imagination)

➤ The need to keep back the flood of feelings we pick up for or from others; regularly maintain our boundaries

➤ The need to recognize any high sensation seeking habits and how they flavor our daily life and challenge us with additional overstimulation that we don't need it

➤ The need to appreciate that we process deeply the work we do, at our own pace

STEP ONE: *Accept Your Sensitivity*

You have to trust your nature. Your talents that may not always earn you big bucks in our society, but they are part of who you are and how you do things. They're also part of your boundaries. If you're in Drudgery work, and in many cases even in Craft work, there may be aspects of yourself that you don't like. If you're in Craft work, within a few years the job may move into Drudgery. This pattern, repeated again and again, might leave you feeling like a failure. Everyone else around you seems to be in a long-term steady job, after all. And you keep changing jobs, changing careers, again and again. "When will I find my niche?" you ask yourself and start berating yourself—sometimes with a little help from others.

The creative, eager mind and imagination needs to be replenished every few years with new challenges. It's possible that you need something entirely new, in an extremely opposite end of the spectrum than the previous few jobs. There's nothing wrong with this pattern, it just means you have to think and plan your career differently. Accepting this part of yourself—the sensitive part—or better, liking it, is an important aspect of your healing and being able to set boundaries with yourself and others.

Many times we think that a low-level "no brainer" job will be a piece of cake and we can come home from it, with brain power and energy to spare on our creative self, our real job hunt, whatever. Yet we still bring all our intensity with us into this job, as we would to any other. The Drudgery culture of these low-level jobs are emotionally taxing on HSPs. Don't stay in them very long. Better yet, don't even go near them. They should be off limits.

STEP TWO: *Appreciate Your Milestones*

We have a tendency to play down our accomplishments. Of course, we have an image in our minds of what we should accomplish, and often we're somewhere between the beginning and the final result of what we picture.

You need to cheer yourself for each minor or moderate achievement you make. These are well-done deeds, and if you continue to beat yourself up for not being at the finish line, you don't like the person you are right now. You want to be the you of tomorrow, but the you of today has taken an important step that will be seen as essential tomorrow. We often like to consider ourselves process oriented. It's important, even while in the process, to appreciate our accomplishments.

STEP THREE: *Knowing and Abiding by Your Limits*

Getting to know and learning to modify one's HSP traits can take time. Often, HSPs tell me that they think they are becoming more sensitive. Or, they just might be becoming more aware of what they once ignored about themselves. These discoveries are wonderful milestones to be appreciated and integrated into our awareness. This can be challenging. Each of us must find our own tolerance level for activity and be selfish about our limits. The better we get at recognizing the signs of being overwhelmed, the closer we come to having effective HSP time management, which keeps us at an even keel while still being productive.

STEP FOUR: *Communicating Your Boundaries to Others*

No matter where we are on the food chain, we need to let others know what our boundary lines are. Some HSPs are better at this than others, and you'll hear their stories of how they held their boundaries.

If it's any comfort, every HSP I've talked to has said that he or she had to work hard at the boundary issue. This includes HSPs from senior management down to file clerks. It takes time, patience, a good sense of humor, and a willingness to be firm when the forces facing you seem pretty darned determined. When we get to the chapters on stress management, being visible and dealing with difficult people, we'll examine several strategies you might find useful.

2

The Worst Kind of Work: Drudgery

I plodded along from day to day, feeling miserable, a failure, that I wasn't trusted, getting paranoid (an innocent remark would set me thinking that maybe the word has gotten around about how useless I am, etc.). In retrospect, I think I might have been sliding into depression; that whole year was colored gray. I think I was fortunate that I got out when I did.

—JANE, SENIOR RESEARCH SCIENTIST

In this chapter we'll examine what Drudgery is all about. I draw from my own and others' experiences, having been in Drudgery and despair, afraid I would never get out, and wondering what would happen to me. When we are afraid, just like children, everything that scares us is frightening and we don't want to go anywhere near it. Understanding what Drudgery is and being able to spot it will lessen the fear. You'll also learn here that it's easier to get out than you think.

There are reasons why HSPs end up in Drudgery jobs. Being "just a job" is not the same thing for you as it is for your non-HSP coworkers. We'll discuss why HSPs experience Drudgery, why it's absolutely crucial that we stay out of these jobs, how to spot this type of job at a company, what to do if we're chronically getting these types of jobs, and what to expect afterward. If you get this much right, you'll save yourself a lot of grief and anguish.

The following checklist gives many of the characteristics of Drudgery. The longer you experience Drudgery, the more extensive the symptoms and the longer the recovery time. If you find that most of the characteristics apply to you, your job is probably Drudgery.

Checklist for Drudgery

If half or a third of the following items are frequent in your work, then you're approaching a danger zone, where Drudgery is not too far away from impacting on your life in a major way.

_____ Do you find yourself fantasizing about all the cool things you'll do when you're not working, but can't get motivated to do them when you have that time?

_____ Has your income been poor for so long that it's beyond being able to support you?

_____ Do you fear that this job will last forever, that you're trapped, stuck, that it's impossible to get out, and that this is the way work will always be?

_____ Do you find yourself agreeing with the comic strip character Dilbert's attitude toward the workplace?

_____ Do you fear that practical considerations are keeping you from achieving your dreams?

_____ Are you overeating or having diet changes?

_____ Do you have repeated colds, flu, body aches and pains?

_____ Do you feel a heaviness, like carrying a burden or being stabbed in the heart?

_____ Do you dread going to work (Monday blues)?

_____ Do you find yourself clock watching—or feel antsy to escape the office well before quitting time?

_____ Do you feel there is frequently no sense of progress, accomplishment, or closure with your tasks?

_____ Is your morale or self-confidence low, or are you doubting your abilities?

_____ Do you find yourself being deferential or fearful toward authority?

_____ Are you finding yourself with very little creativity compared to your normal desire?

_____ Do you find yourself easily getting angry, crying, feeling frustrated?

_____ Do you have post-traumatic stress disorder (past traumas continue to stress you) or burnout?

_____ Are you experiencing depression, or being treated for depression?

_____ Do you have insomnia or a need for lots of sleep?

_____ Are you doing any substance abuse?

Conditions That Contribute to Drudgery

Typically, several factors together are involved in creating Drudgery. It's rare to find one operating alone. Here are some factors:

➤ Continuously long working hours

➤ Ongoing insufficient recognition or lack of meaningful appreciation for your efforts

➤ Long debilitating commutes

➤ Prolonged emotionally negative attitudes or behaviors toward you from boss or coworkers, including bullying

➤ Unpleasant physical setting: fluorescent lights, uncomfortable temperatures, constant lack of privacy

➤ Many restrictions on how and when to do the work

➤ No intrinsic benefits in the work

➤ Boring, unchallenging work

➤ Past traumas that continue to bother you

➤ Feeling patronized, or treated as if you were in a subservient role

➤ Staying at a job out of loyalty, when it is no longer satisfying or enjoyable

➤ No sense of accomplishment or closure to your work

Drudgery Island

On Drudgery Island, home of the desolate, the discouraged, and the depressed, the sun beats down hard on your body and water is scarce. You have to watch out for scorpions, snakes, and sudden rock falls from the cliffs. The water is bitter—what little there is of it—so you never get a cool sweet drink to quench your thirst. And there's little shade. The nearby city is dreary and devoid of healthy vegetation, color, or any aesthetic beauty.

Everyone walks around with balls and chains attached to their legs, like prisoners or slaves. Their cheerfulness seems forced. Housing is of poor quality, and there are no social activities or leisure time to bring people relief. It's just work, work, work, and no one feels as if he gets any benefit out of his efforts.

The workers here often feel at the mercy of another's whims, or worse, under siege. It's as if all they do just gets sucked into the powerful forces of the owner, management, boss, or some office prima donna. The people here are often depressed, exhausted, and some are physically sick as well.

Rescue planes fly overhead, but no one seems able to shout loud enough to be heard. Wherever you go, high walls keep the island enclosed, and to the inhabitants, escape seems impossible. Every now and then someone disappears, and rumor has it there was an escape. But beyond the high walls it is empty space, vast sky and clouds, with no sign of where you'll land. Many want to escape but are too scared to jump, and so they end up making this place their home.

Why Drudgery Is Not "Just a Job"

The above imagery from Drudgery Island graphically describes what many people actually *feel* their work is like, both emotionally and physically. "I feel trapped" and "I can't take it anymore" are common refrains among sensitive people. And you do feel trapped, constricted, afflicted, and caught in a cage from which it seems you can't get out. You can even hear it in the sigh of someone who groans, "Back to the grind." So, if you feel drained, demoralized, or bored, or perhaps excessively challenged, with increasing stress and health problems, you are in a Drudgery job.

Drudgery is often why work doesn't work for the HSP, and probably many of you now reading this book picked it up because your work is Drudgery. Often, people talk about doing work that is "just a job," and they seem to do this "just a job" for a long time. In fact, any job, regardless of income, status, or duration, can be "just a job." Even if someone changes jobs, like changing clothes, it could still be "just a job." And many people do "just a job" because they have to.

You may think you ought to be able to do this kind of work too—but you can't, no matter how hard you try. *For the HSP, Drudgery is traumatizing, often physically and emotionally, and far worse than "just a job."* Just because others in the office can last at this miserable job for a decade doesn't mean you can.

How often have you been in a situation that started out great, and you were hopeful that this would be your Calling, only to have it turn into Drudgery? The forces that make work "work" for us are not for everyone. It has nothing to do with our conscientiousness, our loyalty, our work ethic. It has everything to do with being a sensitive person.

One of the big mistakes that frequently lands us in Drudgery is to take on a job because of a sensitivity need. Here are three examples:

➤ Taking on a part-time, low-level job because we think it won't be very demanding, so we can put the bulk of our energy into something else, like serious job hunting or recuperating from a previous high-stress job, or attending to our creative needs on the side.

➤ Taking on a job out of a need for meaning and our own idealism. These are powerful incentives that can sugarcoat a bitter circumstance enough for us to endure it well past the point where we have begun to pay a price. One friendly person in an otherwise awful workplace can make the days a little more bearable, but won't solve the problem.

➤ We take on a job because of its flexibility, a highly desirable commodity to HSPs. A job with a flexible schedule is another sugarcoating that transforms boring and unchallenging work into a "manageable" burden.

So if a job has even one point in its favor that feeds your particular sensitive needs, and that point means something to you, you're hooked, until the pill has worn off and you start to feel that hook, which by then has wormed its way deep inside you.

Drudgery is traumatic because HSPs stay with it too long. Drudgery can surface for a few hours, or it can last years. Sometimes you can start in a new job feeling great, and end up in a nightmare. While any job can have it's moments of drudgery, true Drudgery will settle deep into the bones of your work and remain there for years, sucking the life out of you. Unfortunately, HSPs stay in Drudgery jobs too long, so the traumatic effect ends up ruining health and self-confidence. It frequently brings on one or more of the following: post-traumatic stress disorder, insomnia, headaches, depression, illness, and burnout. Drudgery is not a place to linger in very long.

Knowledge is power, and the more you understand about Drudgery, the less threatening it will be to you. You can get out.

Recognizing the Drudgery Job

While Drudgery Island is imaginary, it was created out of the words and emotions of many HSPs as they described Drudgery situations. There are two types of Drudgery jobs. Some working conditions are inherently unhealthy; these I call "Drudgery Institutions." And there are personal, psychological conditions within us that guarantee Drudgery. When our sensitivities become the driving force for choosing a job, there's the risk that the institutional and the personal could come together in a way that is virtually codependent.

If we place Drudgery within the framework of Abraham Maslow's hierarchy of needs, which he describes in his seminal work, *Toward a Psychology of Being*,[1] the D level has to do with deficiency. When people are on this level, they're in a survival mode, more dependent on others, less able or willing to think for themselves. They have more fears and insecurities, more self-doubts, are unwilling to take risks, and don't like change. Drudgery is very much a D-level world. In contrast, a more self-actualized person is in Maslow's B (or Being) realm, where people are happier and more relaxed with change and ambiguity. They're more inclined to be open, both to initiate change and to accept changes that just happen. Their creativity is higher, and they have increased acceptance of themselves and others. They're also more autonomous and don't feel dependent on others for their sense of self or survival.

Using Maslow's hierarchy of needs as a model, psychologist Joel Aronoff did extensive anthropological research to examine the two major occupations of Dieppe Bay—cane cutting and fishing—on the Caribbean island of St. Kitts.[2] Dieppe Bay in the 1950s and 1960s had large sugarcane estates, and the majority of the population was involved working in the cane-cutting business. A smaller group of men were fishermen and generally not involved in cane cutting except when the fishing season was slow. Both occupations were seasonal and followed the rhythms of the village and harvest.

Aronoff noted that the cane cutters had many traits of those in Maslow's D level. They were more deferential toward authority figures, more fearful, more depressed, and complained frequently about their problems. Their work gave them little opportunity for personal accomplishment or recognition for the efforts they made. The cutters worked in teams, and it was the team's efforts, not the individual's, that determined the pay received. They knew that every cane cut meant a specific income. Even the manner in which they worked the fields, keeping precise distance from one another—without opportunity to forge ahead and carve their own path—was controlled. The head cutter was responsible for keeping the group moving, so the individuals had no personal responsibility or reward for their efforts. However, they did have the group's companionship and could tell stories and joke while they worked in the heat.

> The difference between the groups appears in the fact that fishermen enjoyed, and seemed to demand, a variety of activities, with no supervision and control, and cutters accepted the unpleasantness of tedious unchanging work under strict supervision for the guarantee of a wage.[3]

The cane cutters were on their personal Drudgery Island. When asked about fishing, they were not interested in doing that work. They expressed their dislike of its unpredictability, the need to save, and the dangers involved in the job. Their reactions characterize the survival mode of Drudgery. The cane cutters were unable to enjoy life the way a more self-actualized person can.

The fishermen, in contrast, were in Maslow's B level. They were more self-confident and saw others as their equals. They were willing to plan and save money to buy equipment and endure the risks of fishing. Their work encompassed a wider variety of tasks, and they seemed to enjoy both the capriciousness and self-reliance of their work. They spent most of their time repairing equipment, playing bingo, or fishing.

The fishermen expressed more self-esteem, an ability to cope with ambiguity, and they were self-motivated, creative, and spontaneous. Their work meant something to them beyond an income, and they enjoyed being self-reliant. These are the qualities that Maslow and others identify with self-actualization.

Institutional Drudgery

Drudgery comes with a certain mind-set, a certain way of looking at work and life that's degrading to the human spirit. This state of mind is common to a wide variety of institutional Drudgery jobs. As you seek to identify unhealthy places with dysfunctional attitudes toward its workers, keep in mind that the mental and emotional conditions within these workplaces is crucial to you.

The cartoon characters in Dilbert have a Drudgery mind-set. They work in a Drudgery world where unhappy people manipulate one another and fight for crumbs.[4] Like real Drudgery jobs, their world includes power plays, victim mentality, ulterior motives (including upstaging and backstabbing), control, patronizing, and manipulation. There is considerable stress and pressure to perform and produce. Not everyone in such an environment is in Drudgery, but there may be enough of these elements to present the HSP with greater chances of falling into Drudgery. Have you ever left a job where the politics or attitudes of others was so upsetting that you felt physically sick? Historically, slavery, prostitution, prisons, mines, and factories qualify as Drudgery institutions. Today we have sweatshops and entry-level jobs, and less noticeable but equally insidious, seemingly ordinary companies with systemic problems caused by unhealthy and addictive cultures. As Joanne Ciulla notes in her book, *The Working Life: The Promise and Betrayal of Modern Work:*

Slavery is a pejorative for work—it signifies human degradation, work at its worst. Even today workers often say, "He treats me like a slave," or "I'm not her slave," or "He's a real slave driver." Slavery represents a repulsive but seductive managerial ideal: total ownership and control of the worker. We associate work with necessity. Slavery represents the most extreme form of necessity. Most people work "for a living," the slave works to stay alive.[5]

These modern jobs might be less physically brutal than institutions of the past, but the same archaic mentality runs these organizations.[6] Generally, the management ideal of progress is to eliminate Drudgery by having everyone doing what they love, with automation and computerization to take care of the monotonous tasks. Yet computerization can itself be very Drudgery producing.

One kind of institutional Drudgery can be seen in low wage and entry level jobs, which I call "simple" jobs—in comparison to professional jobs. The reason they are "simple" is because of what they offer the HSP. With a professional position come more responsibility and demands, longer hours, and more duties, along with increased status. Entry level, menial, or low wage jobs are not as easily subject to increased hours, responsibilities, or tasks. Hourly people can leave at 5:00 p.m. each day, and they don't have to take their work home with them. For the HSP, it means a controlled number of hours, less responsibility, tasks that are often familiar or (seemingly) easy to learn. Many HSPs gravitate to these jobs. You'd be surprised how often I found overqualified people telling me they had jobs as a cook, file clerk, maid, orderly, or stock boy. You'll find out why shortly.

Barbara Ehrenreich, a successful journalist and author of the nationally acclaimed best-seller, *Nickel and Dimed,* decided to live the life of a minimum wage earner. As she explained in her book, she thought she could handle these "simple" jobs, but quickly found them to be physically exhausting and emotionally demoralizing. She discovered that these were jobs where an individual isn't treated well, or allowed to grow professionally, or have any life outside of work.

In a Drudgery job, there are no rewards for "heroic performance"—something HSPs are prone to give. Of course, for those who grew up in a culture where work is something you had to do to survive, the idea of heroic performance is unheard of. In such circumstances, the workplace is an emotional battleground, where the worker resists and the employer inveigles in order to get the tasks done.

Of course, intuitively, everyone knows that Drudgery is not something they would like to do. So all sorts of rules, controls, and psychological balls and chains are created to keep you at this job, because it's a job that has to be done. Kevin Bales calls this psychology "modern slavery." It requires a person willing to see their condition as "part of a normal, if regrettable, scheme of things." Either convinced by others or emotionally fearful enough to believe themselves unable to be self-reliant in the cold cruel world, these people accept bondage, even in situations where they could easily walk away and be free. The other ingredient in such work is a boss or "owner" who sees himself or herself as a parental figure fostering insecurity and dependence.[7]

The key here is the relationship between leader and follower and the attitudes they have about their relationship that binds them together in a healthy or unhealthy manner. In the case of the low level entry jobs, HSPs can gravitate toward menial work because they do not understand how unsimple these jobs truly are; that is, the price such work will exact, and that the psychological environment is emotionally disastrous.

If you're choosing a job because you think it will be less demanding, you run the risk of being bored and eventually depressed. But the values by which these minimum wage jobs are run are also damaging to the sensitive nature. As Ehrenreich discovered:

What surprised and offended me the most about the low-wage workplace ... was the extent to which one is required to surrender one's basic civil rights—and what boils down to the same thing—self-respect.[8]

This Drudgery mind-set is not always easy to spot, but there are some definite red flags that can provide clues, even when a company seems healthy. For example, the standard consensus among workplace psychologists is that stress, and its sinister sibling burnout, are caused by major mismatches between the person and the job. Burnout, as Christina Maslach and Michael P. Leiter write in *The Truth About Burnout*, "represents an erosion in values, dignity, spirit and will—an erosion of the human soul. It is a malady that spreads gradually and continuously over time, putting people into a downward spiral from which it is hard to recover."⁹

The authors believe that when stress and burnout begin to erode company income, the company is also playing a part. They go on to list the conditions that cause stress and lead to Drudgery: overload, lack of control, lack of rewards, lack of community, lack of fairness, and strong value conflicts. While individuals experience burnout, organizations are equally responsible, if not more so, for its cause:

We believe that is not a problem of the people themselves but of the *social environment* in which people work. The structure and functioning of the workplace shape how people interact with one another and how they carry out their jobs. When the workplace does not recognize the human side of work, then the risk of burnout grows, carrying a high price with it.[10]

Personal Drudgery

There are ways in which we as individuals put ourselves into Drudgery without realizing it. We will address three common examples that apply to HSPs.

INFLUENCES FROM THE PAST. As alluded to earlier, Drudgery is not limited to work. Any trauma is by definition Drudgery. Therefore, early childhood traumas, life-threatening illnesses, along with workplace problems, can be Drudgery. For HSPs who had traumas in childhood, those experiences can create post-traumatic stress disorder (PSTD), which occurs when a previous trauma continues to cause you stress for years afterward. Because success in the workplace really requires us to be empowered and congruent, PSTD can interfere with our progress, which means that we can create Drudgery situations.

SENSATION SEEKING. Another type of personal Drudgery occurs with HSPs who are also high sensation seekers (HSSs, discussed in Chapter 1). Once such a person masters a task, it loses its luster and becomes boring—and down into Drudgery we go. HSSs are often on a roller coaster, with steep learning curves and then plunges down into Drudgery.

IDEALISM. This is another attribute of the HSP. There's a bit of Don Quixote in all of us. HSPs often have a farsighted ability to see the big picture and possible long-term consequences. Combine that with compassion and a need to be of service, and idealism can be a powerful influence in our lives. How many times have you wished you had the power to solve the world's problems, or felt an urge to help during a disaster? Unfortunately, idealism is a major cause of burnout and stress. There are several reasons for this. One is that idealism is an emotion, and until recently emotions were not given much acknowledgment in the workplace, though emotions of all kinds play a powerful role in work.

Take nursing, for example, a profession that certainly includes idealistic HSPs. Ayala Pines and Elliot Aronson write in *Career Burnout*:

They really want to help people, and they care deeply about their patients. Yet they burn out after a relatively brief period of time.... The nurses are attentive, become involved, and then their patients die. The stress is enormous.[11]

By now you should have a good feel for what Drudgery is, and you may have been recalling some experiences as you were reading this chapter. It's important to recognize those times when you were stuck in the middle of it. Recognition is good. It's the first step to knowing what doesn't work for you. The next step is to understand why you got into those situations. Then you'll be that much closer to using your knowledge of these painful situations, which you had no idea would end this way, to avoid future Drudgery jobs. If you're presently in a Drudgery job, hopefully this will lead to you getting out—and staying out.

The Outcome for HSPs

If you're in Drudgery too long, as we said, you may experience stress, burnout, and depression. Burnout feels like exhaustion, but it also includes helplessness, hopelessness, and entrapment. You can get burned out from being overchallenged with too much to do, or underchallenged and not well-utilized. As Pines and Aronson note: "The main cause for burnout is the feeling that the work no longer gives life a sense of meaning and purpose."[12]

Our sensitive nature brings information to us from a wider variety of sources and with great subtly. We're quickly overstimulated, and we must monitor that overstimulation if we wish to retain our well-being, not to mention having our highly sensitive systems kept free of all sorts of stress-related illnesses. And we must learn not to compare another's ability to sustain "just a job" with ours. Our needs are different, and our approach to work must also be different.

How Long Can Drudgery Affect You?

One of the things you must contend with if you stay in Drudgery and experience the trauma and stress is recovery. *It takes time.* Jane, quoted at the beginning of this chapter, did not get closure on her particular Drudgery experience until 12 years later, when she was asked to speak at an international conference:

In preparing the talk, I started examining that work and what I had actually done very critically, and came up with the startling realization that I hadn't done so badly at all. The gray cotton wool sense of failure had muffled the reality. However, although I could consciously, intellectually, acknowledge that the work was okay, it didn't diminish the sense of failure; in fact, it probably exacerbated it, because now I felt that if my work was all right, why hadn't I had the gumption to stand up for it and for myself?

Coming to terms with this would take more thought, and Jane then discovered that she was an HSP, which helped her to understand that she wasn't flawed, she just had a temperament that made standing up for one-self hard to do. While you may not need 12 years to resolve the residual side effects of Drudgery, you will have some work ahead to heal yourself. We will address this in the next chapter.

How HSPs Get Into Drudgery Jobs

There are five ways that seem to stand out when we consider how HSPs end up in Drudgery. They're not mutually exclusive, and sometimes several may apply to you:

1. The ghost of drudgeries past

2. The simple stress-free job

3. The idealistic path

4. The Icarus effect

5. The attack from within

The difference between these categories is not always clear cut—you'll see several in here who could easily be in more than one category. What matters is what *hooks you* into Drudgery situations. We'll discuss these more fully after presenting the stories. Three of these are caused by internal Drudgery qualities within the person, and typically, the other two are caused by being in a Drudgery institution.

As you read the following stories, refer back to the above list of conditions most likely to cause Drudgery and see how many you can spot in these events, as if you were a detective, seeking the clues to a mystery—the mystery of your own Drudgery history. There can be a combination of factors happening. Drudgery can sneak up on you, like the frog in cool water, slowly being boiled, or it can hit you like a sledgehammer. How long does it take for these people to get out? What stories resonate the most with you?

The Ghost of Drudgeries Past

Drudgery is not confined to work. Any traumatic experience could be considered a drudgery experience. Because of the ability of the sensitive person to register, if not imprint, experiences into their bodies, emotions, memories, and imagination, good and bad experiences can remain with an HSP a long time.

A sensitive child, exposed to abusive behavior early in life and not given enough love and help to overcome such conditions, may be deeply affected into adult years. This early Drudgery (traumatic) experience can sap an adult HSP's health and emotional well-being, draining away energy that would normally be channeled into developing both the interpersonal and professional skills needed for a successful career. Jacquelyn Strickland, an HSP coach working exclusively with HSPs, calls this type of person a "core issue HSP." I have noticed many HSPs with prolonged workplace Drudgery who have experienced early childhood traumatic experiences.

Here's a description from Joey, an HSP haunted by a past trauma that affected her at work:

I am very noise-sensitive, I hate it when someone starts screaming. It is the last thing I want to hear. I think I was shell-shocked as a child. My father is a screamer—I grew up with screaming, I think I have always been noise-sensitive. I think anytime I hear people screaming, yelling, fighting, that kind of thing—I feel my body freeze, just freeze, and I feel like that little child again. I can't handle it, I just can't handle it.

Yet Joey learned how to overcome this ghost with one of her coworkers:

[He] would have these screaming attacks, he never screamed at me, but I witnessed him doing it to other people. He would just carry on about the stupidest things.... This man began screaming like a two-year-old having a temper tantrum, I began laughing—I fell on the floor from laughing until he stopped screaming. He looked at me and started to laugh, and I said, "I can't believe how upset you are getting about something so stupid." ... Usually, I don't laugh in people's faces when they get upset, I had just had it with that guy. I've seen him screaming at other people, etc. I had a total lightbulb moment the next time he began screaming and thought this is not a healthy environment.

Elaine Aron explains in *The Highly Sensitive Person* that our sensitivities make us more prone to experience everything with great detail, and that intense events, whether they're good or bad experiences, will be stamped into our psyche and body, lingering there for a long time.[13]

These early life traumas can make HSPs more depressed and anxious, more so than a non-HSP who went through a difficult childhood. It may require therapy to get to the heart of these ghosts. With diligent effort, however, HSPs can overcome these ghosts and prevent them from interfering with their lives. Healing your past is an important part of growing as a human being and will have long-term benefits for you in your work.

The Simple Stress-Free Job

There are times when the idea of a new job is so stressful that taking the easiest route is appealing. Basically, there are two reasons why HSPs choose "simple" jobs. Perhaps your confidence, for whatever reason, isn't sufficient to face big challenges, so something moderate to low on the challenge scale is like Baby Bear's porridge—just right. Or perhaps other areas of your life demand most of your energy, so you feel you need a job that doesn't compete for your attention. Whatever the cause, the new job needs to be as simple and stress-free as possible.

Generally, entry level jobs are hourly work, with labor laws that protect the worker from being there more than eight hours and ensure that he or she has a specific time for lunch and breaks. In comparison, on the salaried, management level the expectation is that you'll work sixty or more hours a week, or thereabouts (and you're there because you love it, right?).

Sometimes an HSP will need the reassurance that he or she won't have to work beyond the eight hours or be put under a lot of stress. So low level jobs are "simpler." Among the simple jobs we normally have in our lives are house cleaning, gardening, running errands, and babysitting. Paid simple jobs can be the low level jobs: data entry, filing, taxi driver, maid service, or any job that *initially feels like it may be easy to do*; a "no brainer."

EXAMPLE: The Maid with the MSW Degree

Juliana is a former master of social work, now a Web designer and illustrator, who has done many Drudgery jobs. When she finished her master's, she was exhausted and wanted something simple while she caught her breath and got her bearings. So she became a maid. She recalls:

Being with people so intensively, as well as the content of the psychiatric job, and the stress of writing a master's thesis, just flattened me, in terms of emotional (and even physical) energy. I needed less challenge for a while and took a job as a maid at an upscale gated community for well-known media and other personalities. I thought this would be easy. The grounds were serene and beautiful. I was on my own nearly all the time. No real time pressure, no one looking over my shoulder.

But there were drawbacks, as Juliana eventually found out. Previously, she had been in a respected (and demanding) job, had very high level skills, and as a result, was challenged regularly. Now:

... people there looked through me, as if I did not exist. And, just a month earlier, I had worked in a mental health outpatient clinic, in the community. People there, both staff and clients, had treated me with a lot of respect. Well, one day, I noticed my shoes. They were the same shoes I had worn as a therapist so very recently. Only now they were the shoes of a drained maid, who could not understand why she needed to be in this situation. "Surely I'm nuts," I thought. "Am I the only one with a master's degree who would ever need to do something like this, just to get quiet and a slower pace, with less people-stress, while I earn enough money to keep body and soul together?"

Juliana was feeling the loss of connection with others, the ability to do challenging work, and the subtle demoralization that shadows someone in an entry level job. For an HSP seeking an interlude from a stressful life, a chance to regroup, or to save energy for what one considers true work, or for family, the choice of a simple job brings with it high risk.

The Problem with the Simple Path

It's important to note that "simple" jobs are not as simple as they appear to be. Many of these jobs, especially those considered entry level or menial jobs, are saturated with Drudgery problems and people. HSPs walking into a "simple" job are going to be negatively affected.

HSPs who take these jobs do not usually consider whether the jobs match their temperament (a guaranteed stress creator). Taking on a job like this, the criteria of HSPs seeking "less stimulation" is sensory: lights, sounds, commute time, and so on. What they don't take into account is that these Drudgery jobs are also loaded with emotional stress because of their values and climate.

Many of us grow up thinking something was odd or wrong about ourselves. And because HSPs are frequently conscientious, with a built-in work ethic to boot, we may assume that our moral fiber will be appreciated in these jobs. As Barbara Ehrenreich pointed out, there are few rewards for heroism here. And those who choose these jobs because they might provide less stimulation are frustrated because the innate need for stimulation of an HSP is denied, and thus HSPs find themselves just as exhausted as with a more demanding job.

Taking on these jobs is not unusual. Many talented people end up in this situation. Researchers on the gifted adult find that many baby boomers, currently the largest generational group, have such jobs:

Because of the "bulge" in the career-pipeline caused by the baby boomers, there are far more talented adults than there are leadership positions in the arts, academia, and the business and political world. As a result, many people with extraordinary talents are too exhausted by low-level, low-paying jobs they must hold to survive to be able to practice their primary talent. Counselors need to remember that the most common block to creative productivity is simply the fatigue and depression resulting from underemployment.[14]

If you have any self-conscious doubts and feelings of being "wrong" because of your sensitivities, the way you're likely to be treated on these jobs will leave you feeling less than satisfactory. The key here is learning more about your fear of, or pull toward, stimulation. Sometimes we're so overwhelmed, we cannot imagine doing anything else that would prolong the discomfort. But you can control your stress level far better than you think. Preventing exhaustion at a crucial time by choosing a low level job is not the answer.

The Idealistic Path

HSPs are idealistic and are often drawn to work that has great meaning to them. But joining a company because of idealism overlooks the day-to-day match between you and the job.

EXAMPLE: My Theme or My Boss

Catherine, in her early 30s, is in career transition, torn between her many interests, especially when it comes to the environment and sustainability. When something captures her passion, she gets hyper and ecstatic about her work. "My heart is beating a little stronger," she says, "and maybe I have a little bit of trouble calming down, but I'm on sort of a high. I'm overstimulated, but it's a good kind of overstimulated." Catherine knows she needs lots of challenges that let her make an important contribution, and needs to be inspired and have some control over her work:

I want to know the whole story behind it, the whole picture, why I'm doing something and how that's going to contribute to the big picture. When I don't have that capability, I guess I don't feel fully motivated and fully empowered and like I'm making a difference.

Catherine found a job with a recycling company that she very much wanted to work for. During the interview, she realized her future boss, a kind and smart person, was not the kind of leader she worked best with. Catherine's intuition was trying to tell her something, but, she said:

I was so excited, I so wanted to get into this field of sustainability, and wow, this was my foot in the door, and I wouldn't have to have a university degree, I could just get experience and build on it. My boss was a nice person and I felt compatible with her, so I overlooked those things in her personality that my intuition warned me wouldn't work.

It wasn't long before the job plunged into Drudgery, as Catherine found her needs not being met, felt undermined in her work, and had to hold herself back with a boss who didn't engage her energies the way she wanted. Catherine realizes that many of her jobs start off on an inspiring high, where she likes to be, and ends up feeling that "I'm basically unfulfilled, I have no power in the higher-up decision making, I feel like a peon, an assembly line worker that has no say in anything, and all my best qualities are not being utilized. I basically feel like I'm wasting away."

Choose Within Your Theme

According to Pines and Aronson, who have interviewed thousands of people, idealism is a trait that may well lead to career burnout. They say that people with the highest ideals, unless they somehow manage to develop effective coping strategies on their own, "are likely to experience the most severe burnout."[15]

The struggle the HSP has is in choosing what to do, not why to do it. You know why: because the theme is your passion. And having a theme is a wonderful way to go. Agonizing over which one of the numerous choices within your theme you should take might be made easier if you ask yourself: "What other issues am I affected by?"

Catherine, in our first example, obviously has a lifelong passion for environmental issues, and deciding where to work has been hard for her to do. How does one choose between a variety of tantalizing directions? Sometimes the theme is not clear-cut for everyone, nor does the right combination of job and theme happen easily.

Those of us with a theme have much in common with the next group—the Icarus people. Both groups need to trust the overall pattern and learn to "enjoy the ride"—the learning experience that comes from a multitude of jobs, which vastly adds to our experience.

In the end, hindsight will give us 20/20 vision and the theme's thread will become obvious. But until then we have to stay focused on growing as human beings and letting our true work unfold for us.

The Icarus Effect

Some HSPs are sensation seekers. Like Icarus in the Greek myth, who was thrilled at soaring so high into the sky, they don't pay attention to the downside of this experience. They enjoy new tasks, new opportunities to learn something different, and they especially enjoy a nice big challenge. Repeatedly, they take on a new job that catches their attention. But within a few years, or less, the job is no longer exciting, and in fact has sunk to being boring. Then, like Icarus, the job plunges down into Craft, and then into Drudgery.

EXAMPLE: "I'll Die If I Do Another FedEx Form!"

In his mid-40s, Jim is currently a director of a humanities program at a university. It's a challenging job and he loves the straight-up learning curve. For Jim, most Drudgery jobs happen once he's mastered an existing job and there's nowhere else to go. He has an eager, creative, and restless nature that needs lots of creativity, flexibility, and challenges. He worked widely diverse jobs, mostly in the arts at management level.

I think that I have actually had that happen on several occasions, where I've gone into something that I felt very passionate about it and then over time it becomes drudgery. Maybe two to three years it goes straight down to drudgery. My job at the Hollywood studio started off, I think, really as a calling, it really fit the bill, and then by a couple years later, I felt trapped, I felt there's no way out of this, "I will die at this desk, if I have to approve one more invoice from Federal Express. I just, I will die." And I felt truly trapped and I didn't know how to get out of that job.... By the time I left it I felt I was being strangled. And that if I don't get out of here my health will seriously deteriorate.

From Icarus to Phoenix

The key to the Icarus effect is the pattern. First, there's the exciting, spiking thrill of a new job, which energizes us. Then, as the job is mastered, it becomes more mundane, ordinary, and, eventually boring. When that happens, many HSPs feel like failures, because they're constantly following a new challenge, never staying in one place, never "maturing" in one career, rising up the ranks, like others whom society idealizes.

All high sensation experiences are transitory, even that thrilling promotion you got last year. While there's something about the job that thrills you, once you understand the transitory (and also rebirth) nature of the thrill itself, you have far more control over your experiences.

In the chapter on Calling, we will discuss the Phoenix Calling. I mention it here because it's the same pattern as the Icarus effect. The start is on a high note, a thrilling new challenge, and then, over time, mastery and familiarity replace novelty and newness, and the challenges become familiar, easily accomplished and eventually boring. The difference is that those in a Calling see themselves as always having something new and exciting to learn, a way of reinventing themselves over and over. And that this is good. Claude Whitmyer, the author of *Mindfulness and Meaningful Work,* calls this "beginner's mind" the "openness and eagerness to learn."16

The need for new and stimulating changes, the lack of self-confidence, the need for a wonderful ideal that makes an ordinary job a way of bettering the world, the need for calm and quiet as a respite from too much stimulation—all of these issues and considerations push and pull the HSP out of good situations and into bad ones.

If you're one of those HSPs who's always curious and thinks a new job is an adventure with a learning curve, only to see it morph into Drudgery a few years later, do what Jim did and monitor your career path more effectively. You have to accept that you need lots of variety and lots of challenges, and that most jobs in the marketplace aren't going to be sufficient for your needs. Change and variety are part of what your career will look like. This is not a flaw. It's not a sign of failure that you can't handle staying with one company or one occupation for the duration of your career. In fact, since the workplace is changing so much, staying in one job is becoming less the norm.

If I were you, I'd think about it this way: You are the Renaissance person, a generalist with a wide variety of interests, talents, and experience. Because you're always going to be assimilating new knowledge and experience, becoming comfortable with this Renaissance viewpoint is crucial. You either have to narrow yourself for a company with a single purpose, which could be difficult, or seek an environment where you can be versatile.

Jim for instance, from the example above, now finds that his vast experience in so many different areas of the arts comes in handy with his current position.

The Attack from Within

Another frequent way jobs turn into Drudgery is because of problems within the company: a corporate culture that isn't right for you, an abusive individual, an unethical decision you can't accept. All of these have made wonderful jobs Drudgery, sometimes for a little while, sometimes permanently.

EXAMPLE: A Manager's Story—the Wrong Culture

Long hours, little appreciation or support, and a climate of "constructive criticism" drove away this HSP. Carolyn is an extraverted, fun-loving, and hardworking computer IT professional. She loves skiing and nature. As a teen, she was an extremely gifted guitarist, but chose computers for her career. She sees her work in computers as mostly Craft.

Carolyn recounts a time she worked for a 30-something workaholic entrepreneur who expected the same of his management staff. Working hard was not a problem for Carolyn. She's an overachiever and loves challenges, and had a staff of seven who worked 24/7 a week. She was paid very well and got excellent bonuses and raises, and her staff gave her the highest rating any manager got in the company's history.

Carolyn was in a demanding, tough job with lots of responsibilities, was involved in developing a good team, and was regarded by her staff and senior management as an excellent employee and manager: it sounds like a potentially ideal condition for an HSP who enjoys a stimulating workplace. But there were problems that soon changed Carolyn's opinion of her company.

The owner practiced "constructive criticism," which meant that for every compliment, there must be a criticism, no matter how small. There were other things too:

I had to fire people, and later when I saw what it was like, and saw the ruthless environment, I became unhappy with the long hours in this environment. One of my staff worked a midnight shift, and she had her books open and was studying when a manager came through and caught her. The president of the company said, "Even though it was the midnight shift and she wasn't busy, she can't be studying because that's against company policy, so she's fired."

Carolyn hung onto this job for three years, although by the second year she knew she needed to get out. "It seemed like I could never really be good enough," she says, and she began to lose sleep due to worry. Her self-confidence and self-esteem plunged, and she became exhausted and put on weight because she'd come home too tired to exercise.

Carolyn's boss didn't support her: "When I did resign, my manager, whom I reported directly to, cried and told me he felt really guilty, because he knew he had not been supportive of me. When criticism was going around about me, instead of being supportive, he agreed with the criticism, and then eventually, of course, they told me they weren't happy with me in management and then I left."

Like many HSPs, she stayed in a Drudgery job longer than she should have. Being an overachiever, Carolyn thought, "If I do it better, then I'll succeed. It was a theme from my childhood. If I'm better, then Dad will love me."

EXAMPLE: Love the Job, but the People Are a Problem

Susannah is a middle-age woman who, once she discovered books, knew they were her life's work. Over the years, she had good jobs, a company car, perks, a lot of influence, and won awards. She loved her work and challenged herself to do things a shy person might resist, like sales. "One of the elements was the challenge of having to stretch yourself," she says.

Although easily sensitive to her environment and people's moods, Susannah was a stubborn and strong woman who rode out several abusive situations because she loved the work. But it took a toll:

I felt I had to smoke because I was so stressed. I was probably drinking too much after work. I wasn't sleeping, I was taking tranquilizers, I was meditating twice a day, I was trying to use affirmations, all these things to keep me sane. I wasn't eating properly, I was constantly tired, I would dread going to work. I would work with the door closed to my office—just so I could have some privacy and think without people peering at me or interrupting me. It certainly affected my health very badly. I was depressed a lot. The thing was, the work was so generally wonderful, if I could just get to my desk and do my work, it was all right. It was all this other stuff happening around me that was so horrible. I mean, if you are editing a book, you can't think about anything else. And that was probably what saved me, in a way. I should have gone much earlier, but as I said, I'm very pig-headed, I'm a Taurus, you know, I'm very stubborn.

Getting Out May Mean Letting Go

This is probably the most unpredictable dynamic. We can choose a good company, love the work, be appreciated, and yet still face a wild-card situation. Sometimes the culture, or a bully, causes our world to change.

It's hard to determine a company's culture from one or two job interviews, but it isn't impossible to tell how healthy the organization is. Carolyn, from our first example, worked in a company with zero tolerance for even the most innocent infractions. Yet she hung in longer than her instincts told her was good for her. Susannah faced bullies and was able to survive, but at a price to her physical and emotional health.

Getting out may mean letting go of the desire to change or improve the situation, or being determined to win. Sometimes it's not the time to let out our latent Don Quixote to tackle a windmill.

What Every HSP Needs from Work

Drudgery is far removed from what you really need or enjoy about work. Mihaly Csikszentmihalyi, a well-known writer and psychologist, describes what happens when our psychic energy is being wasted:

When we feel that we are investing attention in a task against our will, it is as if our psychic energy is being wasted. Instead of helping us reach our own goals, it is called upon to make someone else's come true. The time channeled into such a task is perceived as time subtracted from the total available for our life. Many people consider their jobs as something they have to do, a burden imposed from the outside, an effort that takes life away from the ledger of their existence. Even though the momentary on-the-job experience may be positive, they tend to discount it, because it does not contribute to their own long-range goals.[17]

Getting Out of Drudgery

You know what Drudgery is like now, what it does to HSPs and how traumatic it can be when we stay too long. And yet it seems hard for some people to get out. Of course, people in survival mode are under considerable stress, so it's hard for them to believe they can escape. In fact they may feel that it's impossible, even though those around them may be saying, "Just quit," or, "What do you really want to do?" Which doesn't help much.

When it comes to being caught in Drudgery, you'll hear people saying:

"I need the money."

"I'm too tired to job hunt."

"I've been doing this job so long I'm afraid I'll never be qualified for anything else."

"I can't quit, what would I live off of? I have no savings."

"I have a family to take care of."

And so the "walls" around Drudgery Island get higher and higher, until something inside of you snaps and you get out. It is typical that the practical side, the fearful side, makes leaving Drudgery very scary.

The fear of leaving is a natural part of the emotional condition we experience in Drudgery.

Once you make that jump, you will feel much better. And HSPs are *glad* to get out of Drudgery. We need to get out.

You cannot expect to make an existing job better. If the job is meaningless, if the work is boring, if the people are making you miserable, you cannot change the situation. I've tried tinkering with a boring job to make it better, but I was focused on the wrong problem. The real problem was that the job meant nothing to me, and the challenges weren't satisfying. It was so far removed from where my spirit was that there was no material for me to improve, emotionally, mentally, or physically.

An abusive workplace is not a place we can change, and we shouldn't try. Perhaps a different department would be all right, if the company is big enough and the people problems are isolated and not widespread. The decision to stay needs to come from your heart and an honest answer to this question: *What would make you happy?*

However, if you choose jobs for which you're overqualified because your confidence isn't good, or you're seeking a calming environment while you rest up from an intense period, you've got a tough challenge. Here, your challenge has to do with personal boundaries and self-confidence. Now that you know the Drudgery has devastating effects on you, it should be clear that you have to heal before you can go forward in confidence.

Until we resolve the confidence issue and trust our intuition, we'll continue with jobs that don't meet our needs. We will have to have better personal boundaries. They're crucial and will make a difference in your life. Every HSP I've talked to says boundaries are among the hardest things they've ever had to master, but that it's worth it. (There's a chapter ahead on boundaries and how we can improve them.)

Listen to Yourself

How do HSPs get out of Drudgery? We're all different. You might not put up with some conditions for more than two weeks, while I would hang in there for months, and vice versa. Fear of any kind is guaranteed to keep us at an unhappy situation too long.

One of the most important things you need to do to get out is to listen to yourself. Our inner self is always telling us what's working and what isn't, only we don't always listen. In the case of two Drudgery jobs I had, I quickly knew that both were wrong for me. In one instance I left in three months. But a decade later, in another situation, even though I knew within six months that a job was no longer right for me, I held out for year, ignoring my intuition.

In the first case, the incentive to leave was strong because the boss was abusive. In the other, the job was unrewarding but the money was good, and I let money be the deciding factor. In hindsight, I recovered more quickly from the three-month bullying job but had a far longer recovery from the other—because I lost both my confidence and my way. Because I chose to be practical rather than trust what felt right, I had to work very hard, and very long, to rebuild my intuition and sense of direction.

Lee Coit, in his little book *Listening*,[18] has found that there are two voices inside us. One voice is calm, reassuring, wise, and always right. The other voice is a worrier, anxious and uncertain. Just listen to your own self talk, and you can hear one of these two voices.

Over time, I've learned that if the worrisome voice is too talkative, I can just repeat to myself, "There is another voice," over and over for a while, to remind myself to listen more carefully and finally that wiser, calmer voice will come. This wiser part is always there to help us, if we listen to ourselves. We do have all the answers.

Are You Ready to Leave Drudgery Island?

If you can honestly answer these questions, then you'll know that you're ready to leave Drudgery Island. There may be many reasons why you cannot leave right *now*, but the realization that the time is coming is a big step toward the day you will leave.

Have you listened to your intuition before and found it to be correct?

If you ask yourself what feels right for you to do, what would you say?

Are you willing to face the fear of leaving and "jump," even with the stimulus of fear?

If you have a past ghost lurking in the shadows, are you willing to get to know that ghost a little more, so you can heal it and grow as a person?

3

Time Out for Healing

When from our better selves we have too long
Been parted by the hurrying of the world, and droop,
Sick of its business, of its pleasures tired,
How gracious, how benign, is Solitude

—WILLIAM WORDSWORTH[1]

I would like you to imagine that you've just landed on solid ground after leaping from Drudgery Island. There is a door behind you and you pull it closed. There. Now, tug hard on it again, so you can feel that the door is solidly closed behind you. (Rattle the knob if you like, I often do.) The door to Drudgery is closed. Do you really feel it? If not, use some of the planks of wood on the ground and hammer the boards over the door. There are some nice boulders nearby that you can push in front of it if that gives you a better feel. *Do what you need to feel that the door is closed tight and will not open again unless you choose to do so.*

Time to Heal

This is a "feel good" chapter. It has several purposes.

1. At this moment, you may not be in severe distress from a Drudgery situation as some in the previous chapter were. But when people are at that level of trauma, they are more befuddled, and they need to be gently reminded, even nudged, to *stop and get away* from the situation for awhile.

2. We can't be "on" all the time. Whether our high intensity is due to the distress of Drudgery or the thrill of a Calling, we need to *stop* and smell the roses.

3. So as part of our training to increase our awareness of our sensitivities, this chapter is designed to be softer. If at the end of the book, you say, "The 'Time Out for Healing' chapter just wasn't as mentally stimulating, and it was sometimes more informal, than the rest of the book," then the chapter will have served its purpose.

If you feel a shift in this chapter, stay with it, and give yourself permission to relax and have a time-out. With our nervous system hardwired differently, we need to pay attention to subtle shifts that tell us it is time to bring down the stimulation. This is your chance to practice, and remember the importance of doing so regularly.

This chapter is meant to take you to a timeless place, if you will let it. Carol McClelland, in her book *Seasons of Change*,[2] describes life's journey in terms of the rhythm of the seasons: fall, the sign that change is at hand; winter, the time to let go of the old, retreat and reflect; spring, when there is anticipation and excitement of new things; and finally, the summer harvest of our labors. Your own particular life may be in any one or all of the seasons. But for the purposes of this chapter, imagine yourself in winter, the time of hibernation and quiet retreat.

Try to be alone, perhaps in a favorite chair or snuggled into bed with hot chocolate, cookies, teddy bears and pets, cozy blanket, or comfy pillows, while you read this chapter. But any place where you'll be comfortable, relaxed, and not feel rushed will be all right. Put away the clocks and watches. Time doesn't mean anything here. This world of healing is timeless, spontaneous, and safe. You might want to have a notebook handy, just in case something bubbles up you'd like to save.

Larry, a trauma survivor, suggests that in order to reorient ourselves to healing, we need to remember several things: hope, a realistic look at life, being in the moment, and a good sense of humor. We've all been in Drudgery, and some of those situations have shaken us pretty badly. It is possible, though not always easy, to keep diligent in watching our boundaries, to stay out of Drudgery. If it's not possible to take a week to rest after each Drudgery job, then try to find some time each week for special tender loving care for yourself alone.

Hope
Our Inner Garden After the Storm

Remember the story *The Secret Garden,* and how two children restored a neglected garden back to beauty? Imagine overstimulation (whether a great creative burst or Drudgery) as a storm that has swept through our life, and we have valiantly fought to protect our garden. So now we're a bit of a mess: covered with mud and cuts, leaves in our hair. Imagine that we've had a nice hot soothing bubble bath or shower, and now we're clean and relaxed, and resolved to make our garden better than ever. We can brush away the dead leaves, plant seedlings or rebuild fences. That's one of the nice things about gardens—they can adapt, grow back, even move around and be prettier than ever before. But we have to help it get there and fortify it from other storms.

> The delicate, enclosed privacy of any garden also reflects our own delicate, enclosed hearts. They are easily disturbed, as we all know, and therefore require solid stone walls and strong gates...We have to be vigilant, like a careful gardener, to keep out the pests and do regular weeding. This is a great mystery, as the theology of gardens implies: how the heart is stationed in delicate balance at a crucial point midway between nature and culture, between privacy and community.[3]

The analogy of the garden before has been used to describe our inner life. This "garden" is when we can be alone, with ourselves. It's probably one of our freest moments, to just let go and not have to be or do anything. And a *yearning* for a soothing place is our inner self's desire for some quiet "garden" time. This chapter will be our opportunity to work in our inner garden and relax. This garden results in a harvest of nourishment for the soul: joy, hope, love, endurance, peace, capacity for self-control, the ability to discern evil. Thomas Moore, in his beautiful book *The Re-Enchantment of Everyday Life,*[4] sees the garden as a sacred place for nurturing the soul.

We HSPs are easily drawn to nature, and if you ever had a place of comfort and safety, a place where you can find peace, relaxation, it's worth remembering that connection. This can be your touchstone, for those moments when you can't physically get away into nature. The garden is also the place where our inner seedlings grow into our Callings. So it behooves us to break the spell of overstimulation from time to time and let slower energies come in. Consider going back and rereading Chapter 1 about how we ruminate and are so intense. Both with Drudgery and the intense absorption of a loved project, we will find excuses to keep going: "I can't afford it." "I've got too much to do." We must learn to resist the temptation to keep going and step away from the stimulation. There are many ways to do this, but the key is: does it relax you? Do you feel nourished, refreshed, peaceful? And ready to be creative again?

We're now going to go on a journey through time and space, and discover and meet our HSP ancestors, and some marvelous Master HSPs. Are you ready?

A Realistic Look at Life
Let's Pretend: An HSP Culture

What would it be like if you lived in a world where everyone was an HSP? How would people interact? Would cities exist? How about slums, crime, or wars?

Would everyone be as intuitive as we are, and what kind of a society would such sensitivity create? No doubt the arts would flourish. Would businesses be people oriented, and would yelling not be allowed (YAY!)? Perhaps a boss would be supportive of your right to grow in your job, if you wished. And you could work your own hours (YAY!).

Our Ancient Heritage

Many utopian novels or social movements have strikingly HSP-like qualities: a desire for harmonious relationships between people and nature; living with a purposeful life and purposeful work; and having an empathic feeling-nature. If we go back farther in time, we could probably find evidence of HSP cultures among primitive societies. Riane Eisler, in *The Chalice and the Blade*, looks anew at old cultures and provides strong arguments for a goddess culture long before a "masculine, or warlike" evolution of societies.[6] And also, since the HSP trait has a tendency to be associated with facilitation and cooperation rather than conflict and conquest, it naturally gets compared with feminine traits.[7] Older, indigenous cultures operated more from a feeling and sensation reference, compared to modern, intellectually based cultures. In the quote to the left, notice how feeling-focused it is.

> When the tribe members feel good, the individual feels good; when others feel fear or anxiety, the individual takes on a similar affect ... this form of consciousness thrives on its ability to optimize feelings of well-being in the community, emphasizing "heartfelt rapprochement based on integrated trust" and an "intuitive rapport" among all the individuals in a group.[5]

Linda Kohanov, who wrote *The Tao of Equus*,[8] describes how animal sensitivies are vaster than we imagined. She points out the similarities between prey animals and the ancient, intuitive cultures. While all animals are able to sense subtle changes in their environment, the prey animal has the need to pick up information quickly and communicate this information rapidly to the community. In an environment where feelings are picked up via the body, emotions, and senses, prey animals—like humans in older cultures—are attuned to subtle changes in their surroundings. A herd of horses or prairie dog packs, for example, communicate instantly to everyone that there's a shift in the wind, bringing the smell of a predator; or the rustle in the tall grass means an unknown intruder.

With highly sensitive people, there is the strong ability to be intuitive, to sense things through the senses and emotions, to feel deeply and connect empathically with others. The boundaries between individuals and the environment are frequently blurred. Sounds similar to what some animals do, doesn't it?

With that beginning, let me introduce you to a Master Highly Sensitive Being—the horse.

The Master Sensitive

Welcome to the world of the horse, the Master Highly Sensitive Being. With a far greater level of sensitivity than humans, horses feel, communicate, and pick up subtleties from everyone and everything in their world. This is because they are prey animals and, as such, have developed the capacity to tune into their environment and to other members of their herd easily and quickly. Human sensitivity is peanuts compared to the incredible and vast sensitivity of horses.

This sensitivity gives horses an awareness of *all* emotions—theirs and humans. Kohanov explores how horses can help humans develop our own highly sensitive *consciousness*, or the ability to be more fully aware of our sensitivies. She believes this is latent in everyone. And I suspect it's stronger in the HSP. But how can this information help us?

Our gifts are ours for a reason, and we need to embrace them and understand them. Also, we have to learn to use them to take care of ourselves wisely. The key is in feelings. To take care of ourselves, to heal, calm down, or use our sensitivies wisely, *we need to become congruent.* This means that we don't ignore our feelings, stuff them down, or deny them.

One of the things Drudgery does is cause us to get all tangled up inside, so that we're out of touch with our happier emotions. Can you remember a time when someone would ask you what you wanted, and you couldn't say? We're not fully "awake" in Drudgery; our deepest, truest feelings are locked up, so we're not congruent. If we were, we wouldn't be in Drudgery very long or very often.

How many times did you not trust your intuition? (Go ahead, raise your hand.) How many times did you not speak up when something didn't feel right, even over a minor matter? (Hmm, raise your hand.) Or how many times did you stuff your emotions down because you were afraid you'd be laughed at, argued with, or scapegoated? (Did you raise your hand? See, being congruent isn't so hard.)

Incongruence has hurt us in so many ways. At work, many emotions are required for the job, while other emotions are expected to be stuffed away and out of sight, not to show themselves anywhere near the office. Yet emotions are used at work to control, inspire, correct, motivate, and lead. Not everyone is willing to admit it, but it's true. We will discuss this further in the stress management chapter.

After a long haul with Drudgery, it may take some healing time before we're in connection with our emotions again. It's okay to take baby steps back toward connecting with ourselves. One thing we can do is ask ourselves every day: What do we need to feel a little happy? We need to see what comes up, and trust that simple, little step, whether it's an ice cream cone, taking music lessons, or bigger things like imagining yourself doing different work than you were doing before. It's okay to dream and play, after all.

> The horse, who had never encountered a person with a visual impairment, watched Josh's tentative steps for a moment before walking directly to the young man's side and putting his withers in the same position that a sighted guide assistant would take. Each time Josh lost his footing, Dundee moved in close, providing his body as balance. Together, they walked, jogged, and ran....No one has ever been able to explain how Dundee knew Josh was blind, or why the horse was motivated to act as the boy's guide.[9]

Like human children, horses know when you're not in touch with your feelings, and, like children, horses will act out what you're really feeling, deep down inside. *They are congruent.*

It's an intriguing, perhaps even romantic idea, to think of the HSP as having some kindred ties to modern animal species and to ancient, lost, forgotten cultures. There is obviously something powerfully important here for HSPs like ourselves to know.

Horses are comfortable with their sensitivities. In an environment where humans are willing to be open to what horses can do, exceptional things begin to happen. As an example, we've all heard how horses can be gentle with disabled people, but their abilities are far more sophisticated than most of us imagine. In a special program to help humans, horses were involved as therapeutic participants. Josh, blind from birth, wanted to walk around the pen, alone, without his cane, after his riding lesson. His horse, Dundee, had other ideas. Dundee took initiative, led and supported this boy's efforts, and took him places he could not have gone on his own.

Dundee represents our HSP nature, and we are like Josh, trying to make sense of a world that sometimes seems beyond our comprehension. The congruence we need to become fully human (represented by their interaction) can take us places we might not have trusted ourselves to go before. I have mentioned that growing as a person is the most crucial step to finding our Calling. When we are congruent and trust our sensitivities, our capabilities can expand, and our Calling starts to notice us.

Being in the Moment

When you began this chapter, I asked you to place yourself into a timeless world, to relax and just be with the healing process so that your deeply perceptive skills could get back into focus. Wouldn't it be nice if we could take that timelessness with us out there in the world, when we're surrounded by busyness? I was amused to read about an ancient Roman comedy writer, Plautus, who was appalled at the invention of the sundial. This is what he said:

God damn the man who invented hours, who first set up a sundial in this city, and who divided up my day into miserable little bits! When I was a little lad, my belly was my sundial—much the best and most reliable of the lot! When he said it was time, you ate, if there was any food in the house. Now, even if there was any, it doesn't get eaten unless the Sun gives the word. Nowadays, the whole town is full of sundials, and most people are crawling around half dead with hunger.[10]

This quote appears in *Hyperculture: The Human Cost of Speed*, a book about the problems of our modern society written by a classics professor, Stephen Bertman. He sees the pace of life, helped along by our high-tech speed, as not only detrimental to our well-being, but also pushing aside some very basic human skills needed to make society, and lives, healthy. Those skills—depth processing, self-awareness, personal discoveries, building long-lasting relationships with others—cannot be done at warp speed. We need to be in touch with our inner self, our "garden," regularly to develop and use these skills effectively.

We spend a lot of our energy trying to keep pace with life. And we worry about it. We work so hard at trying to keep pace, and feel unsatisfied in the process. That dissatisfaction comes from our need for a time to do our "silent" work, the deep processing we relish. So while others can "do" five things, an HSP can *deeply and intensely process, understand, and create* in regards to three things. It's not doing less, it's doing deeper.

> The very speed of our lives inhibits the possibility of self-discovery; first because a life that is rushed provides few opportunities for critical reflection, and second, because a mind that is wired into the circuitry of its culture tends to lack the capacity and incentive for self-liberation.[11]

This is a qualitative difference, the difference between apples and oranges. It means we cannot compare our abilities at assimilating, processing, and producing results to another. Yes, I know people do this, but for sanity's sake, forget what other people think; we can't compare ourselves to others. HSPs often have high expectations, bordering on perfectionism. We have high ideals and good old-fashioned Martin Luther–like Protestant work ethic determination to flagellate ourselves when we fail. This is part of the intensity.

So how do we develop these deeper processing skills, so that we can expand our capabilities and get the attention of our Callings? Take the time outs you need. Take them regularly. This is personal time for you. No obligations or to-do lists at hand. And as often as possible, make nature, or your own soothing thoughts, or your memories your only companion.

Humor

Remember, Larry said we need a good dose of humor to help us unwind, relax, or heal. HSPs can be so serious! And we need to laugh at ourselves, as well as learn how to deflect criticism with humor.

Here is a joke, submitted by Catherine Post, a very humorous HSP:

How many HSPs does it take to change a lightbulb? Answer: Only one!

However, that HSP must pause to check, before working with the dangers of electricity; a secure and nonallergenic platform must be available, to avoid slippage or other unwanted environmental influences; the HSP may do it in his or her own way, but all the others will talk, for a while, about the difficulties inherent in any proposed approach; the HSP must be careful not to hold on *too* tightly to the bulb as it is screwed out of the socket, or else the bulb will break, the HSP will feel bad, his hand will need some TLC, and the other HSPs, especially those in relationships with non-HSPs, will have to go find the fuse box and render the electricity inoperable, while the HSP gently removes the leftover pieces of glass from the broken bulb holder. The watching group may discuss the meaning of light and process any personal symbolism as to why this light went out at this time.

The bulb itself must also be of the correct wattage, and must not be made of fluorescent or other irritating materials. Having said all of this, the HSP who has had the honor of taking on this job should be one without the massive time and energy constraints of twenty-first century employment and other life, which could render him or her too tired or even transmarginally inhibited before the bulb is ever approached for replacement.

But, having satisfied all of the above requirements, one HSP may change the bulb, and do it in his or her own unique way, regardless of how any other HSP or "normal" person would handle the job. And, needless to say, the job will be done to the utmost in quality, safety, environmental friendliness, and nonallergenic high standards, for all to enjoy for a long time to come. And the HSP who accomplished this priestly task shall then be entitled to rest, in as great an abundance as required, until the next "need" comes up.

HSPs can be so serious! And it's time we laugh at ourselves. Having a sense of humor will help you feel more empowered, more in charge of yourself, and deflect negative attitudes in a positive way that shows you are indeed in charge of yourself.

Keeping Our Soul Connection

This chapter is about rest, and keeping our connection with our soul, which opens the door to our Calling.

When we are overstimulated, we need to step away from the stimulation and regroup. It's not as easy as it sounds, because lots of things distract us but we just keep going. In this chapter, we had the opportunity to practice a time-out ... to attain a softer energy and learn more about our own abilities to sense subtle shifts in our nature. We have traveled through time, visited ancient cultures and modern, highly sensitive horses, and have learned a little more about the importance of rest, congruence, and trusting our sensitivities. All of this will strengthen us, and we will become more receptive to personal growth and to our Calling.

The next chapter, on stress management for the sensitive person, will explore some new developments on emotions at work and the impact of stress on HSPs.

4

Stress Management the HSP Way

HSPs need to be self-aware, selfish, and self-disciplined.

—ROY, DATABASE ADMINISTRATOR

E very HSP I've talked to who is familiar with the book *The Highly Sensitive Person* says that over time, they've become *more aware, more conscious*, of what they're sensitive to and have ignored before. This is because they've learned to use their HSP ability to detect early signs of stress.

Roy, our quote for this chapter, is right about HSPs. We need to be aware of what distresses us. That's the first step.

Second, we need to be more selfish (in a positive entitlement manner) to maintain those needs we have.

And finally, because our natural curiosity is easily distracted by intriguing possibilities, we need to be more self-disciplined. Usually we give up an important boundary for a little while (we might go out on Wednesday instead of Friday) and pay the piper later (dragging and stressed the next day at work). The only problem is, the piper can get bigger and more unmanageable if we don't recognize it as a predator and keep him properly trimmed, leashed, or barricaded from our garden.

This process of getting to know oneself, of becoming more selfish and disciplined about one's personal boundaries, takes time.

Internal and External Boundaries

As we noted in the first chapter, stress can be internal (emotions or thoughts) or external (workplace conditions). Internal, or personal, boundaries help us manage our sense of being overwhelmed. If we can't take care of ourselves and know what's bothering us, how will we be able to communicate any concerns to others? Nor can we expect others to honor our boundaries if we don't honor them ourselves. Dealing with people and setting boundaries with them will evolve more easily as we value ourselves enough to be *aware* and *listen* to our bodies and emotions.

The key to HSP stress management is in developing *good personal internal boundaries*. This includes paying immediate attention when we're becoming stressed and doing something about it. We are then improving our early "detection system."

Most of the time, we don't notice when we're stressed because we're so busy trying to fit in, and we're too accustomed to ignoring and not seeing things as an HSP. For that reason, I urge you to read this chapter *with* your sensitivities, *conscious* of your vulnerabilities. It's a road map for the sensitive person, with signs along the way. We have to trust and listen to ourselves. As we become more congruent, we don't block the signals of stress as much. And then we can say, "I'm tired," or "I'm miserable," or, "This feels awful and I don't want to be here!"

Why Stress Occurs

When Alvin Toffler wrote *Future Shock,* over 30 years ago, he spoke of a new disease, "a shattering stress and disorientation that we induce in individuals by subjecting them to too much change in too short a time."[1]

Indeed, stress occurs when the demands of life significantly tax our emotional, mental, and physical resources, such as overscheduling ourselves even though experience has taught us that we can't do this.

For myself, I've found that I can't do a big "outing"—a long drive to an important business meeting or social event—twice in one or two days, back-to-back. The result is stress, perhaps exhaustion, and being unproductive the subsequent day or longer. I've known this for a couple of years, and yet I have to work hard to discipline myself not to schedule too much.

At the time I'm scheduling, I may feel good and think, "I'm fine, I can do this." But every time I go with that attitude, I fall flat. And I'm the one who pays for it, by falling short during the next day's obligations. I see the same phenomenon in many HSPs. They try to finish a flurry of projects, rushed together, right up to the last minute. And then they require a two- or three-day downtime afterward.

What Is a Personal Boundary?

Recognizing what stresses us and not allowing it to do damage means seeing ourselves as a separate self from others. This defines your personal boundary. These boundaries give us wiggle room to grow and be creative. We are living beings, with enough mixtures of talents, capabilities, interests, and personality style to require plenty of open vistas to sustain a lot of growth.

Remember our garden, our inner self that we're caring for? Every good garden has a boundary of some kind to define what's in and what's not. We are made of many substances that "grow" us: earth, air, fire, water, emotions, ideas, imagination, energy. Each of these requires a space of its own to develop a unique garden identity. A poor border means havoc to the plants from predatory creatures, or loss of identity from inroads by more aggressive plants. Build a good boundary to keep out external predators, water and care for the plants, ferret out innocent-looking vegetation that is really a bunch of voracious weeds, and the garden will flourish and take on a life of its own, with charm, color, warmth, and beauty. But to create these boundaries, we need to know more about what we need, what we are like as HSPs.

HSPs always talk about how much work it is to build and maintain boundaries. "I'm getting better at it, but it's taken awhile" is a common refrain. This is so because we're often tuned in to everything around us, making it harder for us to step away and have distance from our environment. So again, sensing ourselves as a separate being from others—a being with needs and aspirations—is crucial.

Our sensitivity and conscientiousness are positive attributes, but they can get in the way of seeing ourselves as separate people. *It's important that we realize we're allowed to have a separate self, and for our feelings to be val-*

ued for their own worth to us. Which means we have to like ourselves enough to care about our own well-being and to see choices as a benefit to us. Then we can give ourselves a loving protectiveness. This is positive selfishness, or as Roy puts it, a positive self-entitlement.

Here are some examples of personal boundaries:

> ➤ I value myself enough to trust my feelings.

> ➤ I am capable of solving my problems.

> ➤ I have the right to have hope.

> ➤ I respect my body, feelings, and thoughts.

> ➤ I have the right to say that something bothers me, right away.

> ➤ I need to listen to the still, small voice that says something's not comfortable.

For example, I find that closing the door to my office—even when I'm alone or it's late at night—creates an inner sanctum that allows me to relax and concentrate more deeply. I sense a subtle difference in myself when I do that. Otherwise, the environment continues to sap my energy and adds to my stress. Whenever I've experimented with this, I can feel the difference in my body and emotions. It might seem silly to close the door when no one else is up and around, but if a boundary line resonates in your psyche, then it's important to acknowledge it.

This recognition or early detection of potential stressors, would be helpful to everyone, but it's particularly valuable for HSPs because of the depth of subtlety we experience. The better we are at managing our boundaries and taking better care of ourselves, the greater our chances of staying away from Drudgery and moving into Craft or Calling.

When we're in Drudgery, our boundaries have ragged edges from being constantly inundated from Drudgery forces. But being out of Drudgery doesn't mean that our boundaries are perfect, for our inner garden will always need attention: pruning, clearing, adjusting this and that as we grow and new experiences come our way. Of course, if we've been in Drudgery and escaped, there will be some vigorous work ahead in our inner garden before our psychic plants have enough room to breathe, to wave their leaves toward the sky, and say, "Ah, sunshine!"

Early Recognition Means Less Stress

SCENARIO: You're sitting at your desk, late in the afternoon, and someone you like asks you to help her with a project she's trying to get done for her boss. You hesitate, feeling uncomfortable because you had plans for the evening. But you say yes, because you hate to disappoint or hurt a nice person.

SCENARIO: Several unexpected interruptions cut into your day, throwing you off, and you break down into tears or agitation.

SCENARIO: A customer calls and screams at you about shoddy merchandize. You didn't make the product, sell it, or even work for the company at the time. You know you're not to blame and that you shouldn't take it personally, but it does bother you. The upset and sadness remain with you for several days.

We are continuously impacted upon by events, emotions, sights, sounds, and ideas every day. We may have thoughts and emotions about this bombardment, but we often overlook its impact on our bodies. The three above scenarios illustrate the common problems of HSPs at work. They may not seem terribly stressful, but they can surprise us with their repercussions for days, even weeks, later.

Remember the exercise we did in Chapter 1, which called upon us to observe when we're starting to ruminate or worry? The point of that exercise was to catch ourselves before we take off into an intense habit that will add to our stress. That was a personal boundary we were recognizing.

Catching any self-critical comments that put us down and suggest we're helpless, rather than optimistic, is a boundary we should recognize, because it's important that we value ourselves. The idea is to strengthen our self-image so that we can be masters of our intensity, so that we can be observant when we're pushing ourselves too hard. And, of course, we're also striving for greater congruence, so that our heart, mind, and body are in harmony.

It is worth repeating that HSPs who spend many years in Drudgery become incongruent, unable to have a harmonious balance between what one feels and what one does. If we could catch the signals early enough, the problem wouldn't grow so big. It's a lot easier to see the big stressors, but the smaller things can elude us. In fact, even then we often sense that something is wrong, but don't know what to do or how to take care of ourselves.

It's up to us to pay attention to subtle clues—the internal fatigue, for example, that results from trying to stay upbeat during a confrontation in a staff meeting while we're experiencing inner turmoil. If you find yourself irritated, upset—perhaps you're unable to sleep—the event that triggered it was just the *last* straw, not the first or only straw. If you looked back over the last few weeks, you'd see a dozen or so little stressors that were slowly layering themselves onto your body, mind, spirit, and emotions like sludge, tar, or sediment. While we can't prevent stress completely, because we're always growing, we can improve our ability to recognize the signals of stress earlier, to keep out these insidious irritants.

But remember to be patient with yourself as you try to be aware of when you feel uncomfortable and to be honest with yourself about the discomfort. That's a big step toward mastering personal boundaries and reducing stress.

Remember When You're Okay and Recognize When You're Not

When you're experiencing a lot of unhappiness, whether from work or personal issues, when there's so much stress and Drudgery around and in you, it's hard to see the small details. One thing you can do is go back in time to the happiest moments in your life—whether work-related or not—in order to connect again with your best moments of health and well-being. When people feel good, they're centered, calm, relaxed, and happy. They can laugh easily and look forward to being around other people and activities. While they enjoy new projects, they also feel comfortable saying no. This is our ideal state. You need to recall this state in order to realize when you're *not* there … when you feel overwhelmed.

Overstimulation, for us, results in feeling more serious, humorless, and single-minded. We rush about, stressed, agitated by little changes or distractions. Our bodies tense up, and maybe we even throw things. The intensity we may feel at such moments could heighten our reactions to others. For example, if someone is sharp with you, it may seem that you've been yelled at when in fact you weren't.

The sneaky thing about being overwhelmed is that we don't realize when we're hours from hitting the wall. It's easy for HSPs to think, "I can handle it," and keep on going, without stopping to rest—until it's too late. We can endure, but we can snap fast too.

Types of Stress

We will consider the following types of stress:

➤ Acute

➤ Episodic acute

➤ Chronic

➤ Traumatic

These four vary in intensity and duration. It's possible for an event to be both acute, as a singular event, and also part of a long-term chronic condition. Circumstance also enters into it. For example, a situation might be mildly stressful for a person who's used to it and has good personal and people boundaries in a happy organization, and traumatic for someone else, who perhaps is coping with picking up the pieces after a massive layoff. So the stressful events described in each category are roughly approximated.

There may be situations that we've taken on and we choose not to change, such as being a parent of a young child, where our dedication and commitment determine some of our choices. But there are still self-care things that can be done to lighten our burdens.

Here are a few well-known causes of stress:

➤ Long, irregular hours

➤ Repetitive, nonstimulating work

➤ Distasteful work

➤ Isolation

➤ High performance required

➤ Low or no income

➤ Work under pressure

➤ Red tape

➤ Conflicting demands

➤ Lack of autonomy

➤ Low public image

➤ No security

➤ Disillusionment

Whle this list is of common stressors, the degree to which they stress you will depend on the circumstances. Now that you've read about Drudgery, can you see how many you might have had at one time in a job? It is not unrealistic to find one Drudgery job containing almost all of the above stressors.

Acute Stress

Acute stress is very common and can be thrilling and exciting, but only in small doses. "It comes from demands and pressures of the recent past and anticipated demands and pressures of the near future."[2]

Can you recall a moment in your life when an exciting new event was on the horizon? Consider what happens with an important presentation we have to give. We're thinking a lot, rehearsing in our minds in order to be prepared, feel ready, sort out possible problems, and decide what to do about them. This may be calming and it may be stressful, depending on the situation. If you have such an event in your life now, ask yourself: what you are feeling—physically, mentally, and emotionally. If you can be aware of the sensations, it will help a lot.

HSPs who are also high sensation seekers will most likely have frequent moments of acute stress. For high sensation seekers, an exciting event is not a negative "Oh-my-God" stress, or they wouldn't go anywhere near it. They have to remember that even if they're having fun, it is still stress to the body. HSS people have a tendency to want more sensations when things get too quiet. And so they ante up the stimulation, creating more stress and fatigue for themselves.

Doing what we love does feed us, but it has its dark side, and it's called episodic acute stress, which we'll get to next. And the problem for high sensation seekers is that they give full reign to what they feel is a thrilling new Calling. They dive headfirst into all the new sensations, without any thought to the potential for generating stress. If you're a high sensation seeker, you may have to remind yourself of that old piece of wisdom about too much of a good thing.

> I'd only been there two weeks. And she was yelling at me and carrying on and I just melted in tears, I ran to the bathroom and cried, and cried, and cried.
>
> —Joey, in career transition

Another type of acute stress can come from a confrontation, which is always overstimulating. And we may need to run to the bathroom for a moment's privacy to regain composure.

Both the thrill of a new experience or a momentary confrontation with a person at work can add on to a larger, ongoing chronic stress, if that is happening in your life as well.

Episodic Acute Stress

Many HSPs experience episodic acute stress all the time. Day-to-day work can be stressful—being a manager, for instance, and having to deal with the pressures of staffing issues—as can raising a family. One area often overlooked as a component of an ongoing stressful condition is the environment in which we work. Usually it's thought of as a circumstance with a definite beginning and end (such as a commute), until the buildup begins to affect us. Long commutes and traffic jams can become episodic acute stress if done day in and day out for years.

Often, we look to the environment and sensory relaxants to manage the intense emotions brought on by work. But sensory relaxants do very little to get to the heart of the problem. When Susannah had problems with an abusive boss and was under so much stress that she began to abuse her body by smoking and drinking more than usual, she had one thing going for her: She could close the door of her office, in order to focus on work and forget the world for a while. But once she left her office, the problem was out there looking for her. The environment can only moderately help, or delay, your healing.

Environmental factors in the workplace, such as fluorescent lights, overly hot or cold room temperatures, remodeling work in the building, or the hum of machinery, can contribute to episodic acute stress events, even when one is not consciously aware of their presence. HSPs who have had previous traumas, even burnout, will be even more vulnerable to future stress because their system is at risk.

I have a new joke for you: The best place to find other HSPs is in the bathrooms of corporate America! It's the one place an HSP can go when at work and have complete privacy and time to settle down. (Please put a book marker here before you go dashing off, okay?)

Let's look at what HSPs report they do at work when they're feeling overwhelmed. Remember, while the list of nostrums below will help momentarily with mild stress, they're not going to downgrade a severely traumatic event to a milder state. Recovery time needed for people-related stress is very long compared to milder forms of stress.

Workplace Relaxants

- ➤ Hide in the bathroom
- ➤ Nap in the car
- ➤ Play music
- ➤ Take walks during break time
- ➤ Doodle with a box of crayons
- ➤ Play with Slinky
- ➤ Use electric bug massage on your head
- ➤ Sip water
- ➤ Soft lights (avoid fluorescent and orange lights)
- ➤ Get up and stretch
- ➤ Close the office door
- ➤ Lunch by yourself

At Home Relaxants

These can help, but they're not the cure for toxic levels of stress:

- Bubble baths
- Read
- Aromatherapy
- Cook
- Manicure
- Museum visits
- Garden
- Massage
- Homeopathy
- Exercise
- Zone out with the TV for a half hour
- A "do nothing" day

Chronic Stress

While acute stress is new (and therefore easier to spot) chronic stress is unrelenting and enduring, and is around for so long that one starts to live with it and ignore it, rather than make changes. A long-term illness, trying to juggle a full-time job, and going back to school to make a career change (this is an often-used Drudgery escape strategy), or any number of disturbing stressors in the workplace (see the list on page 79) are all examples of chronic stress.

Traumatic Stress

Traumatic events are specific, such as a severe injury or accident and, of course, abusive behavior from another. Judith Wyatt and Chauncey Hare, the authors of *Work Abuse: How to Recognize and Survive It*[3] consider abusive bullying and "mobbing"—originally a European term for when several people at work try to force someone out by humiliation, general harassment, false accusations, and so on—to be extremely stressful and little understood, by both the distressed person and their support system. These types of abusive behaviors can have dramatic effects on the individual, even changing an effective, agreeable person into a "difficult" person.

When events like this happen, a number of personal boundaries are affected. (We will discuss bullies in more detail in Chapter 7, "Highly Sensitive Kung Fu.")

While bubble baths and long walks provide momentary relief, true relief needs to be far more substantial. We are not powerless. Remember, when we find ourselves in abusive conditions, it may be time to leave. This may be scary, but it's important to our well-being.

The authors of *Work Abuse*[4] list four steps of treatment that get us past the "flashback" phase of recovery: Here is a brief description of the steps they developed:

1. *Validation and release,* in which you affirm your experience and vent emotions.

2. *Cause-effect review,* by organizing your experiences to feel you're in control about what happened.

3. *Shame resolution,* by exploring the event to place it in proper perspective.

4. *Developmental understanding,* integrating the experience so you can prevent future abuse.

Health Effects

"Burnout," a popular colloquial term, is a serious problem, especially for HSPs. Thus it is worth our efforts to take responsibility of burnout for ourselves very seriously and to explore what this really means. In *Career Burnout,* Pines and Aronson define burnout as "a state of physical, emotional, and mental exhaustion caused by long-term involvement in situations that are emotionally demanding. The emotional demands are most often caused by a combination of high expectations and chronic situational stresses."[5]

The consequence of burnout is that the individual is more vulnerable to stress, for perhaps years afterward or even for that person's lifetime.

Many people affected by burnout at some time in their lives find that they cannot function at the high level they had before.

The magnitude of this problem for the HSP is worthy of a book of its own. If you're in a Drudgery job or you've just left one and you're feeling slowed down, depressed, and with low energy, low motivation, distressing physical symptoms, or a sense of feeling trapped with no resolution in sight, take careful note of all these things. Learn about burnout and perhaps seek professional help in order to minimize great physical or psychological devastation down the road. If you do seek help, try to find a medical or mental health professional who understands and believes in your experience and who can give you good solid advice. People in burnout do *not* have the energy to champion their own cause. Save your strength and find the best support to help you through this time.

Being "On"—Emotional Labor

Every job requires you to be "on" in some way. You have to "act" grown-up, professional, and so on. And there are even specific emotions required for some jobs. For example, a flight attendant doesn't argue or fight with an angry passenger, and a policeman doesn't give a cheery hello to a bank robber. That would be bringing the wrong emotion to the job.[6]

Sometimes we're paid to express certain emotions at work. A salesman has to be optimistic, a mother nurturing and loving, and a company "hatchet man" able to eliminate jobs without guilty feelings or squeamishness. The honest emotions an individual feels are not emotional labor. True feelings are congruent feelings but may not be welcome at the workplace, especially in a dysfunctional Drudgery institution.

Often when we start a new job, the freshness and excitement gives us the "episodic acute stress" that we can ride with for a little while. In time, however, the fatigue increases and the ability to stay "on" gets harder and harder. We slip into chronic acute stress, and the job begins to cost us.

With a job that requires a lot of "face time" with others, a person will experience stress, even if he or she is an extrovert. And in order to recharge, we need regular breaks from this face time. But that isn't always provided. Such breaks could be time off ("comp time"), rotation of jobs to a behind-the-scenes job, a lounge where employees can rest, or regular debriefing and stress meetings in which employees can discuss their emotions about work.

Matching the Job and the Emotion

Whenever the emotions you're expected to bring to work are not what you really feel, you're being incongruent. When that happens, you and the job no longer match. Then staying with this job is stressful and will increasingly shift you into chronic and eventually traumatic stress. Staying under such conditions is also damaging your intuition, the inner radar that you need to navigate through life.

Let's reiterate the difference between learning and loving a task and actually doing it. For example, many HSPs love law; that is, they love the mental exercise, the complexity, nuances, and creative strategies available to the lawyer. But the actual practice of a specific area of the law may not be harmonious with a particular HSP's temperament; litigation lawyers are trained and need to be aggressive. They're paid to do that. This is their emotional labor.

Psychologists and consultants dealing with the workplace are starting to pay attention to emotions—how they are managed and how they're used at work! We all know emotions go to work along with the rest of ourselves, but this has often been ignored or played down.

This new development has given us some basic concepts pertinent to our experiences and needs. We'll discuss two of them: emotion management and emotional labor.

We all have emotions, and how and when we use them is our "management" of them. Everyone does some kind of emotion management every moment of the day. Religious and secular holidays, for instance, are times when certain emotions are expected of us. The "work ethic," for another example, is a term that conveys information about the combination of behavior, emotions, and values expected at work.

The culture of a company—its values, beliefs, stories, and ambience—may favor certain emotions over others. A company with mostly single individuals is going to have an entirely different emotional atmosphere than a place where the majority are family people with plenty of photos on the desk, company picnics, and a company baseball team.

While businesslike behavior is expected on the job, the culture of the company usually includes "water cooler" time, when we just gather around and chat during working hours, and it's not a formal break or lunchtime.

Progressive companies see this as part of a natural process of bonding and communication that helps employees build relationships with others in the company. It's informal (suggesting the emotional labor of one's job has momentarily been set aside) and serves a subtle but important service. This is where we learn who is a team player, who is a loner, who is the real power behind the boss in the lab department, who's working on a special report and is struggling with information that Joe in a department two floors away could solve quickly, who has a new baby or just lost a parent. Daniel Goleman, author of *Working with Emotional Intelligence,* would call this the "social radar" that's needed to develop our political smarts, in order to survive and thrive in the workplace.[7]

Some social attributes of a job are overlooked by HSPs. Since most HSPs are introverts, we're not drawn to socializing behaviors at work as quickly as extroverts. We're slower to become one of the group. It's important to make small efforts to fit in and develop some connections with others. It helps to lessen any perceptions that a person is a loner or is standoffish. This is particularly significant for HSPs since, being different from others, we're easier targets for scapegoating.

What often happens is that HSPs enter a field or a job with certain expectations. A particular job may inspire an emotion in us—the initial feelings of idealism, adventure, or glamour. But the work itself is not the same thing as the values held in the workplace.

In *Career Burnout: Causes and Cures,* Pines and Aronson examined the emotional problems of nurses who were working with terminally ill cancer patients. These nurses began their job feeling "incredibly idealistic. They really wanted to help people, and they care deeply about their patients. Yet they burn out after a relatively brief period of time."[8]

The nurses started out fresh, with a loving and wholesome faith that they would be able to bring caring and compassionate emotions into their job. What they weren't expecting was the incredibly high stress of watching painfully ill people—with the accompanying psychological stress from having to inhibit normal reciprocal emotions—and so they gave their deepest feelings but received little in return. The authors discovered that the nurses gradually distanced themselves from their patients, displaying more calloused emotions—shocking idealistic new nurses with these behaviors—and feeling guilty about the changes in themselves.

Nurses try to look "crisp, efficient, and cheerful" while feeling terrible inside. Starting out in Calling, these nurses descended into Drudgery and burnout. Being idealistic, say Pines and Aronson, puts one at high risk for burnout. And this is because the emotions expected at work are not always what one experiences from the work.[9]

An HSP Nursing Aide and Stress

Rachel is a tender-hearted young woman who loves older people, who loves helping them and doing healing, nurturing activities with people and animals. Like the nurses in the study mentioned above, Rachel is idealistic and has a strong work ethic. So she took a job as an aide in a nursing home, making minimum wage, and stayed there for six years. She would like to leave and go into a new career.

Rachel described the job's office politics as a bomb about to go off, but what she didn't see was how many different "bombs" there were. Based on the conditions when she took this job, Rachel's description of her situation and the distressing nature of her job, and her steadfast efforts to take care of herself, she is probably in Drudgery.

Usually I am so drained from work and my life is mostly about work—I really don't want to do anything else.

I am very bad about that [boundaries], I've gotten a little bit better at it. It helped after I read that book [*The Highly Sensitive Person*], because I know that I do need time to myself. So I've gotten a little better at saying no, because I know I can't function if I'm always giving in to other people, because I don't have any respect for myself. My body can't take it if I overload it. I have a very large problem with that at work, because we are so short-staffed and I live right across the back door from where I work. So when they are short, they come and knock on my door.

Having the type of work one loves to do, as Rachel does here, with values that one admires as well can leave us open to personal boundary loss. Some of you may be familiar with the term "codependency." Overall, it can describe a situation where, for whatever reasons, we have the experience of functioning and feeling as if we were a "satellite" revolving around another person, or around a profession or a job. This kind of overcaring has great ramifications for the HSP.

We need to be very careful that our love and our values also reflect our need to care for ourselves and to preserve our boundaries: the sense of being a separate self. Otherwise, if we let a codependent relationship with a person, profession, or job grow within us, it comes to rule our lives. And then we're in for more suffering, emotionally and physically, than the average non-HSP in a similar situation, because of the resulting stress. When that happens, we lose some of the richness of our HSP traits—the depth processing and the attendant values that give our lives such richness.

Let's look at Rachel's struggle, which can represent the struggle many others in helping professions have. The major stressors on Rachel and the emotions involved are:

> ➤ Minimum wage. (This is not good for morale.)

> ➤ Performing an entry level job: management has a perception of entry-level workers as Drudgery people who are not of a status to be treated with much regard or trust. Little control, meaning, or satisfying challenges. (This is demeaning.)

> ➤ Conflicts between her need to get out of this situation and her loyalty to the people she cares for; there are other aides she would not trust with her people. (Her feeling of conscientiousness.)

> ➤ Rachel's lingering idealism and aspirations. (Her desire to help the old and sick.)

> ➤ The distress of working with those with illnesses associated with aging. (Giving a lot but not getting much back from those who are ill.)

Showing kindness and empathy are all qualities likely to be found among self-actualized individuals, who are the most likely to be idealistic. These emotions cannot be regulated by a job (especially a Drudgery job); self-actualization must come from within. In this type of work, where serving and helping others is so important to HSPs, our idealism and well-being will be at risk.

Staying Calm by Retaining Control

HSPs need calm. Feeling calm is crucial if we want to minimize painful overstimulation. The need for calm is so ingrained in us that our search for it can be unconscious.

Sometimes we need things to be done a certain way, to happen at a certain time, or our distress rises. And controlling a situation is one way to keep things as calm as we can get them. We often need to be in control, since there are so many unpredictable possibilities. This behavior can be seen when we fuss over tiny details, like needing to have the fabric of a shirt feel just right or our files a certain way, or otherwise our anxiety goes up.

Does this mean we're "control freaks"? Yes, we can be insistent that things be done our way or not at all.

Diana, a manager in a large public library, explained why she needs control for her own comfort:

Once you are out of control by being so overwhelmed, it is harder to calm everything down. Some people think you are too self-involved or that you are a control freak, well, I am—because if I don't control things, I suffer, so I have to be a control freak! I have always been a control freak, I just didn't know why. I realize now, looking back on my life, that I was a control freak because I was trying to keep things from getting to that point where I was just overwhelmed. But other people don't see it that way. Most of the time I was only controlling things that affected me, I wasn't controlling other people's lives, I was trying to control my own life.

Letting go of being in charge is not easy. It may mean putting aside our curiosity about the work and also putting aside our desire to be challenged by the task. Someone else gets to play in that sandbox now, not us. As long as we hold some interest, curiosity, a need to learn from this task, the harder it will be to let go of control. If it is essential that a task be done a certain way or one becomes distressed, then it's useful to let the other person know how they can help you stay calm.

It's worth repeating that needing to be in control stems from a need to be calm. When things are overwhelming, they are already out of control. First, we need to acknowledge that what we really want is calm. If we're worrying about the ethics of a job, that's not calm. If we're afraid of losing a client by turning down a project, or we're afraid of hurting an employee's feelings by telling her she needs to get her act together, that's not calm.

Keeping calm is not about controlling external conditions, it's about being aware of what overwhelms us and how close we are to being upset. The more diligent we are in self-care, the better manager we'll be and the less controlling.

Juliana's Log: Staying on an Even Keel

Juliana is a middle-age HSP who has experienced lots of stress in life. At one point her work style was a go-go-go crash, which she did for years, only later realizing what she was doing to herself with stress. Eventually she became bedridden for two years and learned that life would go on without her. It was an important realization that she didn't have to do everything. "Life is messy," she said, "and I don't have to clean it up!"

Juliana has learned to trust her own judgment about what she needs in terms of pacing her work. She's an extremely intense worker, pouring her whole enthusiasm into whatever she does. She's developed a sophisticated method to help herself monitor her own stress levels.

Using a word processor, she tracks her work and how she feels on a daily basis. In order to prevent such a buildup again, she created a log to monitor her stress level (see Figure 4-1). Juliana explains how this log works and how it has helped her:

Tiredness is something that creeps up on you, gradually, and when I get into going postal, an upset, a crying jag, being angry at others or critical for some reason, if I look at my log, *I find that I've ignored little signs of being tired.* For me, it's a process of learning to pay attention to when I'm tired. You would think you would know when you're tired, and act accordingly, but I never have and I've kept on going, and I'm not doing that now. It took looking at my log to realize how much work I've done, and that I didn't have a clear emotional awareness of where I was. The log makes real for me my whole process; it wakes me up. I've noticed that other HSP friends have more ups and downs, and I'm staying more level now.

Now, every day she'll check in with herself throughout the day and ask two questions: "Am I tired?" and "Am I happy?" If she's not honest with herself, she pays the price, in the form of exhaustion, or worse—anger, crying, or a dreaded form of withdrawn depression. Juliana works hard and demands a lot of herself. But now she strives to pace herself more efficiently so she can be more productive while also feeling good and reasonably happy on a consistent basis.

She uses colored fonts or background lighting to highlight important moods or reactions so that she can get a sense, like an early warning radar system, of what is building within her. The log is wonderful, a graphically accurate and honest feedback too, for her ongoing self-care. The Feeling column is where she notices her reactions throughout her day.

FIGURE 4-1. Juliana's Log

DAY	FEELING/CIRCUMSTANCES	TOTAL HRS	WORK ACTUALLY DONE	HOURS
Thurs	**Calmer, happy, feel good from sleep!** Good idea to go to bed early —I needed that. Excited about new client's project, but **uncomfortable** with his attitude about the project. Tired by 5th hour on Mike's project but kept going—that was a mistake. What will I tell Mike about not finishing, even though I worked more than I know I should have? Uncomfortable. **WARNING: too many hours**	6+2.5	AM: Computer maintenance 2 hrs Planning animation project also Afternoon: Mike's project 6 hrs. Too many hours for me, but I got it all done. **Need to watch my hours, rest in evening.**	26.5

DAY	FEELING/CIRCUMSTANCES	HRS	WORK ACTUALLY DONE	TOTAL HOURS
Friday	Didn't sleep well, bad dreams. Started new Sam project, he called 3 times. Pain in the butt. Feel like I'm barely keeping my balance but am still okay. By p.m. back on track.	3+2	AM: Sam project 3 hours. Noon nap and lunch 3 hours. PM: 2 more hours on Mike project.	31.5
Saturday morning	Morning: **Tired.** Got talked into doing a short project that I really don't want to take. **Caught by surprise.** For crying out loud, Isn't it still Friday? Oh well, I was caught off guard. All in all, though, I did pretty well this week. Not exhausted. Going into the weekend. Hooray!	7.5	Short project for Celia. Afternoon longer, but enjoyable stuff, so it was okay. Later, I **cheated myself:** did 30 min phone calls, after my stop time. Groan. Oh well. Still, I feel **cheerful,** reasonably good.	39
Saturday later	Played catch-up, trying to be like everyone else, with their 40 hour week. Man, I am tired. I did so well all week, keeping my balance. Darn it!	5	More junk I did not have to be doing. Golly. Why did this happen again?? ACK. Tomorrow for sure will be entirely free!!	44
Sunday	Ha! **I did nothing!** **Loved it!** Need more of it! Need to remember the world will not collapse without my constant effort.			44

There are a number of ways to do self-monitoring like this. Journaling, either in a personal journal or in your day planner, or put red dots by extra stressful days and green by restful days, so you can view a month at a glance.

Gaining Control

Workplace stress is one of the most troublesome problems for HSPs. Teasing out some of the causes of those problems gives us more control over our lives. There are two major areas that cause us stress discussed in this chapter.

First, we need to define and understand stress. We know that we need to pay attention to the intensity of the stress and to be aware of *when* we're stressed, and closer to the present moment than in the further past. And we need to know more about *what* stresses us. For each person, these stressors may vary, but generally, people at work cause us the greatest level of stress. The proper method of dealing with increasingly intense and long-lasting stress can make a significant difference in our well-being. The more intense and longer lasting the stress, the less likely relaxants like bubble baths and nutrition will be effective. Stronger measures are necessary.

Second, up till now there were vast unexplored areas of emotions associated with specific jobs and conditions in the workplace; and emotions can cause stress. Some research is being done in that area. At the moment, however, many occupations don't prepare potential employees for what emotions will be required of them. Most of the time we learn through the hard knocks school of life, and by then our stress is rising, and our unhappiness along with it. If we can discern what emotions are part of our job description but are distinct from our temperament, we will have isolated a major stressor.

So you, dear reader, need to use your depth of thought and careful analysis, along with savvy assessment of yourself, to know where you fit in all of this. We cannot get rid of all workplace stresses. But where you meet the world and it meets you, use the information and skills you have in hand now to find a way to be more reasonably comfortable with your situation.

Be patient with yourself. As I mentioned in the beginning of this chapter, HSPs acknowledge that they are continually learning and growing in their assessment of themselves and in monitoring their boundaries and self-care. They are generally happier with themselves, but they also realize that the learning continues.

5

Craft: The Confidence Builder

Most of my law work is like that. You know, it's neither drudgery nor fun, it's just grinding it out. Of course it's crafting, in effect. Lawyers use that word "crafting" in a document. But ... on an average day there's drudgery, there's fun, and there's craft, and it all mixes up and you can have, you know, 50 different variations of that in a given day and even more!

—ARTHUR, ATTORNEY

C ongratulations! You have entered Craft! You are officially on your way to finding your Calling. You may have thought you were looking for your Calling while in Drudgery, but here, you'll feel emotions that are clearly signals from Calling. There is still a close proximity to Drudgery and some Drudgery thinking in Craft, but Craft radiates greater confidence and a more positive attitude toward life that goes far beyond the Drudgery world.

Craft Checklist

If you find yourself experiencing most of the following items, it's more than likely your job is in a state of Craft.

____ Are you challenged by the job?

____ Can you walk away from it?

____ Do you have some exposure to Drudgery on a regular basis?

_____ Do you have some exposure to Calling elsewhere in your life on a regular basis?

_____ Do you find yourself agreeing with the comic strip character Dilbert?

_____ Is your self-confidence strong?

_____ Do you do clock watching?

_____ Your income is very good, but the work isn't that satisfying?

_____ Do you experience some dissatisfaction and frustration?

_____ Do you have some enjoyment of your work?

_____ Do you experience long spells of joy for your work?

_____ Does your work feed your mind but not your heart?

_____ Did you choose the job for some specific, practical reason (it pays the bills), but it's not emotionally rewarding?

_____ Do you stay at the job because the people provide happy social times, yet the work itself, or the commute, the boss or others in the office is _blah_?

_____ Did you choose the work for the wrong reason but get some moderate satisfaction?

_____ Have you tried to make your job more interesting, but found it doesn't work?

_____ Does the work provide you with moderate to low meaning?

_____ Do you have some autonomy but not as much as you'd like?

_____ Is there some flexibility and control, but not as much as you'd like?

_____ Does the income sustain you?

_____ Once in a while, do you get a decent or exciting project?

_____ Is one aspect of the job very satisfying but another _blah_, or worse?

_____ Is your philosophy: Developing skills and the right attitude, will help you find a job, but work is still just a job to pay the bills?

Conditions Likely to Contribute to Craft

__➤ Enough income to save for fun things

➤ Using skills of some complexity

- ➤ Variety and challenge in the work

- ➤ Employees are generally treated with courtesy

- ➤ Responsibilities, a level of trust, and more freedom than in institutional, low-income Drudgery jobs

- ➤ Great job, lousy boss

- ➤ Great boss and coworkers, boring job

- ➤ Interesting job, lukewarm people environment, and long commute

And to Slip from Craft to Drudgery

Finding your job changing from Craft to Drudgery is very upsetting. Here are a few things you can watch for to be sure you're monitoring your situation carefully.

- ➤ The more you enjoy strong intellectual stimulation, the less likely a low level entry job will keep you interested

- ➤ The constant need for intense "spiking" passions that fizzle out in a couple of years. It's important to understand the duration of your passions

- ➤ The need for a different topic but with some type of challenge. For example, an editor edits many books and he or she might well enjoy the editing process. But his or her interest might wane if the topic is always the same. Thus, a change in topic might help.

- ➤ A high-low mixture; a part of the work is Calling and another part is Drudgery, creating Craft.

Craft Island

This time we'll journey to an imaginary island quite different from the "Drudgery Island" in Chapter 2. It is filled with towns, marketplaces, playgrounds, trails, and farmlands. Everyone is learning and growing new skills and abilities. You can observe a hustle and bustle among the denizens. Large kettles of soup and baking bread emit inviting odors. Dickens's *Great Expec-*

tations or Covey's *The Seven Habits of Highly Effective People* are read and studied religiously. Everyone is full of big plans and projects. Sports teams have a waiting list of hopefuls; schools and universities are filled with eager learners of all ages. The newest guru of some fandangled management theory always talks to a full audience. The towns are pleasant and the people seem healthy and busy.

The people on Craft Island have an entirely different attitude about work and life from those on Drudgery Island. You can sense some "Dilbert-think" still present, but not with the pervasiveness of Drudgery. That's because the people in Craft realize that self-confidence is the key: No one can motivate you but you yourself. You're the one who has to make an effort to succeed. If you don't like the work, get out.

This is the land of the achievers and doers. Always productive, they're eager to try out new things and master new skills. Yet while there is a generally positive feeling about work, it is still *just a job*. Nevertheless, you can perceive lots of learning, growing, and challenge on Craft Island. It's not a bad place to stay, by any means.

What Is Craft?

The above allegory is what the world looks like when people, freed from Drudgery, are in Craft. Clearly, a lot of creativity is released. Admittedly, this is an overly admiring vision of Craft, based as it is on a contrast to Drudgery Island.

Here's another: Imagine, if you will, that someone puts a plate of sandwiches in front of you. The bread, hot out of the oven, smells aromatically enticing. But the filling is of wilted lettuce and stale meat. This is Craft too.

In fact, Craft is a *hybrid* of Drudgery and Calling. The more I learn about Craft, the more it reminds me of Dante's Purgatory, right smack in the middle between Heaven and Hell. Never too hot nor too cold, it lacks both the vast passion of Calling or the acute pain and suffering of Drudgery. Millions do very well here, and HSPs will also do fine in Craft, but we will not be soul-satisfied here, and we're still at risk for a slide down into Hell.

Intuitively, I'm sure each of you can spot Drudgery, Craft, and Calling in your work. And I'm certain you could list all the Craft jobs you've had, even those with aspects of Drudgery and Calling in them. While your intuition is undoubtedly right, do you understand why this work and these jobs are Craft?

Part of the challenge in this chapter is to helping you fine-tune your ability to spot the finer points of Craft. Growing as a person means recognizing what isn't working for you and moving toward what does. In talking with HSPs, I've found that our intuitive sense of each of these places is quite good, but our ability to know *why* we're in Craft is harder for us to sort out. This could be because our society blurs Craft. It seems tepid in contrast to the melodrama of Drudgery or the magical bliss of Calling. We see the Calling in our work and we're encouraged to do Calling, but knowing why something isn't really Calling—and, more likely, is Craft—is not always clear.

The Smorgasbord

Because Craft is a smorgasbord of bits and pieces from both Drudgery and Calling, like the meal that looks good but is unsatisfying, this chapter is a perfect juncture to discuss the interactive dynamics between these two. And like cooking a stew, knowing your ingredients makes a lot of difference in how the soup will eventually taste.

Often, a job has elements of all three—Drudgery, Craft, and Calling—frequently with one dominating. Arthur, a self-employed attorney quoted at the beginning of the chapter, is a person whose profession is his Craft and whose hobby is his Calling. The work pays the bills, and he has complete control over what he does and how much he does. There are challenges to the job, and his skills allow him to work efficiently. His real Calling is in his life-long hobby, exploring how to create a better society.

The challenge in juggling all three in your work is knowing why this is happening. So often the work changes, downward, sometimes slowly, sometimes quickly, but down it will go. And the frustration is in not understanding what the heck happened. Why did a decent, if not exciting, job not work out? Why couldn't it get better? Where there are several Drudgery and Calling elements together in one job, it's often hard to understand the dynamics. You'll encounter a lot of information about Calling, before we even get to that chapter, and rightly so, in the following brief history of how Drudgery, Craft, and Calling have evolved over time.

History of Drudgery, Craft, and Calling

Drudgery Gives Way to Craft

Let's begin way back to Neanderthal times, to humanity's early history, when Drudgery was the most common condition of life. Life was hard, unpleasant, and work was a means of survival. As human intelligence sharpened, work began to be more than just mere survival, as building cities, cultivating farmlands, and creating written language and rich cultures flexed intellectual muscle and the need for specialized hand- and eye-coordinated skills. Drudgery continued to exist, mentally, emotionally, and physically, but was destined to be replaced by Craft. In Western Civilization, the sense of Craft pride blossomed on a large scale out of self-employed artisans and bourgeoisie. They, in turn, "crafted" social change, foreshadowing modern democratic societies. This growing segment of the population was proud to be self-reliant, original in its endeavors, and free to create its own lifestyle. But at the same time, much of the populace was still bound to a hand-to-mouth existence, if not to outright servitude.[1]

Craft today still reflects that quality of independence and pride in how a job is done. And the "Dilbert-think" that is so sharply accented in modern Drudgery is softer in Craft, as the individual begins to experience his or her own self as an independent being with skill and abilities.

Emotionally, Drudgery does not meet the needs of the head or heart. Craft is the place where both become involved and enlivened by work, though they're still not fully engaged. That changes when you're doing your "bliss"—your Calling. At the same time, a major *emotional* difference that separates Craft and Calling from Drudgery is that both require higher levels of personal empowerment, self-confidence, and happiness.

Remember our cane cutters and fishermen from Chapter 2? The cane cutters were in Drudgery. The fishermen were more self-actualized and in either Craft or Calling. They were creative, enjoying new things, willing to be venturesome and experiment with life.[2] To be in Craft, we need to be free of any large "chunks" of Drudgery in our work. We will always have to keep growing if we want to stay out of Drudgery. And our true work will grow toward us.

It may be that we'll always have some Craft in our lives, personally, physically, or professionally. It's a never-ending journey, and a rewarding one, because we will always find something wonderful about ourselves to learn. So when we leave Drudgery behind, and we begin to build good boundaries for ourselves, we start to enter Craft. Our respect for ourselves, which also involves liking ourselves and others, increases. Likewise, there's a progression beyond Craft to Calling—the more intellectual challenge and emotional satisfaction our work gives us, the closer we get to being in Calling.

Craft Think

For millions of people who work in modern countries, Craft would best describe where they are. We're prepped for it from childhood and encouraged to think about getting a *practical job* "that you like, of course" and that will provide an income and a livelihood. The work ethic could be the motto for Craft, and so any job, no matter how low or how high, can be ennobled with work ethic values. Craft work, by its nature, is a place to learn new skills so it will stimulate you, provide reasonable challenges, and, hopefully, provide a decent income.

In our modern society, Craft is all around us. It is reflected in the businesslike, work ethic attitudes we're expected to cultivate. In the management section of bookstores, you'll see many books on honing your "craft," your career, salesmanship, even the craft of managing multiple careers in this new age of job transitions, globalization, and outsourcing of work. A lot of the Craft quality is "how to" and practical, with an upbeat attitude. Think of a workroom where a craftsman has his tools, benches, and wares. It's his skills and products people want.

From Craft to Calling

Because the distinctions between Craft and Calling are not as great as they are in comparison to Drudgery, it's easy to mistake one for the other. So what *is* the difference? Arthur, the attorney quoted in the beginning of this chapter talks about this. As I've pointed out in the Drudgery chapter, for HSPs, the highest risk factor of your work that can quickly turn Craft into Drudgery are people issues. The risk is that while a supportive few may bolster you in an unhappy job, the Drudgery elements, whatever they may be for you, keep chipping away at your psyche, creating tension and stress.

Loving your job is one of the signs of being in Calling. In Drudgery, neither the head nor the heart is involved in the work. With a Calling, both head and heart are committed to the work you do. Craft is in between. In Studs Terkel's book *Working*, this person is in Craft:

A lot of people, it's drudgery to go to work. Not me. I don't say I love work, I don't say I hate work. It's a normal thing for me than just not doing anything. I figure I'm kinda needed.[3]

These are typical Craft attitudes.

"I could walk away from it and never look back."

"Intellectually stimulating but emotionally draining because of all the people issues."

"The work is only mildly bearable, but the people are why I go back every day."

Compare these statements to anyone in a Calling, who says, "I adore what I do," and, "I love my work." Calling engages so much more of yourself, your talents, passions, and enthusiasm. Consider the words of Kahlil Gibran in *The Prophet*[4] when he says, "Work is love made visible," and you will know what a Calling is. You can hear Calling when someone says, "I have fun, I love my job."

Drudgery, Craft, and Calling Within Business

Do you work in a company that is Drudgery, Craft, or Calling oriented? If you were in Calling, and you worked in a Drudgery company, how would you be perceived? Remember that Callings fuel the individual. Our composite picture of a person with a Calling is someone charged up and motivated. No one has to prod him; he is the natural "self-starter" that companies crave. And the self-starter—as long as he's in a Calling—has a deep well of energy all around him, in other people, to encourage and sustain him. Those "called" seem magnetic because they're happy and charged up, and seem fresh, vital, alive, and healthy. It's a nice package. There's a little extra sparkle with a Calling, and a willingness to go the distance to make change possible.

I'm sure you can recall one of those fantasy movies where two people trade bodies and find out what it's like to live and work in the other person's life. In the same manner, I'd like you to join me in a little fantasy. Fairy tales can be used to sharpen distinctions and make the vague crisper to the eye.

Suppose one of our Calling Island residents decided to go to Drudgery Island for a visit and to work awhile. Imagine the people on Drudgery Island, with their Dilbert-think, their balls and chains, sour attitudes and snipping, and me-versus-them approach to management. In comes this happy, pleasant, energized person who smiles as she works, pays attention to details, and says how she thinks and feels. She's friendly and helpful but doesn't let others encroach on her boundaries. Sometimes she comes in early and willingly works late to get an order finished on time. What do you think the denizens of Drudgery are going to suspect? Will they think she's for real or some spy sent by senior management? Will they welcome her with open arms, as a long-lost buddy, or wonder if she's loosing her marbles?

Okay, switch gears and pretend that by some happenstance a Drudgery Island person wakes up and finds himself on Calling Island. He's got the same job he had before, and gets up, moaning and groaning, about another day at work. He's muttering and complaining while driving in, arrives at the office to find things are a bit off. He gets defensive when someone suggests changes to his department, and he's certain that another manager wants his job. He criticizes the work of those who report directly to him but offers little help in how to do a better job. Later in the day, he gets angry (for no apparent reason at all) and yells at his secretary. How do you think his coworkers will take this? Will they ignore his behavior or make comments? Will they think he's overworked and underpaid?

The point of these two scenarios is that:

➤ Moods, attitudes, and values are reflective of what "island" you're on.

➤ Change has to take place in you in order to get to the next place. And change takes time. You can't just leap from Drudgery straight to Calling. Wanting a Calling and being in a Calling are not the same thing.

➤ A company can have a Drudgery, Craft, or Calling "mood," and if you're not in the same space, you'll stand out.

➤ If they want someone with Calling energy and you take the job just to get a job and don't like it (but said you were crazy about it in your interview), it will be apparent that you don't fit in; you can't fake Calling. You may be a wet blanket, a damper on the enthusiasm of others around you. You won't be able to sustain the highs the company wants of their employees. And if you started out loving the job and find yourself in Drudgery two years later, you won't be able to completely hide your changed emotions.

Everyone is in predominately one of the three modes: Drudgery, Craft, or Calling. We often fear (and rightly so) that we don't fit in. Of course we may not, if we're there because this is just a job, or worse, Drudgery. You won't be fooling anyone, *can you be honest with yourself about that?* When this feeling of being out of place happens, we need to think about leaving. Since HSPs stay in Drudgery too long, the sooner we get out, the better, for our own health's sake as well as for the benefit we gain by being in an environment where our mood matches everyone else's. When we're in the right place, a place where we can be more in sync, we'll be more productive than if we were in the wrong place.

The Work Ethic

The work ethic, not unlike the "Puritan ethic," is a deep part of the American psyche. It says that work is good for you and builds character, even if the work is difficult and hard—perhaps particularly if it is. You learn responsibility, duty, and conscientiousness, and you also learn how to take work seriously, develop a sense of community, and become more self-disciplined, especially in the face of hardship and struggle. Struggle is seen as an opportunity to elevate oneself and humanity, refining oneself and others out of selfishness into selflessness. So, according to the work ethic, work has an ennobling role in society. Therefore it's good.

So, you might ask, what is the relationship of the work ethic to our three modes of work: Drudgery, Craft, and Calling?

The work ethic emerges very strongly in Craft, for instance, as something that should be inside you, internalized and accepted as part of who you are. And there are some important societal assumptions about Drudgery jobs (low-income, menial, and entry level positions), or where the boss is in Drudgery and treats the job and others in a Drudgery way.

One of these assumptions, on the part of companies, is that people in these jobs do not have a work ethic—it has to be *imposed* on them. The thinking undoubtedly is: No one would want to do this type of work, so we have to make them, and therefore help them become better people. Another belief is that either you've got the work ethic or you don't. While a job can build your character and help you advance if you've got the ethic latent within you, none of this will help if you haven't an ounce of work ethic in your nature.

When you're in Drudgery, work feels like a cage, trapping you inside in order to get the most out of the day. In Calling, there are no cages, but the work is so much a part of your identity, it's almost indistinguishable from you the person, and you need to constantly uphold your own boundaries so that you do not become lost within the work.

For example; in Drudgery, you're given time cards to punch; how long you go for breaks and lunch is monitored; and there are chits to remind you if you're late or appear to have a cavalier attitude about your job. In comparison, in Craft the boss or company will be more subtle about saying, "Be on time, do a good job, put the job first above other priorities," but you will be reminded. And when you finally reach a Calling, where you, the job, and the work ethic are assumed to fuse into one seamless whole, there is no need to discipline and shape you into a mold. Remember, Drudgery is quantitative work, but a Calling is qualitative.

For a conscientious HSP who has internalized the work ethic and finds himself in a Drudgery job, there's the agony of both *feeling* and *trying* to be loyal, conscientious, and dutiful with a job that is making you miserable. Others around you in this same Drudgery job who don't have a work ethic seem to shake off the stress of the job better than you. That's because they're only daily visitors to this prison, while you, because you've internalized the work ethic, find yourself carrying your prison around inside of you! *The loyalty you feel, the conscientiousness, perfectionism, and idealism that's so naturally a part of your temperament, is now anchored to a job that is not nurturing your spirit.* There's a lot to be said for doing a Drudgery job and not having a work ethic. It makes for less angst.

I Work Hard, But I Don't Do Hard Work

Let's clear up the fuzzy communications surrounding the emotional meaning of working hard. There are two ways to work: the Drudgery way, and the Craft or Calling way.

> **I'll be doing a project and look up and it's nearly midnight. I work hard, I work long hours, you bet your life I do, but I don't do hard work. —Anonymous HSP**

Hard work only makes sense when it has a purpose that means something to you. That meaning puts it into a context of your own values. Have you noticed that once you enter Craft, work is not as hard? You may struggle, but the *emotional pain* is less. This is because, by definition, Craft gives more freedom of control to the worker. It may not be as much freedom as in Calling, but it's enough to diminish Drudgery.

Choice allows us to prepare ourselves mentally and emotionally for the work at hand. We can then assess if it fits within our abilities and has enough interest to make the experience worthwhile. When you have no choice in doing hard work, there's an emotional struggle going on inside of you and that exponentially increases the trauma.

As you explore the difference in yourself between Drudgery, Craft, and Calling, the magnitude of difficulty will help you discern the presence or absence of Drudgery in your work. You can work hard in a Calling, but it doesn't feel harsh. What happens is flow, because now you have more choice, and thus the challenges are interesting.[5]

Drudgery	Craft/Calling
Repetitive	Absorbing
Tedious	Stimulating
No choice	Choice
I hate it	I like (love) it
Detesting	Fun

In Drudgery, hard work is assigned to you; you don't have a choice. It's not pleasant at all; it's tedious, difficult, and uninteresting. In Craft or Calling, hard work is absorbing, even fun. We get lost in thinking, exploring, looking forward to the next step of the process. We want to do it and are free to do it as we wish, and we may have to be dragged away in order to get us to stop. We can be digging ditches or doing our taxes. The task is not important. What's important is whether we have a choice, our comfort with the task, and the level of difficulty it presents.

There's the chance, of course, that someone in Calling takes on a new challenge that would seem to be exciting and steep, only to find Drudgery emerging out of the experience. This can be very confusing. What went wrong? Thinking back to the stress management chapter, when we know ourselves and monitor our internal states, we do not find ourselves head over heels in Drudgery down the road.

While you have more control, challenge, and/or variety than you did in Drudgery, you're still not as free in Craft as in a Calling. Peter Drucker, writing about the modern "knowledge worker," describes the person in Craft and what happens when he's not allowed to perform his Craft, and his attendant plunge into Drudgery:

The knowledge worker cannot be supervised too closely or in detail. He can only be helped. But he must direct himself, and he must direct himself toward performance and contribution, that is, toward effectiveness.... The motivation of the knowledge worker depends on his being effective, on his being able to achieve. If effectiveness is lacking in his work, his commitment will soon wither, and he will become a time-server going through the motions from 9 to 5.[6]

Can a Drudgery Job Be Salvaged?

There's one final note about the interactive dynamics between these three work experiences.

For the highly sensitive person, Craft becomes a potential gateway into Drudgery. This is because it's very hard to take an existing Drudgery or

Craft job and transform it into Craft or Calling, since the meaning, control, or challenge may be too low to correct.

The two strongest factors that make a job Drudgery for HSPs are people and the tasks we do. If we're having people problems, we obviously don't have the social skills to get us out (or we wouldn't be here to begin with). With the tasks, HSPs can often focus on improving the job, finding new or different things to do, and so on.

But HSPs will try. I can recall a Drudgery job, for example, that bored me, but because of the work ethic, I wanted to transform the job into Craft. So I tried to do things with my tasks to make them more interesting. I was trying to change an existing *task* without any changes in the circumstances. For a few days my imagination could seek improvements. But the enhancements could not overcome the presence of Drudgery in other forms. I was not addressing why I was there; the job had no meaning for me and I was not taking care of myself the way I should.

The moral here is that you'll have a very difficult challenge to leverage a bad job out of Drudgery and into Craft, or Craft into Calling, without a major change in the psychic income you need.

Teasers of Calling in Craft

One of the things you should come away with from this chapter are the "teasers" in your Craft work that point to a Calling. There are three common teasers: curiosity, talent versus passion, and theme. Let's look into them.

Curiosity Killed the Cat, Satisfaction Brought It Back

We HSPs are quite curious. We respond to even a little curiosity and will check it out. This can be risky. If you read the introduction to this book, you know that right after finishing my Ph.D., I took a month-long job delivering fast food in a T-shirt three sizes too big for me. And I hated it. I was *curious* about what an entry level, straight-off-the-street, we'll-take-whomever-comes-through-the-door job would look like. I discovered I didn't like it. I knew it would be a temporary job, but I was surprised at how immediately the Drudgery affected me. I did it because, on an impulse, I followed my curiosity.

We have to keep in mind that what really satisfies us (and keeps the cat alive and purring) is not curiosity, but interests that match not only our abilities, but have meaning as well. It's not bad to explore and be curious. Just be aware that there may be Drudgery too—a nice painful-size chunk of it. If we're willing to go in, learn something—for example, I now know what entry jobs are like for teenagers—and once you've found the lesson, get out, then the experience will have served a purpose. And we learn every day. Even writing this section has given me a closure on my fast food experience. I now see that it served its little purpose in the scheme of things, let it go, and move on. So I can't say it was wasted.

Talent Versus Passion

As I mentioned above, it's not curiosity that keeps us satisfied, but the interests that match our abilities and have meaning. But how do we know when a talent fits the bill?

Craft is a great time for us, when we're mixing and matching values and talents to experiences and coming up with all sorts of crazy looking experiences. Because we HSPs have a dislike of making mistakes, we need to see these events as *learning experiences* and allow ourselves time to evolve. Talent can be with us all our life; if we could draw as a child of 10, we can probably draw when we're 50, even if we never picked up a crayon during that 40-year gap. But interests come and go, and change as we grow. Interests are like symphonies: They can flow from crescendos to staccatos and even fade away. So picking a job based on an interest, let alone a career, means paying close attention to how we use and experience both our talents and passions.

> I don't know how much aptitude drives interest or interest drives aptitude; I try to look at my past history, my work history. Jobs where I've really had interest and I've also maybe had an aptitude, I've done very well. If the interest wasn't there but I had the aptitude, it still maybe wasn't a good fit. And if I didn't have the interest or the aptitude, it was a disaster. —Max, workman's compensation specialist

HSPs are often multitalented, and our different potentials rise to the surface at various times in our lives. Sometimes a smorgasbord of talents are obvious early in life; other times they unfold gradually as we mature. If you took assessment tests, the results would indicate that HSPs could do a number of things. But the riddle for the HSP is how to tell the difference between a talent and a passion, if we're constantly evolving and growing. To tackle this riddle, it's important to bring in a third ingredient: values. As Dr. Barbara Kerr put it:

Traditional career counseling techniques which emphasize matching clients' abilities and interests with job characteristics may be of little use to the young gifted adult. Instead, an approach based on identifying the most deeply held values, and planning life goals which actualize those values, may be the treatment of choice. Career development then becomes the search for meaning rather than the search for a job.[7]

We're often original, complex, and talented, and can handle blending several different talents together in unconventional ways. But you may have to go out on your own to do this, since finding a job where you can apply several skills may require considerable patience in the search, and strong social skills to cultivate a situation to your liking. Craft and self-employment (also known as "self-reliance") are closely linked.

For the HSP, the work ethic will require you to walk a delicate line. True motivation to do a job comes from within; we all know that. What we miss is determining what motivates us. In our society, we're encouraged to follow our interests, our dreams. But for multitalented HSPs, there will be many interests, small and large. And having an interest doesn't mean you're going to want to do it.

The thrill of a new idea—a form of sensation seeking for the intellectual—is just that, a sensation, a high. I have a lot of interests, and I love learning all about them, but over time, I've become aware that if I'm halfhearted to resistant to doing them, then this is not a job for me.

And so we're fooled by the constant societal encouragement for us to follow our interests. Remember that we are enrolled when *all* of ourselves are interested, not just one (mind, emotions, values) part. Some people can just go in, punch the clock, do the job, and go home, but HSPs do not do things partially well. We can't leave parts of ourselves at home—we're a package deal: heart, mind, imagination, creativity. The other part of the wonder that can become a frustration, especially for middle-age HSPs, is that our talents don't stop emerging. We're still discovering ourselves and wondering what to do about it.

The Theme Behind the Work

Themes are usually big and broad topics. Health, history, nature, the arts, music, medieval studies, etc. When you have a theme that stays with you a long time in your life it could be the "background music" for your work, while you explore various jobs. The problem for some, is choosing. Catherine has one dominate theme, and there are just too many exciting things to do and she can't do them all at once, which she'd love to do. Others, have more than one passionate theme and find themselves torn this way and that.

However, a theme can be one of the easier ways to work toward your Calling. As long as your fundamental values and interests are the goals of the job, you can still keep circling around the theme, testing out new paths to see where you can go next.

Dissecting a Craft Job

Because Craft is in the middle, I often find that it takes more work for someone to notice what her Calling and Drudgery qualities are. Often, for example, people mistake Craft for Calling.

As mentioned previously, we're comfortable in Craft, but it's still "just a job" and we aren't really crazy about it. This is because while Craft captures either one's mind or heart, it doesn't get both. Drudgery has neither our heart nor our interest. And a Calling commands both heart and mind.

If you recall, at the end of the chapter on Drudgery there were three things I mentioned that have a lot of influence on whether we're in Drudgery, Craft, or Calling:

➤ Control over what, when, were, and how we do our work

➤ Work that means something to us

➤ Challenges that we like

The less you have of these three, the deeper you are in Drudgery. The more you have of all three, the deeper you are in Calling. So if you've got a mixed bag, you're right in the middle: Craft.

To reiterate, it's not just what you do that's important, but the value it has for you. We need meaning, we need control, and we need challenges.

Take a look at Figure 5-1. This is what Craft might look like: The glasses are half full, right in the middle between nearly empty Drudgery and brimming over Calling.

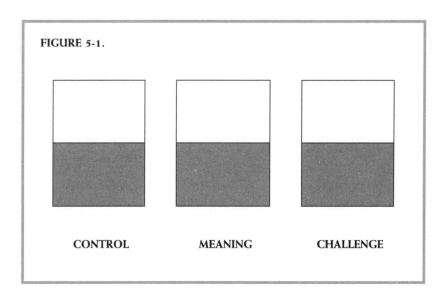

FIGURE 5-1.

CONTROL   MEANING   CHALLENGE

Drudgery Emotions in the Craft Stew

Listen carefully to what people say, and evaluate the words they use to determine which of the three working categories they're in. Words that express dread, apathy, fear, anxiety, worry, frustration, hard work, burnout, and helplessness, are telltale signs of Drudgery.

Marki is currently a webmaster. She's been in a wide variety of jobs, from clerical to classified ad selling. She loves trees, birds, and Jungian psychology. Marki explains what was different about these jobs that made them Drudgery, Craft, or Calling for her. I've italicized certain words to lend them emphasis. We'll look at two jobs she had.

Marki's Classified Ad Job: Drudgery

The classified ad job was *difficult* because of the cold calling ... *I hated cold calling.... It's like you don't really want to go to work in the morning* and you're sitting there saying, *"Oh no, not another phone call." Nothing gets completed* because you always have to stop in midstream. All these details hopping around that you just really *don't have much control over* because *it's not your decision.* Even though I got to design a book cover and some of those really creative things I enjoy doing, *the clerical part was hard.* We were supposed to file everything we did immediately. I'd be on my way to the file cabinet and somebody would stop to talk to me and I'd forget what I was doing. They told me if I didn't improve or get more organized, I wouldn't get a raise. So I left. *I knew I would never be able* to get to the file cabinet without being interrupted.

Notice how the language is very much Drudgery. There is one moment where she gets to do something she enjoys, but the company doesn't find that crucial to her job, which to them was the clerical office work and cold calling.

Marki's Drudgery Language

I hated cold calling.

It's like you don't really want to go to work in the morning ...

Oh no, not another phone call.

Nothing gets completed ...

... don't have much control ... it's not your decision.

... the clerical part was hard.

I knew I would never be able...

In this Drudgery job, did you notice Marki's intense dread and dislike of cold calling, and the lack of closure with each project that creates so much frustration in her? Notice how these unpleasant characteristics of her job seem pervasive in her work. This work doesn't sound very meaningful, does it? She's challenged, but not in a way that is rewarding.

Remember, we need control, meaning, and challenge. So how much control does Marki have over her work? Some of the most important tasks (as far as the company was concerned) were those she knew she'd never get done the way they'd like. And she didn't like the work she was doing. In addition she found the challenges unpleasant and hard. It doesn't matter that these challenges were clerical, for Marki (note this folks) they were *hard work*. What she enjoyed doing was obviously not her boss's idea of what was important. *And her boss doesn't think she's working hard enough at her job*, because he gave her a warning.

Given our three glasses, with Drudgery having the least amount of water and Calling the most, where would you put her? The "glasses" in Figure 5-2 graphically illustrate that she has very little control, barely any meaning, and not much of the right kind of challenge.

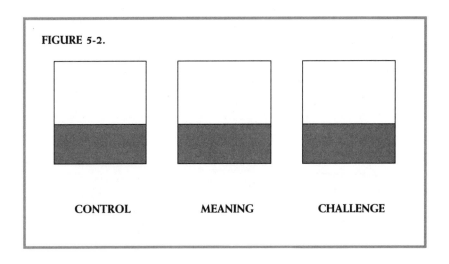

FIGURE 5-2.

CONTROL   MEANING   CHALLENGE

Marki's Textbook Publishing: Craft

I could contribute my ideas to the bosses. *I did have some control.* The textbook publishing job, *I really didn't have a lot of control.* That was *very frustrating.... These kinds of things were really important* although *I wouldn't call it a calling.* It would still be craft, *but the job was not too bad.*

I'm doing what I was trained to do and what I *enjoy doing,* but the *subject matter is pretty dry; I wasn't passionate about it. It didn't excite me,* and *the politics was very hard.* When I was doing desktop publishing, it was drastically important to me to have a pharmaceutical textbook be right, but [the topic] was not a calling for me. It might be for a pharmacist.

Notice how different this job is for Marki. She has a mixture of things she enjoys (Calling energy) with activities that are not as appealing (Drudgery energy). I've made two lists, so you can see how many references there are to qualities that are Calling, versus Drudgery, and results in that wonderfully aromatic bread with stale meat and wilted lettuce. These are the situations that can fool us. How many times will we stay longer because the bread smelled so good, and we forgot about how stale the meat and lettuce were?

Calling Language

I could contribute my ideas ... (*This means something to her.*)

I did have some control. (*Ah ha! Control is important here.*)

These kinds of things were really important ... (*She needs meaning.*)

I'm doing what I enjoy doing. (*Something fun.*)

Drudgery Language

... but the subject matter is pretty dry. (*The fun is not in the topic.*)

... I wasn't passionate about it. (*It's not something she loves.*)

It didn't excite me. (*She says it again.*)

... the politics was very hard. (*Oops, people problems.*)

For this job, the glasses have much more in them (see Figure 5-3).

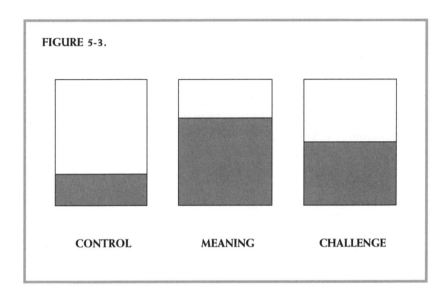

FIGURE 5-3.

CONTROL   MEANING   CHALLENGE

These can fluctuate from day to day, but over time you can see a pattern. Sometimes there's more meaning but not much control. Other times, the work is meaningless and boring, but there's the freedom to do it the way Marki wants and when she wants. There's more than just Drudgery. There are some elements of Calling, but not enough to bring Marki into Calling all the time. So she's in Craft.

Why do HSPs find Craft jobs turning into Drudgery? You can see it happening here. Curiosity is a Calling energy, and if it's too mild, it won't take you very far. This is why two people at the same job might have very different feelings about the work. The person with a strong passion for the work will be sustained by a strong inner fire. The little fire in the individual with mild curiosity will eventually die out. Marki gives a clue here:

I had a *curiosity* about other businesses and who they were.... It was *interesting* just to be around newspaper people. *I like newspaper people, they're a kick.* It was a different environment than what I was used to, it was fun to be able to write ads ... *I always went in just a little curious about what the company does, but the problem is, it wasn't interesting enough to hold me.* Pretty soon the company wasn't that interesting and all this drudgery work was *drowning me.*

As I mentioned earlier, curiosity is good for experimenting and testing out where you might go and what might work for you. But in itself, mild curiosity is not a sustaining energy. Marki is also a high sensation seeker, and so many things will be of interest to her. Curiosity will give you adventures, but it won't support a Calling.

Craft and Calling: Different Needs

Now that we have a sense of what makes Drudgery and Craft different, let's tease out Calling from Craft by focusing on some people who are exploring the difference between the two—Julie and June.

Julie runs a family business, and her work is mostly Craft with some Calling. Her dilemma is what she needs to feel satisfied with herself and her work. June is by day a technical writer and by night a freelance writer. She's spent enough time with her freelance work to know how differently she feels in Craft versus Calling.

The Family Business

Julie is a third-generation manager of a family retail business selling pet supplies. In addition to her love of animals and nature, she's also interested in Reiki and tai chi and would love to explore those more deeply. There are lots of challenges in the job, with a constant need to fine-tune the products and services as the market changes. It was Julie who shifted the business's focus to keep it competitive.

For her, this business is alive, like a living being, but the challenges in terms of family and business boundaries cause her stress, confusion, and wonderment. While she loves her work, she has a hard time balancing her work and personal life. Her family is still involved in the decisions, so the business is not fully hers to control.

At the same time, Julie wonders what it would be like to go into an entirely different area and leave retail behind. She has lots of control and challenges in her work, but her "meaning glass" is confusing. She's devoted much of her life to preserving and cultivating a heritage that serves something important to her, yet is still seeking what is meaningful for herself. In the end, of course, the meaning must be *your* meaning, not someone else's.

My father is looking at retiring soon, and I'm looking at possibly buying the business. And I'm trying to establish what would be ideal for me given my temperament. I deal with so many sales people and customers and telemarketers and the people I supervise or work with, that's a lot of contact with a lot of people. My home life, a lot of times, suffers. I'd like to have more balance between my work life and my home life as far as having people in it. I've been finding in the last year or so I've been doing more things in my personal life, but now I'm having more problems in my work life dealing with everything that's going on. It's like my brain short circuits. It's too much.

....So as for who am I? I'm somebody who wants to do something positive in the world. That's why I'm focused on energy healing, tai chi. Something that's going to be healthy and helpful to me, but also hopefully helpful to other people. That's a big focus for me. That's part of the reason I created the wild bird pet supply business, because I could help pets in the human/animal bond. The pet industry has changed so much in recent years that some of the joy of that has left the industry.

Deep Meaning for Calling

June has a Craft day job as a technical writer, and in her spare time does her Calling as a freelance writer. When she's in her Calling, her work is so absorbing and fun that she doesn't mind the solitude. But when doing Craft work, June needs to be around people; it keeps her buoyed. Her Calling feeds her so well that her needs are entirely different when she switches to Craft. Here's her description of what she feels about what she does (emphasis added):

I don't know exactly what this means, but when I'm writing, even if it's for two to three days straight and I haven't been around people very much, I don't even notice it or miss it or crave it. And I think because of how full I feel from my writing and what I get out of it—because I never feel lonely—rarely do I feel lonely, I should say. *I guess so many of my basic needs are being met with my writing* that I can go for days and not feel like I really

need all that much contact with other people. Part of what makes work work for me are the people! If I was totally alone having to do that work, I don't think I could survive. They keep wanting me to telecommute and do work, and I keep resisting.... One of the things I get out of work is the interaction I have with other people, because at some level that makes work tolerable ... *because the work doesn't [fill me], it's the interaction with other people....* **So just being around other people, being around their emotions, helps to fill that need in me so I don't feel empty.**

Julie's energy is draining and she doesn't know who she is. Her work invokes powerful, Calling energies, but she's not growing. June, also in a full-time Craft job, knows what her Calling is and gives it a place in her life. She is sustained emotionally and is growing, in different ways, by both jobs. Now, given all you know so far, what do you think is going to happen to these two ladies?

Why HSPs Get into Craft

Craft is a mixed bag blending bits and pieces of Drudgery and Calling, and the ability to maintain this state is dependent on how long the Calling qualities remain strong enough to resist the downward pull of Drudgery. Remember, the heart or the head is involved in Craft, but not both to the same degree.

And then there's the "lure of the new," which we encountered in the chapter on Drudgery, when HSPs are drawn to new things and find them exciting. Recall, in this chapter, Marki's situation: The novelty of a new job drew her in; and Julie, for whom the novelty of running the business her way provided interesting and demanding challenges and stimulation for her mind but no personal deep passion. But novelty alone will not satisfy most HSPs, and it's something we need to watch carefully about ourselves. HSPs need more than a lukewarm mental curiosity. We need our heart, imagination, creativity, and values to be fully engaged, because we are intense and creative beings.

Another occasion we HSPs find ourselves in Craft is when we take jobs for which we're overqualified—sometimes in a job that is institutionalized

Drudgery, as part of an attempt to reduce the intense stimulation in our lives. This is the "simple path" discussed in the Drudgery chapter, where low level jobs are thought to be less demanding havens from the highly pressured workplace. But the job's Craft nature is an illusion that is swiftly shattered.

Still another way a job becomes Craft for the HSP is when it starts out as Calling and, due to changes at work, the conditions deteriorate toward Drudgery, pulling the HSP down, out of Calling and into Craft. Many of us will fight hard to stabilize in Craft, because of our instinctive work ethic nature and the need to retain some semblance of well-being.

Consider Henry, an HSP who loved his job of 20 years or so. He felt he was making a difference, and it suited his intellectual and creative temperament. But when a new manager came in and brought with him an abrasive and micromanaging style, Henry felt hurt, and demoralized, and the job plunged straight down. He's still trying to salvage that job and keep it going in Craft, and you'll hear more about him later, in Chapter 9, "Psychic Income."

This is not to say that Craft is always a transient condition. Many people, including HSPs like Julie, can stay in Craft a long time.

Invoking the Journeyman

Let's return briefly to history and the middle ages. During these centuries, the European landscape was under tremendous changes. New kinds of businesses and careers were emerging, the governance of human life was evolving toward the ideas of modern thinking, and the middle class, birthplace of considerable self-confidence, self-reliance, and self-employment, was being born.

The image of the journeyman of this period is a good symbol for Craft, being between the indentured servant (who was often in Drudgery) and the master (who, while not always loving what he did, did have the tremendous freedoms of a Calling).

The journeyman had a valued skill, and for a few years was free to work with masters while improving his craft. Journeymen traveled, changed jobs, and honed their skills. And once he'd undergone the obligatory years of training and apprenticeship, the journeyman could advance to master.[8]

As a modern journeyman, the HSP can participate in the workplace in a way an employee cannot. The business world is changing constantly, and HSPs need to consider how this affects them and how to make the most of the new circumstances. These changes will require the average worker, who desires greater control over his or her career, to learn how to leverage him- or herself in and out of new kinds of working relationships, such as traditional employment, freelancing, self-employment, and virtual businesses. But regardless of whether you're an employee or self-employed, as William Bridges says in his book *Job-Shift*,[9] you need to see your career as your business and think like a self-reliant self-employed person. This is one "job" you can have total control over, if you so choose.

Leaving Craft for Calling

The differences between Craft and Calling, to a person who is in either one, are obvious, but they are not always clear to an outsider. The island we will see in the last chapter is of incomparable beauty. That's what a Calling should feel like. And like leaving behind Drudgery, a leap of faith is necessary. The "jump" is not quite as painful as it was from Drudgery to Calling. And by the way, you cannot go from Drudgery straight to Calling. You need to build self-confidence and lots of other social skills, before you can tackle a Calling. If you've been in Calling before and stumble into Drudgery, then it's not so difficult to return to a Calling.

6

Being Visible as an HSP

He said, "Oh, you're just too sensitive!" And it wasn't true, he was being a jerk. "Oh. I guess I'll have to treat you with kid gloves now." I started crying, and he says, "Oh no, you're gonna cry," and I just looked at him and I let him have it! *I said, "I'm releasing emotion, and if you think your anger is not emotion, I don't know what you think it is because it is. You are emotional yourself." Anyway, that kind of finished the conversation and we got along better after that. He respected me for speaking up, but he made it hard for me.*

—CAROLYN, IT ADMINISTRATOR

We've come to an important juncture. We've left the debilitating life of Drudgery behind and entered the world of Craft, where we're more confident and self-assured about our abilities to be in charge of our lives. But as a Calling glows on the horizon, it's time to explore certain important HSP attributes we need to bring forward for the next steps.

When we do things we love, we are being our true selves. What we love is special and vitally important, and it's one of the things that is singularly *unique* and no one else can claim. A Calling also makes us unique, along with being happy, vital, and alive. When we find our Calling, we're more visible. And people who notice us want to interact with us.

Are you ready to be noticed? To be seen by others? Are you ready to speak your truth, like Carolyn, in the quote at the beginning of this chapter? How does the idea of being seen and interacting with others (including a number of new people, possibly authority figures along with those who might work with you) feel to you? In this chapter, we'll explore ways to prepare for greater visibility in a manner that is comfortable with the needs of HSPs.

An HSP Legacy

Henry David Thoreau was a highly sensitive person whose life and thoughts left an exquisitely poignant stamp on American history and culture. He was an introvert, more at ease alone in nature or with some close friends. And to many in his community, he was a failure at holding down a steady job. He dabbled here and there, teaching for a while, working at his family pencil business, surveying, and giving talks. And he lived meagerly and close to the land, so he could devote as much of his time to writing.

While he was well known for his part in the Transcendentalist movement, communicating wasn't always easy for Thoreau. He hated being misunderstood. But Thoreau had something to say about life, nature, people, society, and spirituality. And he found a way to do it: his way. He didn't push himself on society, and he didn't put himself out there a lot, but in his own way he was able to be visible to others.[1]

There are choices as HSPs that we can make to put ourselves out there, like Thoreau did. And you control how much you do about this. When you read about him, you see a man who cared deeply for nature, who was thoughtful, sensitive, passionate about justice and integrity—values that mean a lot to HSPs. Thoreau let some of his HSP nature shine through for others to see.

There are many ways you can communicate your sensitive nature to others without feeling too vulnerable, too open and exposed; to communicate, instead, in a way that feels safe and manageable. There are ways to do this that *enhance* your ability to connect with people at work, retain your privacy, and still feel safe. The goal of this chapter is how to give others *quality* information about us that can clear away confusion, doubts, and misunderstandings, and that cannot be done by hiding. We'll look into little ways of "doing a Thoreau" and letting others see us a little more clearly.

Do We Have to Give the Whole Enchilada?

So how do HSPs become more visible? Many think they have to explain the whole HSP "enchilada." That certainly shows all the ingredients of the

HSP temperament and how we "cook" at life. But in reality, spoon-feeding small morsels works a lot better. Giving someone the whole enchilada, although it imparts a lot of valuable information, it also can lead to "indigestion" in the form of resistance to what you're trying to say. Plus, it also only requires you to narrate what you know, not what you actually *need.* So, instead of the whole enchilada when it comes to explaining who we are, it would be better to keep it simple and take baby steps, for the benefit of others as well as ourselves.

Remember, other people are also overwhelmed at work. They're busy juggling several things at the same time; and yet, they still can say no or speak up and ask for things when something doesn't sit right with them. HSP or not, isn't this what you want? To be able to express your needs effectively and professionally? To get a softer lamp instead of fluorescents or to stay calm when someone yells at you over errors in a report?

The real challenge comes in saying what you think and feel from a place of peacefulness about yourself. That's powerful. *This is the heart of being visible.* The result is a change that lets you feel freer to be yourself. Carolyn, quoted at the beginning of the chapter, was certainly visible. Yes, she cried when overwhelmed. But she wasn't ashamed of it, and she didn't let someone else belittle her reaction. She held her ground and moved forward with a better working relationship. *Sometimes, that's all you have to do.*

Sharing a bit of ourselves with others, being authentic and real to them, is empowering.

Making Ourselves Visible

In order to be understood, we must be *visible.* And part of being visible includes communicating on one's own behalf. Often, I've heard HSPs debate the pros and cons of explaining ourselves to others and how to go about it. Do we divulge our strengths *and* weaknesses? If so, how much do we reveal? And how about what we need: A quiet workplace, no fluorescent lights, and so on?

In this chapter we'll focus on successfully asking for what you need, without feeling *ashamed* to do so. Being visible as an HSP at work means you're comfortable enough with yourself that you'll let others see you as you really are, so you can deal more effectively with people you encounter nearly every day. This is the best way for you to thrive in an ever-present, often invasive workplace that can cross boundary lines daily.

It's surprising just how much others discern about us, even when we think we're not "visible" to them. While we may need privacy and time away from others, there's tremendous value in being present too. As we let ourselves be present with others, we become more real to them. It's amazing how easy it is to fool ourselves and think that if we're invisible, others can't possibly see through our invisibility cloak. But they do. The problem is, they may misunderstand us (which is dismaying), or see to the heart of us (before we're ready for them to do it).

The Benefits of Quality Information

There are many benefits to letting others see a little more of you, or a lot more of you, depending on your comfort level. For one thing, being visible makes us feel good because we're meeting some of our needs by speaking up, and that alone lightens the burdens of Drudgery.

As we leave Drudgery and get ready to enter Craft, self-actualization begins. One striking difference between HSPs up and down the corporate food chain is the level of self-confidence those in Craft and Calling radiate compared to those in Drudgery. Sometimes the former also rush to the bathroom to have a good cry when overwhelmed, but they're generally comfortable being who they are, taking charge, giving their honest opinion, and holding their own with others. They have found the secret of what it means to be visible and present. Doing so regularly prevents a backlog of unmet needs from welling up and causing problems.

There is an unspoken struggle in our hesitation to ask for what we need. This is important; if we want to find our Calling and do work we truly love—and even ask for the kind of money we want—then we need to accustom ourselves to be relaxed and happy around people, in order for us to communicate our needs. We can't hide too much and also do our Calling, because by definition a Calling connects us to others and causes us to grow. We may be doing a lot of quiet time alone with our work, but there will also be connecting time. So, by definition, those who are doing work they love are also connecting in a positive way with others.

West Coast therapist Gary Linker, who works with highly sensitive people, says that many HSPs lack positive self-entitlement to express their needs. This is the belief that you and I both have rights, to be negotiated, understood, and appreciated. To hesitate to stand up for what you need because you fear it will infringe or bother another demonstrates a lack of positive self-entitlement. In contrast, to believe the world revolves around you is exaggerated self-entitlement.

To have positive self-entitlement means knowing you have a right to:

➤ Work in a reasonably comfortable emotional environment.

➤ Be treated in a respectful kind of way.

➤ Express your thoughts and feelings to the same extent that management allows all other employees to express them.

➤ Do your work in a environment that is not detrimentally disruptive and undermining.

➤ Communicate it with confidence.

When we doubt ourselves, we lack this positive self-entitlement. Then, for instance, you might feel:

➤ Like a *fraud*, because you don't fit in the corporate workplace.

➤ *Torn* between the discomfort of the office temperature or the discomfort felt in trying to do something about it.

➤ *Ashamed* that you cry or that you need much more than just a moment to yourself.

➤ You have to *avoid* saying something you *fear* will hurt another person's feelings.

➤ *Embarrassed* to tell your boss that you took on too much and now you're drowning in work.

➤ *Ashamed*, because you feel like a late bloomer, with no retirement plan, and a history of job hopping.

➤ *Guilty*, because you want to take lunchtime by yourself.

In fact, these are normal and acceptable feelings and needs we all have, but that we HSPs feel more acutely because of our intensity. And we have the right to ask and negotiate a solution—not in a timid way, as if ashamed of the value of our request, nor under extreme duress, making demands from a place of panic and an urgent need to bring calm to an overstimulated body and psyche.

Positive self-entitlement lies between the extremes of the timid person asking for what he or she needs, which comes from learned helplessness, and the negative, demanding self-entitlement of those who are only too willing to push their way around. With a sense of positive self-entitlement, you can state your needs from a place of inner peace and calmness. To be ready for our Calling, this is where we have to be.

If you're unsure about what rights you have, try asking some personal friends (it's a judgment call to ask someone at work, because of the unseen politics), and consider what they have to say about it. Sometimes we just don't know what *is* right, and for that reason we're hesitant. This is the HSP's way of pausing and checking, to fine-tune information, calm our emotions, and move forward better prepared.

A second, and practical, benefit to being visible can be seen in the experience of gays who come out and let others truly see them. "Coming out," of course, is a way of being visible. The research of Kirk Snyder, author of *The Lavender Road to Success*, a career book for gays,[2] revealed that gays who came out at work have, on the average, a 50 percent higher salary than those who didn't!

Snyder says there are two basic, practical reasons. Those who didn't come out spent too much time at work *hiding* and *worrying* about being discovered, and so weren't as productive because they couldn't concentrate on their work. And secondly, the dynamics in communication was interrupted because the other person knew that the unannounced gay individual wasn't totally authentic. You need good communication to connect, so when these individuals became *accepting of themselves and less afraid of others' reactions*, when they were no longer holding back, confidence radiated from them. Therefore they could ask, communicate, and be authentic and productive. And the difference had a strikingly measurable outcome in dollars and cents, promotions and recognition.

This is something we can learn from, in our own way and according to our specific needs, as HSPs. It's empowering for us to work at being visible—to have the courage to be ourselves.

Why Do Sensitive People Hide?

The opposite of being visible is to hide. And we regularly vacillate between these two, as we struggle with the attraction or dread each can offer. Knowing why we hide and how to be visible is the core of preparation for our Calling.

Consider what it's like when change comes along. New people and experiences enter our life. One moment, it feels exciting and fun, and the next, we're running for the bedroom to turn off the lights and pull the covers over our head. There have been times when I felt I was taking two steps backward for every one step forward. As we grow, our world changes. We'll have mixed feelings about these transitions, and we need a safe harbor during this time. (*Transitions*, a book by Bridges, is a good source on this topic.) It's very easy to imagine the potential of a new direction, and the images can be both captivating and overwhelming.

But hiding is distinctly different from the safe harbor, or resting place, we need when we're overwhelmed. Although the need for rest may send us into retreat, which can look like hiding, the emotions blur the distinction. In the chapter on Drudgery, we saw that HSPs often retreat to a less demanding job to avoid being overstimulated. It may be entry level position, or something so easy that it surely won't be demanding. Rest is when we need a break from stimulation. Hiding is when we're afraid, embarrassed, and/or perhaps ashamed, that our flaws will be seen. So we seek invisibility for a while, until we're ready to be seen again.

Here's a story about what happens when rest and hiding are mixed together in someone's choices:

That master's program had been really grueling. There was always much more work to be done, things to be learned, new avenues to try, than I could do, even if the allotted time for it had been doubled. Having pushed myself, because all the new learning was exciting and fun, I found myself at graduation time feeling exhausted and spent. I was not alone in that. But my difference was, I required rest to a degree that I saw others did not. I took a job as a maid, thinking that the mindless nature of it, and that getting away from the new field I was in for a short time, would help me to regain my energy and perspective. I didn't feel good about it, even though it did afford me some rest. What I see now, with many years' hindsight, is that I was not only resting; I was hiding, as well. I didn't quite know how to be comfortable in being out there, in my new career. I loved what I was doing, but felt a bit out of place. Some of this was my introversion; I knew that. It had been hard to be "out there" for as long as I was, during the master's program. I needed a safe harbor in which to rest. Unfortunately for me, that safe harbor provided not only rest, but a chance to hide as well. I also became, through hiding, less connected to what it was that had originally given me a feeling of being alive.—Juliana, Web entrepreneur

---

Consider, as well, Scott, an easygoing HSP who grew from a quiet, behind-the-scenes job to one where he was quite visible. His story is different from Juliana's. Scott loves to write and spent many years alone, in a small room, happily writing speeches and communications for his boss. As he advanced, Scott knew supervisory roles were not his forte, and took a different advancement track and—with help from his mentor-bosses—he eventually became Director of Communications with almost two hundred people reporting to him. "I'm good as a number two man," he says, "because I can see long term, and together, my boss and I cover more ground."

Notice that Scott, now self-employed, recognizes the advantages and disadvantages of his nature and found a direction that let him grow. He took his time and knew when to stop hiding and become visible:

My personal experience has been that my HSP tendencies constantly pull in two directions: one that is very effective and provides a long-term direction/perspective; the other is pulled by day-to-day noise. Hiding the clutter and unhiding the depth of perspective is the trick. (Other people sure don't want to know how I sometimes feel like a raw, exposed nerve; but the vision that comes from discerning a wealth of detail that surrounds me lets me make more meaningful decisions—at least, that's the way it seems.)

I'm suggesting that we take the time to ask ourselves: "Am I hiding because I need to rest from the stimulation, or am I really avoiding new experiences, the unknown, because I doubt myself and feel overwhelmed by the challenges that I imagine lay before me?" It's all right to take time to sample various directions. And time is relative. Back in Chapter 3 I quoted an ancient Greek who felt that the sundial was ruining his life and everyone around him was on a fast track. Your challenge is to grow toward a level comfortable for yourself, and that may take time. But when you get there, you'll be happier than if you rushed.

Summarizing the Value of Visibility

Remember, being visible means you choose to provide others with quality information about yourself. You can give them as little or as much as you want, at your own pace, and in your own time.

The process of being visible means *accepting yourself*. If you don't believe that anything about yourself is good and valuable, you cannot give that level of quality to others. To give, you must believe you are of quality. It means being more *true to yourself*, and trusting your instincts, judgment, gifts, and self-worth.

Think back to the chapter on stress management: We need to set *boundaries* with others, such as *speaking up* when we don't agree, or *leading* and not being afraid to have greater responsibilities. This separates us from others at that moment, so that we're more clearly delineated against the landscape. And this is what a Calling can do. If that sounds scary, remember, we are in charge of how much we show others. And we can give others quality information.

While the stories in this book can be uplifting and reassuring, I encourage you to use your support system and discuss what being visible means to you with a trusted friend. This can be beneficial as you discern what draws you toward being out there and what leads you to hide.

Claiming Reverence at Work

Since highly sensitive people are value-driven, values are the cornerstone of an HSP's energy and productivity. Defining our values will help us tremendously to improve both productivity and relationships with coworkers. Claude Whitmyer and Salli Rasberry, who write about self-employment in *Running a One-Person Business,* say that those whom they found the most productive individuals were those who continually clarified their personal visions and values: "Your interests and perseverance are greater when you pursue goals you believe in."[3]

One of the big challenges in prioritizing values is the workplace itself, which will challenge you to find a balance, a harmony, between your values and those of the company. It's a good exercise, since it makes us more articulate and more expressive, as well as imparting a deeper understanding of the living dynamics of the workplace.

As HSPs, we value many things, including the need to:

> ➤ Help others in a meaningful, life-affirming way

> ➤ Do quality work

> ➤ Stay calm, relaxed, and happy

> ➤ Accomplish new things

> ➤ Interact positively, without exhaustion

> ➤ Gracefully say no, and have it stick

> ➤ Make a point clearly and effectively

> ➤ Not feel rushed into making a decision

The challenge is how to communicate these values to others at work.

Paul Woodruff, an ethics philosopher, explores the role of reverence in our lives in a book with that title: *Reverence*.[4] This is a cardinal (universal) virtue common to all humanity regardless of race or creed. Far more than just a religious feeling, we can experience it when we make eye contact with another, or when we participate in a choral production, for example, where everyone works hard together to produce beautiful music. It needs to be experienced to be understood. Reverence is about human relations, especially those of unequal status, and the emotions that invoke our common humanity. These emotions include awe, respect, and appropriate shame, and they are often expressed or reinforced through ceremony.

As to reverence: Thoreau knew and wrote about it extensively. It is often found in abundance in HSPs, who have a tendency to be empathic, compassionate, respectful, and giving. As a result, it's sometimes assumed that we're too soft, too sensitive. This clashes with how many characterize the world of business, where it can appear that the business world as a whole appears to be detached, even insensitive, when it comes to its demands upon and expectations of its workers. Of course, this attitude isn't uniformly adversarial, but there is something to the generalization that says the world of business values expediency and efficiency, in the service of productivity, and puts personal considerations second.

HSPs regularly experience awe. Our capacity for intensity, and the ability to see a wide range of subtleties, easily creates feelings of awe and respect for the world around us. And we are capable of shame. Woodruff says "you cannot feel shame without feeling respect for something larger than yourself—family, society, or moral ideals."[5] In essence, he believes that life would be disastrous without shame. But we are also capable of shame when we need not feel it, when we berate ourselves (with a little help from our imagination) for our presumed failures. Reverence involves self-respect. It's similar to positive self-entitlement, which is an intellectual understanding of what our rights are. Reverence is also about our rights, but experienced through specific emotions that bring out our common humanity. And it's in the emotions of the workplace that it presents us our greatest issues. Together, the intellect and the emotions give us a balance in knowing what we need to say, plus the feelings needed to experience connectedness with others. From this flows strength and the clear-sightedness to see who others really are, and thus to take a stand and assume our own proper place with them, in an esteemed world. Reverence, with its capacity to bridge relationships across generations, races, and hierarchies, is an essential part of becoming visible.

But the greatest power of reverence comes in how it reconnects those of unequal status: boss to employee, adult to child, wealthy to poor, and so on. It takes only one person to create the experience of reverence and hold it so others can experience it too. Like positive self-entitlement, which is a psychological way to talk about the same thing, reverence establishes a feeling of humanity between individuals.

Indeed, work is about emotions as well as business. Reverence, being the great equalizer virtue, has the power to connect in an emotionally satisfying way. Business is about making connections, although not necessarily with the sensitive touch of the reverence experienced by HSPs. But it could be.

HSPs often feel awe, respect, even shame (when we don't live up to our own expectations), and I'm suggesting that we see this in a new light. We need to own our reverence, our capacity see our humanity. In a Calling, we have the self-confidence to see how we're all connected as human beings. And our Calling involves us more fully in life in a happy and rewarding way. We need not be afraid to own this capacity for awe and appreciation of life, which is highly likely to come up in a Calling. Gregg Levoy, in *Callings: Finding and Following an Authentic Life*, puts it well when he writes:

In saying yes to our calls, we bring flesh to word and form to faith. We bring substance to dreams, to passions, and to the ancient urgencies. We ground ourselves in life and bring ourselves into being as alchemists and magicians in their finest hours.[6]

Practicing Reverence at Work

Now that we have an understanding of reverence, let's examine how we can experience it in our workplace. As we practice reverence in our dealings with people at work, we're practicing the quality of interaction needed for a Calling and, at the same time, we're practicing visibility.

The Boss and the Mentor ...

The boss is the single most crucial person in your job. Good communication with him or her helps you get accurate feedback on how you're perceived, and allows you to renegotiate an out-of-control overload of work to a manageable flow. And knowing who this person is will help you with your communication and your interactions, because reverence does its greatest magic between individuals of unequal status. So it's useful to know how to create that relationship with those above and below us.

Your boss is the person to whom you report and who assigns you work. If you're an employee, he or she represents the company, and has a lot of say and influence in your work and what you do. Depending on the relationship we have, the boss may not be someone you feel comfortable being honest with, or feel comfortable revealing more about who you are, what you need, and what you want to do.

If you're self-employed, by the way, your "boss" is your customer. In healthy situations, the relationship with your client is egalitarian, with each bringing to the table what they need and what they're able to do, and both go from there in an honest and responsible manner.

As mentioned previously, while we can have a mutually reverent relationship with our bosses, reverence is not expected of the manager's position. The job of the manager is to get the work done, on schedule. The worst managers—with the most emotionally insensitive style—are going to upset HSPs more than others. While we can have a mutually reverent relationship with our bosses, reverence, unlike managerial skills, is not expected of the manager's position (think of emotional labor). Time takes precedence over all other factors—time is truly of the utmost essence. And the worst managers—with the most emotionally insensitive style—are going to upset HSPs more than others. Given this, there are so many possible ways we can work well with our bosses, if we keep in mind that Drudgery darkens the emotions, and makes reverence harder to achieve, but not impossible. Reverence doesn't have to happen out of the blue, it can be built into the relationship, gradually, over time. And fortunately, as we grow, our abilities to be unaffected by difficult behavior improves.

Another working relationship, usually between an experienced professional and someone growing into a career, is that of mentor and mentee. There are certain similarities to the usual scheme, in that both bosses and mentors typically have greater personal experience and professional knowledge than their staff. The mentee, like the employee, seeks to advance his or her career and wants to do it well.

Where the mentor-mentee relationship and that of the boss and employee diverge is that the boss is practically and legally our superior and has the right to tell us how to do the work. The mentor, however, has no direct binding employment relationship with us, although this person might be in a different department in our company. The difference creates the possibility of different relationships.

... And How Relationships with Them Differ

The relationship with a mentor allows more opportunities to cultivate reverence than with a boss (although not always). A true mentor helps us grow as human beings, and ultimately grow our Calling.

What is a mentor? Mentoring is much closer to the type of arrangement suited to the creative and sensitive HSP nature. A good mentor only gives what the mentee asks for. Because the ulterior motive of controlling the work is gone, he or she is more often flexible than a boss, as well as attentive, nondefensive, a good communicator, supportive, resourceful, and open to new ideas.[7]

In addition to not controlling us, a good mentor is not invested in using us to fulfill his or her own agendas. Since we don't work for a mentor, a mentor can have a hand in encouraging our career development, point out the landscape in which we wish to grow, and give us clues about the pitfalls and opportunities. Lacking, ideally, a boss's ulterior motive— to preside over our job—mentors have a greater luxury of time to relax and help us look at all our options. Sometimes they can serve as a networking resource, opening doors for us to others who may provide mentoring. Sometimes mentoring is an informal relationship and may last only a little while. Or we may change mentors as our career changes. Implicit in all this, and unlike most employee-boss interaction, there's a strong egalitarian quality in the mentoring relationship.

The mentor is involved in a bigger picture of our career, the boss in the details of our work. He or she has a vested interest in the quality and timeliness of our productive activities, and has the social and legal right to instruct us on what to do and how to do it. Rarely are mentors our boss, as bosses have more complex relationships between the work and their employees and can't be expected to keep a mentoring role separate.

A mentor is someone I respected who was smart, able to really understand what I was doing, and what I was going through and help me in a direction that was beneficial. A mentor is someone who has the ability and takes the time to understand what is going on inside a person. If someone is writing a report, there are two ways to approach it. One way is the external way and one may say, "This is what we need, you need to rewrite and it needs to look like this" and you impose the way you would do it. It's more difficult to look at what people are doing and to make suggestions that let them accomplish what they set out to do in their own voice, their own tone, and in the direction they've taken.—Scott, Web entrepreneur

---

However, there are ways a boss can incorporate some of a mentor's role. The more respectful a boss is to an employee—listening, taking time to explain things, and not micromanaging—the closer that person comes to resembling a mentor.

It would be nice, of course, if all bosses were mentors. But that's not always possible, and there could be conflicts of interest in mixing those roles. It takes more effort, as Scott points out, to be a mentor. And as much as a boss might like to, he or she may not feel comfortable doing so, because the roles are different. But it is possible to improve communications with one's boss so that a more reverent relationship can be established, with some of the mentoring style emerging. You may be the one to set the pace.

The following section shows how to translate our needs, spoken and unspoken, into positive self-entitlement language, or to foster a more reverent interaction between you and your boss.

Creating a Reverent Dialogue with the Boss

I asked lots of HSPs what they'd love to tell their boss or any boss. Here are some of the things they said:

> "We should listen to each other's ideas and don't dismiss so many things right away."

> "Get in touch with those underneath you."

> "Follow the Golden Rule: 'Do unto others as you would have them do unto you.'"

> "Don't ask people to lie or do anything ethically wrong."

> "Trust and respect are vital."

> "Allow an adequate amount of time for me to do my job properly and well."

> "Give me an environment that's colorful without being overdone."

> "Give me the freedom to be as creative as I possibly can be in doing my job."

> "Don't try to manipulate me with kindness."

> "Lighten up! Unless you're a policeman or a fireman, unless you're in the E.R. at a hospital, the world does not live or die by what you do."

"If one of your employees says it's physically impossible to do such and such a task in the amount of time you're setting for it, listen to that person. They're the ones who are out in the trenches doing the job."

"Communication is important. Tell the same thing in a variety of different ways until you actually are getting through."

"I want to know from my boss that I've done a good job and from the people who work for me too."

These are wonderful needs, aren't they? But we need to recognize that these statements are in their raw, interview form, and are focused on what we want *the boss to do*. If spoken exactly as they're worded here, they would probably put the other person on the defensive and would be unlikely to encourage the boss, much less to engender reverence on his or her part.

Understanding that when we feel the need to criticize, it's not necessarily a reverent situation, how can we improve upon the above presentations? Remember, the first step is *accepting yourself*, which is a positive.

HSPs indicating the above as part of their wish list for the boss have a specific need behind each request. Can you catch the heart of the need in each? If you can see that core need, you've taken the first step toward being visible. So, what do these statements tell us about what we as HSPs need? Below are some examples of how to translate the above listed statements that are more positive toward the listener, invoking reverence while at the same time making our needs known. It's important to practice creating our own reverence dialogue, for it can be quite useful. The next list refines what our needs are, and make good topics for discussions with trusted friends, or a mentor, but may not yet be ready for the boss.

"I need to be treated as an equal, not someone to control, manipulate, or berate."

"I need to be trusted that I know how to do my job and will do it responsibly."

"I need to take a break when I'm feeling fatigued and not feel apologetic about it."

"I'm more productive when I can give reasonable attention to each project."

"I need to be able to renegotiate the work if I find that I'm overestimating what I can do within a given time."

"I need to lighten up and not have everything and everyone be so serious, especially my boss."

"I need people to communicate with me without micromanaging me."

"I need people to not talk down to me."

"I need reasonable deadlines."

"I've never been able to come up with good ideas right away, but I come up with great ideas after I've played with it a little."

"I need a mentor to guide and support me, not a boss who just orders me around."

Now, this list encourages reverence by acting as if reverence is there. In these needs, we're respecting ourselves and asking others to do the same.

Applying Reverence in Workplace Communications

Now that we know what reverence is and what needs we need to communicate, how do we take this one step further, into daily on-the-job activities? Here, we'll get some ideas from HSP bosses. We'll also look at positive ways to say no and some creative solutions from other HSPs on getting what they need. We'll also look at how to use humor as a communication tool

Advice from HSP Bosses

Several HSPs who are supervisors had a few suggestions about dealing with bosses. Notice how the language encourages the other to regard you with respect, because you regard yourself the same way. Diana is a managing librarian in a big city public library.

People understand medical conditions but not emotional conditions. For an HSP employee, the main thing is to understand what your limitations are and to be willing to put yourself out there and *tell* your supervisor what your limitations are.

"So it's up to you to speak up for yourself," says Diana. It's better to let them know in a timely manner, than wait too long because you don't want to look bad.

Here are some ideas from other HSPs who have been in management positions:

> **SAMPLE LANGUAGE** *(instead of using the word "depression," which is nearly always viewed negatively and with suspicion in the workplace, use "fatigue"):* "I am having trouble with fatigue. Is there some way to structure this responsibility a bit differently, that will work for both of us?" *(Mary, therapist)*

> **SAMPLE LANGUAGE:** "Sometimes I take on too much because I want to do a good job, but I overestimate how much I am emotionally and physically able to do, so could I have permission to renegotiate assignments?" *(Diane, library manager)*

Successful Two-Way Workplace Language

When we talk to others at work, whether it's our boss or coworkers, one of the most important things we have to do is communicate in a way that allows us to convey our needs while also acknowledge the other person's.

A Word About Saying No

How good are you at saying *no?* Are there times when you can do it easily, and other times when it's extremely difficult? What could be happening that makes it easy or difficult for you?

Before we can even begin talking about how to communicate your needs, you need to be able to say no, because that may reflect a need. The chapter on stress management is important for refreshing your memory on how to monitor your overstimulation and watch your boundaries. The better you get at watching and taking care of your stress level, the better you'll be at saying *no*, politely and firmly.

No is about communicating your boundaries in some manner. The workplace is so invasive of our time, energies, and boundaries that it takes careful attention to notice when this happens and then adapting, if you need to. You may need to tell someone no for different reasons. Even renegotiating your workload midway through a project can be a form of no. *No* is often tied into our early experiences, to our self-image as a separate being from others, with our own needs and feelings.

> ➤ Saying no is *feeling good* about yourself.

> ➤ Saying no means *changing* something uncomfortable.

> ➤ Saying no is a *healthy monitoring* of your stress level.

Saying No Is Feeling Good About Yourself

There are many ways to say no. Some work better than others. *No* is an important word, and requires a loving protectiveness toward yourself in using it on your behalf.

Saying No Means Changing Something Uncomfortable

HSPs are eager to learn and grow. We're attracted to stretching our minds and creativity. Sometimes we take on a new project only to find it growing like a weed, spilling over into our lunch hours, our weekends and evenings. We become overwhelmed, frustrated, and exhausted. While many people at work will thrive with a lot going on, HSPs can only tolerate this for short periods of time.

No one will know what your tolerance level is unless you tell them. But the timing and manner in which you announce your tolerance limits could be perceived as trying to avoid work, being irresponsible. Or it can be seen as being mature and organized. We all make mistakes in planning our schedules; it's only human.

Saying No Is a Healthy Monitoring of Your Stress Level

One of the most valuable things you can do for yourself is be consistent in your boundaries. Communicate early when you have problems, try to assess your limits and honor them. It's so easy to be attracted to a new project, a new idea. I've watched an HSP start her own business, help her spouse start a business (and try to manage most of it too), begin brainstorming about going back to school in order to have more credentials for her career, take on another job to supplement her income while the business is still in baby stages, and, in addition, work in a volunteer organization. She continues to add and add and add. Being on her own, she can easily drop something if it's not right, but for those in the workplace, with this tendency to constantly consume new things, what would you do?

If you need to say no, don't forget to compliment or thank the other person, to be sure to let them know how they can help you achieve your goal and what it will mean to you.

Some Ways to Say No Without Saying No

"I want to get this work done in the next couple of hours, and I need to ask for your cooperation to give me some time to myself to do this. That will really help me get the job done."

This way you ask for their help, instead of rejecting them with a Greta Garbo style: "I want to be alone." Then they can feel good about what they're giving you. Be appreciative when asking for their help, and let them know you will connect later.

"I'm a quiet person, I need to go home and kick back. I can't work overtime as much as Karen."

This tells them that you need to unwind quietly. It can be part of a general conversation about what we do after work hours.

"Yes, I tend to be quiet, but it's usually because I'm concentrating hard on my work."

Here, you're explaining that the quietness is not a sign that you don't like someone, but that you're doing something constructive with your time.

"I do enjoy being included in the luncheon, but that project just fried me and I need to kick back a bit and be quiet before the next wave hits this afternoon."

Everyone can appreciate needing a breather, especially during a time of intense pressure to get a lot of projects done.

Two Strategies for Influencing a Boss

Are environmental factors, such as lights and temperature, a problem? This is a variation, of sorts, on saying no—two strategies on how to request an improvement or change.

Therapist Gary Linker gives an example of how to address specific problems with temperature:

Once they know that about themselves and what they need, if they can then negotiate that with bosses and take it to the bottom line in terms of productivity, oftentimes they can sell that issue to their boss and get some success. I've had people who complained about being under a fan, being cold all day, and were finally able through some role-playing to practice that. Something as simple as that. To be able to speak up and say, "This fan really makes me cold and I'm spending half of my time trying to get warm and not being very productive. If I could just move it, it would really, really help."

Here's what Roy, a database administrator, did to get rid of the fluorescent lights in his office. Notice how he patiently requested a reevaluation of the lighting needs every time he moved, so that over time his needs were accepted and properly documented.

At that point I proceeded to remove the ceiling lights and just use my desk lights. Well, that definitely set a pattern. It helped establish a condition.

...I contacted our safety and health office, and they sent a guy up with a light meter so we could help get a baseline for how much light I needed to work with. It was so low that it surprised everybody. That was the other half that helped build a foundation for documenting the need for a low light environment. As the months went by, I moved a couple of more times, but each time the need was revalidated and I was able to get the low light environment that I needed.... After five years I've got the history, the pattern. This is what I need to work well, even when I wear dark-tinted glasses when I'm working. Dark glasses in a dark place because I'm working on a computer.

Business Language and HSP Sound Bites

In the years I went to business networking meetings, everyone had a brief statement that described what they did, and perhaps how they did it. These "sound bites" are a personal calling card for a business. We can take this idea and create personal sound bites for your workplace. They can be little ways to educate people on specific traits you feel need to be acknowledged.

Keep the language cheerful, nonthreatening, and informative. Trust your intuition if something doesn't feel right. You might even ask a few people for help in creating the message, and benefit from the combined creativity. Notice how the first two examples say similar things, but the top one is more uncomfortable. It could put off some people, making them feel rejected and that you think negatively of them. It could eventually even result in rendering you a scapegoat. The second lets others know you still welcome them, but that right now you need to work quietly. You could even add a "sticky" message with the time you'll stop the project and reconnect with your coworkers.

QUIET IS PRODUCTIVE—INTERRUPTIONS ARE DISRUPTIVE

or

QUIET IS PRODUCTIVE—PLEASE COME BACK LATER

Do you wish to be seen as someone with a particular style, like doing careful methodical work and preferring to not be under extra pressure? The following examples convey a message on quality and the cost of mistakes that result from hasty work. While you may appreciate, even crave, a chance to take a project at your speed and no one else's, the workplace is by nature a place of compromise, constant change, and the testing of limits. Be prepared to compromise on the pace of your work. There are other ways, such as using your creativity to *see and point out* the next step, rather than taking the extra time to do the next step.

CAREFUL QUALITY WORK DONE HERE

QUALITY IS LIKE FINE WINE—IT IS *NOT* A RUSH JOB

TAKE TIME TO DO THINGS RIGHT,

GO TOO FAST, LOSE YOUR CASH

Perhaps you want to encourage a good-natured mood and cheer in others. If you have a natural tendency to humor, a sense of play and fun, and feel that your workplace is too serious at times, the following might help release tension and stress. Extroverts with a sense of humor could help you craft engaging slogans like:

FOUR LAUGHS A DAY KEEPS STRESS AWAY

GOOD HUMOR FIGHTS STRESS

These ideas are intended to help you explore different ways to give others around you a chance to see more of who you are, and in a positive and interactive way.

The Courage to Be Visible

To summarize, we HSPs need to take charge of our attitudes toward work, using reverence toward ourselves and others, and honest and prudent communication, to gain a safe sense of visibility. It is the inner experiencing and the outer sharing of reverence that will give us the self-confidence to which we aspire if we're to live closer to our true Calling. And, in claiming our right to reasonable self-entitlements, we accept the courage to be visible—visible enough, that is, to claim our rightful place in the working world.

Our visibility and our self-respect, which takes *all* of our HSP needs into account, will pay off handsomely in our working life, as opposed to hiding, which some confuse with meeting our needs for rest and relief from overstimulation. We HSPs, whether employees, mentees, or self-employed persons, can only benefit ourselves and society by creating a safe visibility for ourselves.

7

Highly Sensitive Kung Fu

She yelled at me and made derogatory statements, unrelated to what was being discussed, and later, in a passive manner, asked for my help on a financial matter. I was still reeling, and said yes. With anyone else, I would have immediately said it was a conflict of interest. It's like I'm punched one way and rebounding another way. Clearly I lost my balance with what to do.

—PAM, CERTIFIED PUBLIC ACCOUNTANT

G ather around grasshoppers.

This chapter is about confusing, difficult, or, worse, serious people problems you face at work. We all face events like these and they seem uncomfortable, sometimes unbearable, at the time. But we need to know how to deal with a variety of people situations if we want to make work "work" for us.

In the quote at the beginning, Pam makes a keen observation in recognizing the emotional impact that threw her off balance. Highly sensitive people will usually have the same reaction. Somehow, you have to regain your mental focus, and retain your boundaries and hold them against the pushing and turbulence coming at you from others. This is where your HSP nature can either help or hinder you.

Solving these problems requires disciplined mental focus, even courage, which is why I have given this chapter a martial arts title, in the spirit of the old 1970s television show, *Kung Fu*. That's where the "grasshopper" reference comes from as well: Grasshopper was the childhood memories of the adult hero whose quest was to find answers to his life. How he came to make choices and decisions all stemmed from his childhood training as

"Grasshopper." He had a disciplined, calm manner, moving through problems and danger without losing his peaceful "center." It occurred to me that the adult hero approached life very much like an empowered HSP: aware, wise, and yet compassionate.

This chapter is also intended to be a crucible to help you grow. The dictionary defines *crucible* as a "searing, searching test," and when emotions are very intense and a problem faces you, it is in fact a lesson in disguise. The lessons start at a mild level of difficulty (even if the example doesn't seem easy) and become increasingly challenging. But you can solve them. Even if you've never successfully solved your people problems before, even if you feel so overwhelmed that you can't imagine you could stop the train, you can. I'm sure of it, and I will be reminding you that you should be optimistic too.

You can learn optimism, by the way, just as you can learn helplessness. If you need to refresh your memory about this, turn back to the first chapter, where we discussed the influence of the past.

You'll meet HSPs who have faced serious workplace challenges. Craft, Calling, or Drudgery—it doesn't matter. There are difficult people problems everywhere. HSPs in Calling or Craft do have an advantage over those in Drudgery, however, since they know how to adapt and put the breaks on a slide into Drudgery by holding their boundaries. That is, they've at least learned some of the things that will enable them to better handle people problems.

Using Your Sensitivities Positively

What we want to do to deal with people problems at work is create positive actions for using our temperament. As mentioned often, our sensitivities can be an asset.

Whenever we feel uncomfortable, for instance, it's a signal that something isn't right. Your anxiety should tell you: *stop*. Then, wait and see how you feel, and evaluate what the behavior of others feels like to you. *Avoid obliterating your own anxiety by reassuring the other person.* If, out of discomfort, you focus your attention on *their* feelings and immediately reassure them, you take yourself away from—and blur your awareness of—your own feelings.

To stop, and not immediately react, is not being insensitive, nor does it mean you shouldn't be sympathetic to others. The point is that you shouldn't shift your attention away from your inner state until you know what it's trying to tell you, so that you can acknowledge the message and promise yourself you'll deal with it, even if you have to temporarily postpone reacting. Your HSP-self, which needs precious time and space to make good decisions, will love you for it.

The following HSP traits can be a disadvantage when working with difficult people:

- ➤ Strong empathy concerning the feelings of others

- ➤ Being afraid of hurting another's feelings

- ➤ Becoming discouraged or overwhelmed too soon and wanting to give up

- ➤ Often not trusting your own feelings

- ➤ A tendency toward learned helplessness

- ➤ A tendency to ruminate and intensify worst-case scenarios

- ➤ Difficulty switching from flight to fight during a crisis

Six Lessons to Learn

For most everyday difficult situations, the first five lessons will be sufficient. The sixth lesson—deals with bullies—will be about a Drudgery problem that can ruin an existing Craft or Calling situation. Bullies are also manageable, as all the experts say, once you know how to deal with them. And specific information and strategies will be presented for this lesson.

Each of the HSP "kung fu" lessons is explained and discussed by drawing upon the experience of an HSP on the "front lines" who has dealt with difficult people. Most of these lessons build on what we've covered in previous chapters.

Any HSP currently in a bullying situation should consider finding supportive people to help them cope with the overstimulation. Nevertheless, as noted above, bullies are manageable once you know how to deal with them.

To deal with the problems posed by difficult people, you can use certain tools to help you with a wide variety of situations. Most of the time these difficulties you encounter will be manageable; perhaps they'll make you uncomfortable, but they'll still definitely be manageable.

The lessons are:

1. Practice makes perfect

2. Use your horse sense

3. It's all about learning

4. Hold your ground

5. Recognize the pattern

6. Don't be someone's snack

LESSON 1: *Practice Makes Perfect*

We've all heard stories, or may have told them ourselves, of what it was like when our little ones first started to say no. *No* is still an important word, even for grown-ups. You need to develop your skills at saying no, firmly, comfortably, and politely. The more you do this, the better you will get, even when under duress. You can stall, ask for time to consider the idea, which is a polite or diplomatic way to say no, and then come back with an answer.

Most of the people you'll meet in life are ordinary people with ordinary problems, just like you. Your mission, should you choose to accept it, is to create a strategy for yourself to become comfortable with *No* in a manner of positive self-entitlement, as we discussed in Chapter 6.

Patty Holds Her Boundaries

For 13 years, Patty's job has put her on the front lines with lobbyists, senators, aides, and staff in her state's capital. Six months of the year it's a high-paced, intense, and demanding job that may require working 48 hours in one shift, while napping on the office sofa for a couple of hours, as bills are being crafted down the hall. The second half of the year is very slow and gives her time to rest and regroup from the intensity.

Patty loves having an influence, even in a small way, to see legislation being formulated and passed. Her boss is a difficult state senator who is brusque, frequently abrasive, and rude to her and other senators, lobbyists, or staff. This is a challenge for Patty, an introvert who's never had assertiveness training and is completely self-taught on dealing with difficult people. Her job, which involves a lot of emotional labor, requires her to:

> ➤ Think fast on her feet daily

> ➤ Be quick-witted and noncommittal while fielding savvy and smooth-talking lobbyists

> ➤ Calm the ruffled feathers of other senators when her boss gets difficult and harsh

> ➤ Coach her boss during meetings regarding bills

> ➤ Let her boss know when he's pushing someone too hard

> ➤ Let her boss know when he's been rude to her

This is a demanding job for an introverted HSP. Patty feels that she's held her own well, but she's starting to experience the fatigue that a long stint at the same job can sometimes bring.

The emotional and mental games of politics, negotiations, and the pressures of deadlines require advanced skills in monitoring her boundaries, and Patty knows she can't slack off. She's had fair warning about that from the experience of her predecessor, a worn-out soul who never stood up for herself with this same boss. "I've learned that I'm not going to survive if I don't stand up to him," she says. So Patty has learned to successfully manage her boundaries by *regularly* letting her boss, and others, know when they're out of line.

It took Patty time to develop these skills, and she learned by doing. She doesn't catch every time her boss is rude—sometimes hours will go by before it dawns on her why she's upset. But when she does, Patty will tell him politely—or occasionally with a touch of sarcasm—that she doesn't want him to talk to her that way. And he'll accept it, for a while; but he's the type who has to be reminded, all the time. Since she faithfully monitors herself and his behavior, if Patty misses from time to time, it doesn't erode the standing she's already achieved with him.

The payoff has been that Patty has a reputation as a mediator for smoothing over problems her boss causes others by his behavior; she can alert him in meetings and knows he'll listen to her. So for Patty, constant repetition—reminding him firmly and politely that she doesn't like being treated abusively—works in a demanding environment.

LESSON 2: *Use Your Horse Sense*

Remember the story of the Master HSP, the horse? The horse has a very important lesson for us: be aware. Now and then, something sneaks by us because we don't see the clues. A sweet smile and an arm around our shoulders and a plea for help, a dig one minute and praise the next, stonewalling that delays our work, leaves us haggling to get a straight answer ... It's that the individual with whom we're having a problem may be acting out of habit, not realizing how emotionally loaded and violating these behaviors can be. Or they might be deliberate and manipulative. But in either case, we feel them and react to them, and perhaps make decisions that cause us even more problems.

Judi Does the Payroll

Consider Judi, who worked in the health field for nearly 20 years. In one job, her boss came up to her, put her arm around Judi's shoulders, smiled and asked for help with the payroll; they had no one to do that job. Judi felt honored to be asked but had a knot in her stomach too. She'd never done payroll before and knew nothing about it.

But Judi took on the job anyway, and the rest of the year was a nightmare for her. She had to manage the busy front desk—with constant interruptions and no privacy—and do the payroll at the same time—which, for accuracy, requires quiet and no interruptions. Sometimes she was even doing both jobs simultaneously at the noisy front desk. *And she wasn't given any training, nor did she ask for any, but they kept giving her more work and she kept saying yes.*

Judi didn't listen to her intuition, her horse sense—that knot in her stomach. She went with the nice feeling of being needed, the illusion of being the one person who could do the job right. She hung in there longer than she should have, because she was stubborn, and by the time she left this Drudgery job, she'd paid a price for it with health concerns.

Judi is self-employed now, and has learned to say no when something is asked of her beyond her comfort zone. She says that all the questions she asks a potential client she *should* have asked her boss, way back then.

By now I trust you can see that I'm a firm believer in listening to our intuition. If it tells us that what's being presented is not right, say so. Saying no isn't rocket science. It just requires listening to our feelings and intuitions and trusting them.

> I want to know what their needs are, what they expect, and so on. In those days, I didn't ask enough questions. And I didn't know what my rights were either. I listen to my gut now.

If there is some trauma early in life, it may obstruct our awareness of what's safe and right for us, but the signal is still there if we trust ourselves and are willing to listen and accept it.

LESSON 3: *It's All About Learning*

Who's to judge which lessons you learn from? It's better to focus on the lessons learned rather than if you win or lose, according to your original agenda. It's the same as being process oriented rather than goal oriented. It's in the process that one grows. The goal is an ideal, but the path one takes to the goal provides lessons, and all paths are lessons.

Gretchen is a retired claims representative for a Social Security office. For twenty years her job allowed her to work directly with the public, helping individuals put their lives in order. It's a difficult job. Working for the government, there's a lot of stress, and a public bias against government employees. She's faced difficult clients and difficult bosses. But she's found ways to use her HSP sensitivity. What sustained Gretchen was her wonderful sense of humor, a love of nature, her faith, and her values.

> I've always been able to sense how people feel ... and the minute they find a willing listener whose thoughtful and courteous and who reflects back to them what they need, they'll latch on to you like a barnacle on the hull of a ship and they will talk and talk and talk.... There were so many days I felt frustrated because I couldn't do more.... You had many clients who would yell at you, too. Who would physically threaten you. I've been hit a couple of times.

Gretchen loved her job, had a good reputation, and, with good self-care, endured the bureaucracy. Five years before her retirement, a new manager decided that all work must be monitored down to the minute. Gretchen represents the many HSPs who do speak up and confront the problems they face. Here's what she has to say about the very difficult conditions in the last years of her job:

At that point [the supervisor] said no longer, we don't care if you're a claims representative, you will answer the phones, you'll man the front desk, but you'll also do your regular job as well. So we were being pushed to the point of literally scheduling by minute. We'd do one task for maybe five minutes and switch and do another task. We could maybe do that for a half an hour, in the meantime we were trying to juggle conflicting appointments because absenteeism just skyrocketed after this went into effect. The pressure just got to people.... I don't think a compassionate human being could have survived under those conditions.

Gretchen stubbornly fought against the change for the next several years. She tried showing management why their approach wasn't working and couldn't succeed. What helped her through this time was her sense of humor and solid self-confidence built from years of healing.

It stems from a very strong, ethical background, plus experience as an abused child. At first I was just a very timid child [who was] always very terrified of authority figures. Terrified to rock the boat. Nobody spoke up for me, but yet if I have the ability to help someone else, I'm going to do it, and the Lord gave me a mouth and I use it. I don't care what kind of abuse I get from people.... I will speak up for those who have no voice. I truly believe that the more life experience you have, the more ability you have to speak out.

In the end, she retired, and the office remained unchanged. Sometimes, no matter how hard you try, you are unable to effect the meaningful change you seek.

Gretchen is starting a new career to become a therapist, working with federal workers. She understands their problems firsthand and has both the compassion and the life experience to fully relate to their struggles.

Gretchen may have lost the battle in her office, but she's found a new mission helping other government workers because she understands the vast range of their problems so intimately. Sometimes a lesson prepares us for a new direction that harnesses our gifts at a deeper level than we were capable of using before.

LESSON 4: *Hold Your Ground*

Barbara is in her 30s, and at the height of her career had as many as 50 people reporting to her. She traveled, gave presentations, and did high-level work as a CFO, dealing with lawyers, venture capitalists, and such. She loved her job and made lots of money.

Business is a game Barbara loves and excels at. She cares about people and adheres to the strict ethical standards of her profession. The crisis for her comes when her standards are not the standards of the company. In one job, her boss provided venture capital to smaller companies and insisted they had to do business his way or lose funding. Barbara wanted to find a middle ground that would make both sides happy, but her boss was adamant. While not unethical to insist on a specific business agenda, it felt harsh to Barbara and it would be her job to tell them they were being cut loose. This was extremely painful for her. She relates what happened to her during this crisis:

I guess cutting off funding was cutting off a lot of people's livelihood. I would try to work with people. How bad my anxiety would be is, I could remember times of closing my door and just having to lie on the floor because I was just so doubled over in pain. That's pretty stressful ... and at that point just telling my administrative assistant to hold all my calls, I don't want to talk to anybody. And just having to sit there on the floor, doubled over, until it passed.

Barbara quit the job. Later, another boss wanted her to lie about the financial data, and she refused and again left. While Barbara had the advantage of some savings to cushion her while out of work, the stress of being put on the spot to violate her ethics was extremely painful. Now, she's self-employed, freelancing, doing bookkeeping and financial work for small companies. She misses the challenges of being a CFO, but not the intense and questionable pressures, and she wonders if she'll ever find a place in senior management again, where her ethics would be appreciated.

Like Barbara, Samantha loved her job with all its challenges and demands, and had risen high into senior management. She was a marketing director for a European company. But Samantha draws the line when it comes to her children.

When her two-year-old son was ill, she stayed home with him, working every spare moment, feeling guilty she couldn't do more. And so when her boss scolded her for not getting a sitter for the child and returning to work, that ruined the job for Samantha. She left to find a place where her family priorities would be clearly built into her job description.

Draw the Line and Stand by It

Both Samantha and Barbara had values that mattered a great deal to them. And it was painful having these values rejected by their superiors. Neither were ashamed to cry or hole up in the office, if it came to that. And both were willing to practice what they preached. If we ignore our values, we will experience pain. Once both women made their decisions to stand by their values, they felt much better. We may not always be called upon to renounce a job for a value, but our soul will not take it well if we ignore that value or let others of consequence ignore it.

Our challenge is to find what we can do that honors our values without sacrificing too greatly. Both women had a financial situation where they could afford to leave these jobs; not everyone has that luxury. The pain can come from not defending yourself and feeling hopeless; we need to search our soul for the level of action that we can do comfortably and draw the line and stand by it.

LESSON 5: *Recognize the Pattern*

You remember Pam from earlier in this chapter, a cheerful and extraverted CPA who also does volunteer work for her horticultural society. She's served in several capacities, including president and general board member. Pam says there is an aggressive woman on the board who throws her off balance and then asks, pathetically, for help with something.

Once Pam recognized this woman's pattern and knew that her loud, abrasive, critical style preceded a request for help (presented in a passive manner), Pam was no longer emotionally reacting to the negative message.

This woman really used to bother me, and I'd have to feel I needed time to prepare myself to being around her. Now that I know more about what's going on, I don't feel as affected by her. And I know what to watch for, and what's going to follow, and then I'll respond the way I want to respond.

This type of passive-aggressive behavior is common in life. Many people do "crazy-making" things, say one thing and do another, yell at you, and then ask for help. Your job is to stay calm, see the pattern, and hold your ground for what is appropriate for your situation.

Pam faced a pattern many of us encounter in life, in various degrees of intensity and subtlety. As much as you can, try to focus on the pattern and see what it's telling you. We'll say more about this in the next and final lesson.

LESSON 6: *Don't Be Someone's Snack*

Most of the time the "difficulties" you will encounter at work are everyday events common to ordinary situations. Bullying is different. It is emotionally violent behavior toward someone. The impact for most people, but especially for the HSP, is hellacious. The bully has a habit of "pounding" on his or her target, and the intent is to win by any means necessary. There is another, similar problem called "mobbing," a term coined in Europe to describe the actions of a group within the workplace who is trying to force someone out.

If you're in a crisis right now, with a bully or mobbing, remember this: *Fear and helplessness are not the same thing.* We may be afraid of a bully, but we are not helpless. We can do many things to take care of ourselves, including, depending on your circumstances, successfully pushing the bully back.

There are many good books and resources emerging now to help the targets of bullying. My goal here, as part of this final kung fu lesson, is to educate you on what the "landscape" looks like, so you're better prepared. The highly intense level of pain HSPs can experience, and the nature of bullies—while not frequent in the population—and their personality traits, make dealing with them a challenge.

Concerning this, there's some bad news and some good news. Let's get the bad news over with first. Research has shown that HSPs are often *targets* for bullies and for mobbing. The following are the typical traits of a bully's victims:[1]

Talented	Dedication
Conscientious	Competence
Moral	Nice
Shy	Bright
Kindhearted and polite	Creative
Eager to please	Self-assured
Integrity	Nonthreatening

These traits sound familiar, don't they? I'm not trying to scare you, but just to give you some solid facts to help you prepare and defend yourself. The good news is that you can manage these situations without sacrificing yourself or your values.

What Is a Bully?

All of us know how to be manipulative. We may do it with siblings, our children, or with friends. Most of the time it's done without malicious intent, but because some controlling behaviors have been part of all human societies and we all pick up a few. The passive-aggressive style, as seen in Pam's story in the previous lesson, is a common, widespread example of this among ordinary people in ordinary situations. But a bully is more relentless and is intent on winning at any cost.

In this lesson, we're dealing with a type of individual who is a master at manipulation and interacts with others in very unhealthy, abusive ways, which can be either overt or subtle. As gleaned from various experts on workplace abuse,[2] here are some well-known traits of the bully:

➤ Pleasant as long as we go along with them, threatening when we resist

➤ Habitually cruel to others weaker than her- or himself and, who won't fight back

➤ Uses intimidation, brusque language, sometimes anger

➤ Unwilling to admit weakness or put themselves at a disadvantage

➤ Frequently are women who bully other women

➤ Don't hear what you're saying

And here are some of the bully's tactics, as cited in the book *The Bully at Work*:

➤ Blames others for "errors"

➤ Makes unreasonable job demands

➤ Criticizes your abilities

➤ Inconsistent compliance with rules

➤ Threatens job loss

➤ Uses insults and put-downs

➤ Discounts or denies your accomplishments

➤ Yells and screams

➤ Steals credit

Another form of bullying, mentioned above and called "mobbing," is done by a group of people at work. It's more complex and not easily recognized. And the goal is to force the targeted person to leave. From the book *Mobbing: Emotional Abuse in the American Workplace*:[3]

And, as in the case of those who are bullied, mobbing targets have these traits:

One of the key factors we found is that many mobbing victims love their work. They are identified strongly by what they do, they feel a great commitment to their work and derive purpose and pleasure from it.... People who do not have a strong commitment to their work often view a job more as a necessary means to earn a livelihood. It does not serve as fulfillment, an opportunity to be challenged and to grow. In a mobbing, these people may more easily turn their backs on the organization and go someplace else. They leave without great remorse.... But employees who are committed to their work are often very loyal. They believe in the goals of the organization. They care about the organization's reputation. They keep quiet, are ambivalent about taking action, and may not readily seek assistance.... They suffer for a longer period. Rarely do such individuals reveal their personal agony. And often they do not understand the complex reality of their situation.[4]

No matter what style of aggressive behavior is used, our intuition and emotions will be our "radar" that something is wrong. When people make us feel guilt, fear, confusion, doubt, stress, and/or anxiety in spite of the kind words they might use, *something is wrong*.

Standing Up for Yourself

Those who have dealt successfully with bullies all stand up to them in some way. With unusually difficult people, Jane, a senior research scientist, is firmer and more protective of her boundaries because her instincts tell her that, for herself, she needs to do this:

I don't confide in people, unless they are close friends, or people I'm very, very sure about. If someone does see I'm upset about something, or react strongly or "sensitively" to something, I will pass it off, present an explanation ("I didn't need that/I'm sorry: I've got an awful headache/I've

just discovered my car needs major repairs/my computer bombed and lost half the data, etc."). I simply don't let people see that I'm vulnerable.

Charlotte, an artist, has made a conscious effort to stand up for herself, despite any fear she has:

I get confronted too. Usually by people who only have noticed the silk, but not the steel underneath. Many people believe I'm nice and easily scared, as I quite often can let people have or do what they scream so loudly about as being important to them. But when my line is crossed, I don't budge. I may very well be scared and feel threatened, but then I attack and fight to death. I am slowly learning that I must draw the line much earlier than I have done, as that lessens this kind of confrontation.

I've also learned a trick or two about how to handle confrontations and accusations. Rule number one is to stick to the truth. And never to answer any accusation, but to pose questions of my own. Keep an outward calm, and speak with a low voice. After the confrontation, I can go home and collapse into a heap of quivering jelly, as it is intensely disturbing and highly arousing.

Charlotte pointed out that at first, when we confront, the stimulation we feel will get higher, but it will also lessen, and the relief we feel afterward is worth it.

But sometimes we don't take care of ourselves very well. Eve is a quiet, sensitive, middle-age woman. At heart an artist, Eve has worked secretarial and administrative jobs for decades. She's always done well, received praise and recognition from her bosses for her excellent work. She believed that if she focused on doing a good job, treating people politely, she could stay out of any office politics or issues. But Eve did not know how to handle a bully and this strategy didn't work in her new job. There were warning signs when she started, that the previous secretary had reported Eve's boss to a state organization for bullying. Slowly, over time, her boss became abusive. Eve just wanted to hang in there until she was vested and then quit to follow her dreams; she feared unemployment and its accompanying insecurities.

While working at this job, Eve said:

All these years with the job stress, I've had chronic illnesses, and I've finally learned to deal with it and gotten much better....I do everything I can to take care of myself...yoga, I have a new program that is helping me with my energy, I'm constantly learning how to improve my diet.

Her physical and emotional health were affected. So she began to take care of herself, as she has described. We know from the Stress Management chapter that none of these strategies will reduce the type of stress Eve, or anyone in her situation, will have. Finally, after several years of enduring this, she took firmer self-care steps, got a medical leave and therapy, and decided not to go back. Eve is now working on starting her own business while holding a part-time job.

We humans, HSPs and not, often want to think that things will be different in our case. We don't want it to be bad, so we ignore the lurking problem. Some people, like Charlotte, know instinctively how to handle the problem, but sometimes we can be broadsided, like Pam, and thrown off base. It helps to learn from the experiences of others who stumbled a bit, to see how simple it is to get lost or fooled and not even realize it, like Eve, who chose to trust her good work, her quiet professional demeanor, and her HSP reticence. These are wonderful traits, but as we will soon discuss, they don't work with bullies.

And this takes us to our next section on the skills we need to deal with bullies.

If You're in Crisis

If you're reading this while in the middle of a crisis, perhaps everything feels like it's moving too fast. The pain is very high, and you need time and quiet to calm down, digest, get past the confusion and fear, ask questions and get help. But you're not getting anything you need, and the next attack comes before you've barely had a chance to breathe freely or have a good night's sleep.

Perhaps you're thinking it will stop on its own if you wait it out, that the other person has said all he or she is going to say and will leave you alone. Perhaps you have a hard time explaining the situation to others, and their advice seems to ask more of you than you feel capable of doing. Perhaps you try some of their suggestions and they don't help, but on the contrary, make things worse.

If you're in this situation, what can you do?

The answer is somewhere inside of you. Go back to Lesson 2 in this chapter (or Chapter 3, if you need to practice slowing down) and listen to your body, emotions, and intuition. Depending on your circumstances, you may not come out of this free and clear. But you can take back control of your life by starting to pay attention to what your self is telling you. Consider this a tough lesson, an advanced lesson, one that requires all your courage, determination, and some degree of guts and willingness to step out of your normal mode into a more "warrior"-like stance for a while. And don't be alone. Find encouragement and advice from those who are able to help you.

Taking on a Bully

Sam Horn, author of a number of books on dealing with difficult people, was herself bullied. Her newest book is *Take the Bully by the Horns*. Sam and I discussed the HSP temperament, and the problems we face when it comes to bullies, and she made several suggestions for HSPs.

First, let's look at exactly what kind of person we're dealing with. A bully is acting deliberately and choosing those most likely to not fight back—and HSPs do fit that mold. Avoiding, not responding, or running away from a bully is like dinner running from a hungry predator. *It will pursue.* You're "it." You must stand up to bullies in order to get them to stop.

Now, you may not know when someone who's being difficult is a bully, at least not right away. Lots of things that happen will be used by all kinds of different "difficult" people. That's why I structured this chapter as a series of lessons to be used for all ordinary circumstances. If you've been doing what normally works well for you to maintain your boundaries, and it seems that you've managed well, but you suddenly encounter a situation where the person is *not* responding as everyone else, you need to take stronger measures. This would then be an unusual case.

Being an HSP under these circumstances is disastrous. First, we want the painful stimulation to stop. Confronting the bully, standing up to her (or him), seems an unbearable idea. But as I noted earlier, HSPs who have done so say that though the stimulation will increase for a little while, it then subsides. And bullies back down when there's resistance. Remember, bullies unconsciously or consciously are looking for *easy targets*, not those likely to resist.

Why You Must Stand Up to Them

Sam Horn says that our HSP strengths, taken to an extreme—our empathic, sensitive nature, even our loyalty—will be used against us by a bully, for whom such traits are seen as a weakness. We are not abandoning our principles or our integrity by going on the offensive with a bully. A bully *intentionally* will mistreat us. We shouldn't be intimidated by how hard it may initially feel to do something that goes against our nature. Rather, we should consider adopting a special skill set—like the kung fu lessons in this chapter—for a bully problem.

In our conversation, Sam Horn stressed that bullying is an unusual situation. As a result, the usual HSP approach, of using empathy to understand another person, will not work. Our HSPs traits will be used against us.

When we're talking about bullies, I want them [HSPs] to take it one step further when they are knocked off balance. When somebody does say something that's offensive, the first question is to ask themselves, Is this a pattern with this person? Do I frequently feel like this with this person? Is this a habitual way of them treating me? And if it is, for them to perhaps switch responsibility. Instead of thinking "I'm responsible for this sensitivity," to understand that it very well may purposely be perpetrated on them and to start thinking "If I'm off balance that's exactly what this person is trying to achieve," and when they start realizing it is a tactic used against them, that also empowers them because they understand what's going on, and they're better prepared to respond to it rather than react to it.

Remember, listen to your intuition and don't ignore it. To that end, review earlier lessons in this chapter.

Horn, on the challenge of an HSP confronting and going on the offensive by adopting a special skill set:

[HSPs] have the right to go on the attack. Now, those are very strong words, however, it is very freeing for [HSPs] to understand that they are not abandoning their principles or their integrity when they come back strong to someone who is *intentionally* mistreating them. The reason why I'm emphasizing this is because [of] ... how tough it is for them to do things contrary to their nature. However, if they understand, if they reframe that, instead of seeing it as being tough, if they see it as adopting a different skill set that is going to serve them and is going to remove them from being victimized by aggressive individuals, then they will embrace it rather than shrink from it.

Just like you'd never dream of using a fingernail clipper to cut away carpet, consider the lessons in how to deal with a bully as special skills for special situations.

What Skills Do You Need?

Here are a few samples from *Take the Bully by the Horns*[5] that might be helpful when it comes to dealing with a bully. However, don't use anything randomly without thinking about it. Take time to read and discuss these ideas with others, *to strengthen your emotional understanding of what you have to do and why.* Take the time to think out what matters to you, how you've dealt with problem people before, and what you'd like to accomplish. Listen to your intuition, not someone else's.

> ➤ Document, in an intelligent and thoughtful way, what happened.

> ➤ Interrupt. This is a great tool. It gives you something physical to do, which distracts the other person and gives you a few precious moments to gather your wits.

> ➤ Use *you* not *I*—you don't want to debate with a bully. The *I* word implies fairness, and fairness, remember, is a weakness to a bully. *You* returns the focus back to the bully.

➤ Put on a brave front. You may have to wing it, but nevertheless you can do it.

➤ Never say yes on the spot. This gives you time to collect yourself and decide at your own pace, perhaps privately with no distractions.

➤ Be brief. Explanations might be construed as an apology.

➤ Be prepared to make a scene—it doesn't hurt to have attention if you need it.

➤ Appeal to their need to save face. Logic won't work. Think of negative consequences they will have.

A bully could change a great job into a nightmare and lead to a plunge straight down into Drudgery when we don't understand what hit us or how to deal with it. If you look back over the stories in these lessons, even in other chapters, you can see that HSPs have stood up successfully to taunts, unethical behavior, abusive behavior, and the daily stress and strains of their jobs because they used their HSP nature effectively. Remember, bullies seem to notice who is using their sensitivities in a self-defeating way. As Sam Horn mentioned, our sensitivities, when taken to an extreme, or when we devalue ourselves, can be a liability for us. Are you ready to put the odds on your side?

The Secret to Surviving

Those HSPs who survive—whether it's a onetime crisis or an ongoing situation in which they are constantly surrounded by abrasiveness—learn valuable skills. We hold our boundaries. We speak up and say what matters to us, and we do this even if overwhelmed. We can do it with or without being emotionally intense. We can have some calm and wit about ourselves, and we can get mad too, and speak angrily.

No matter what our situation, we will encounter difficult people. We don't know if they'll just be someone who's basically decent and has a crusty way of communicating discontent, or is someone with serious psychological problems. And it really doesn't matter, because in the long run, we still have to maintain our boundaries and continually strive to be congruent and honest with ourselves. That is the best thing we can do.

Congratulations, Grasshoppers!
You have finished your "kung fu" lessons.

Allow yourself time to savor the information and the realization that if you really desire to improve your ability to deal with difficult situations, you will manage to do so. If you look back at past chapters, along with this one, you will see many examples of HSPs who were in difficult situations. Each HSP had his or her own way of dealing with them. As you assimilate your own experiences and those of people around you, you'll start to pay more attention to your inner signals when things are bothering you. You'll start to speak up more frequently on your own behalf, and you'll find that you are holding your own, comfortably, clearly, firmly, and with good humor.

8

Self-Employment, the Alternate Path

I have to create an end result, but I'm starting with a blank piece of paper and imagination. I'm convincing other people to back me, and I have an audience I'm trying to serve on a theme I believe in. All of that is basically on my shoulders to try and figure out, but I don't know that I'm going to be able to do it until it's done. There are stresses in that. And I have to deal with a lot of people when I don't want to deal with a lot of people. I'm selling and convincing and cajoling people all the time, and that much goes against my nature, I believe, but it's a skill I've picked up. This is my magic carpet, my path to get out and do things I want to do because I'm passionate about doing this stuff.

—ERIC, FILM PRODUCER

There are so many things to say about self-employment. The basic, overall message I wish to share is the need to balance one's HSP nature with the outer work of building the business.

In this chapter I'll address some of the areas where our HSP nature could be challenged. You will undoubtedly discover others. HSPs can do very well in self-employment. Some go beyond into entrepreneurship. Others struggle. We are not unique in that regard compared to the rest of the self-employed population. We differ when we don't pay attention to our HSP needs.

The world of business is changing. It's more fluid and malleable than it once was. Business experts see the stereotypical long-term employee who works in one career being replaced by a cadre of unusual working relationships as more work is "outsourced," and more temporary and "virtual" work is offered to meet changing economic and technological circumstances. The thinking now is that everyone needs to become more self-reliant and learn new skills to navigate through the changing landscape.[1]

You don't have to want to be self-employed to benefit from this chapter. Self-employment is indeed a *state of mind.* It's a way you relate to work that requires you to have a strong center and a strong sense of direction and purpose. William Bridges, author of *Job-Shift*, calls it "the self-managed career."

> You must see yourself as a self-contained economic entity, not as a component part looking for a whole within which you can function. This is why it is so important to see yourself surrounded by a market, even when you are on the payroll of an organization.[2]

Self-Reliance and Self-Employment

Self-reliance is at the heart of self-employment. It has to do with making your career your mission along with your vision for personal and professional growth. When you look carefully, there is no clear demarcation between the self-reliant employee and the self-reliant self-employed. Except that employees don't usually give a lot of thought to the business side of doing things.

Those who have a traditional employee lifestyle can benefit from knowing something about self-employment. The skills involved in keeping an eye on your own working life would also be helpful for those employees who want to keep an eye or two on those forces that may directly impact on their careers. And given that often HSPs change jobs and careers many times in their lives, in the ever-changing workplace landscape, the idea of a self-managed career is ripe for our use.

In this chapter, we'll discuss what's involved in creating an independent, self-reliant state of mind, and we'll discuss how self-employment can serve certain HSP needs and how it hinders others. But keep in mind that both the self-employed person and the employee have strong needs for interesting challenges, meaningful work, and some control over what, when, and how their work is done. And there are many shades of gray as one migrates from employment toward its counterpart—entrepreneurship. Each permutation pulls out other attributes in you.

Mahatma Gandhi

Many years ago I read an article about Gandhi's thoughts on economic freedom for India. To do this meant going back to an economic system that existed before the British were in India, when each village was economically self-sufficient. Gandhi's particular method for helping India achieve self-sufficiency was the spinning wheel. Much of the world remembers seeing him quietly spinning, a practice he kept up on a regular basis. It was both a philosophical message as well as a practical step toward his vision.

When cotton was spun and wound into a four-foot loop a specific number of times, and then tied and twisted a certain way, it was called a "hank of cotton." Gandhi wanted the hank of cotton to be the basic economic unit, which could be created by anyone with a spinning wheel. This not only preserved the self-sufficiency of the village, but also retained the village's emotional and economic dignity.[3] This image has stayed with me for many years, as a symbol of personal self-reliance and a reminder that each of us has within us the spiritual, mental, and emotional resources (our own personal hank of cotton) to provide for ourselves.

What Is Self-Employment?

As I define it, self-employment is a single individual who has no full- or part-time long-term employees and who prefers to stay "solo" and run the business alone.

In the business world, the self-employed are seen as the "first step," or a transition, toward having employees, shops, and larger capital outlay, rather than a viable established path in its own right. If you went to classes on starting your own business, you would find that almost everyone there sees the "growth" of the business in terms of dollars and in physical and/or personnel expansion. Quantitative growth is encouraged; it is a definition of success.

But there are vast millions who enjoy being "solo." Self-employment is the most common form of business worldwide. In the third world, it's a way of lifting populations out of poverty. Self-employment was once more prevalent in America than it has been in the twentieth century. The work culture has strong roots in the pioneer and entrepreneurial spirit that shaped the early colonists who, in addition to having a fiercely independent spirit, valued self-reliance, the work ethic, and originality.[4]

To give you an idea of the range of skills and talents possible in a solo business, they include: lobbyists, oil traders who buy and sell drilling rights worldwide, accountants, professional tennis players, paralegals and lawyers, street vendors, word processors, astrologers, therapists, piano teachers, gardeners, writers and editors, artisans, and a host of cottage industries. Self-employment is extremely versatile and plastic, easy to shape and reshape, according to your needs.

Solo Is Not Solitude

Being on our own today is not the pure solo life. We're not working like the grizzled old trapper in the nineteenth century who would disappear into the woods for months and surface a few days a year, with barely any social skills, to sell his furs and buy tobacco. I know of HSPs who would love to have an e-business and disappear into the electronic woods and be safe from the difficulties being around people brings. But if one craves solitude that badly, it's more likely that recognizing the influence of "old ghosts" and then attending to healing oneself needs to be taken care of first. In fact, rather than complete solitude, self-employment often involves creating new relationships with others. For introverts especially, having a large pool of business and networking contacts of any kind is unnerving, since they typically do not have a lot of casual acquaintances; small, intimate friendships are the norm. For the self-employed person, this casual group is not necessarily made up of good friends, clients, or staff, though there might be some elements of all of them. Indeed, these casual contacts can be interesting and friendly, help solve problems, give valuable information, and perhaps provide a project or two. But expecting this group to deepen into friends or clients is unrealistic. We are expected to bring a lot of enthusiasm when interacting with this group, and this energy needs to be sustained regularly. For the introverted HSP, remember, this is a special group that can help us on our journey without needing these ties to evolve into anything deeper. Developing a comfort level with this group will take some creative thinking and good stress management, particularly for introverted types.

The Gray Area Between Employee and Self-Employed

In certain ways, being self-employed is not as big a transition from being an employee as you might think. Many employees who have autonomy in their work resemble the self-employed. If you love what you do, have a schedule you're delighted with and the freedom to do your work your way, you're almost the same as a self-employed person. The only major difference is that you don't have to market yourself to generate money. The company does that for you.

Types of Employment

The transitions and gradations to being self-employed shouldn't frighten you. HSPs can be found at all points of the continuum between working for others and working for oneself. There are some "stopping places" along this continuum, however, that are more comfortable than others. Let's note and define the various points and distinctions between working for another and being completely on your own:

➤ Employee and teleworker

➤ Independent contractor, subcontractor

➤ Self-employed

➤ Small business entrepreneur

➤ Large business entrepreneur

Employee and Teleworker

An employee or teleworker works for a company. The work and the money are given to you in exchange for your daily presence and, essentially, for your being at a company's "beck and call." Telecommuters share many of the same personality traits and work ethics of the self-employed yet they are employees (i.e., self-starters who can work well unsupervised). While the idea of telecommuting is well known, the activity is not well-established in business. Drudgery, Craft, or Calling work can be telecommuted (data entry or working on reports). While there may be some benefits to doing telework, be prepared, that if you take Drudgery or Calling work home, *that is* what you're taking home.

Independent Contractor or Subcontractor

An independent contractor or subcontractor is someone who wants the independence and flexibility of hours yet retains some of the employer-employee relationship without the demands of building a business. While this can be a true self-employed situation, there is a gray area.

The independent contractor is sometimes a hybrid of sorts between an employee and a self-employed person. Independent contractors can have steady work for long stretches with the same company, working side by side with the employees, only they legally cannot be told how to do the work. This is because the law has certain specific rules that define independent contractors.

Some contractors even subcontract, and that person is also self-employed. Some people prefer freelancing/subcontracting jobs because they don't require the same heavy emphasis on marketing and selling of oneself to others. The problem begins when the job ends and there are no other clients. One must hustle for business or become an employee. Some people see contracting as a way to get their foot in the door to a full-time job. So it can be used to get in, or get out, of employment. It is a way to slowly get the feel for being on your own. There are legal issues, though; be sure you understand IRS rules.

Self-Employment

True self-employment is a creative place, and many enjoy just being self-employed without growing in the external way: employees, shops, products. Many times I've heard people describe how they've teamed with others, freelanced, subcontracted, soloed, depending on circumstances.

Small Business Entrepreneur

The small business entrepreneur starts a business that grows, in terms of the number of people employed and the capital involved. There's an implied expansiveness to this category, and the implication that one has the desire to make an impact on the community.

Large Business Entrepreneur

The large business entrepreneur also starts a business in which the number of people employed increases, as do the capital expenditures, and there's also expansiveness implied in the venture and an ability to make an impact on society or on an industry. The major difference between this entrepreneur and those who maintain small businesses is in magnitude and the demands on those involved.

Gregory, a multitalented HSP with two Ph.D.s, has a business doing IT project management, which at times spans both self-employment and small business entrepreneurship. He uses independent contractors who work with him on various projects. Becoming self-employed wasn't something he planned on; it evolved out of his needs. He likes helping people solve their problems.

Being able to help them understand how everything works, how they are going to benefit from the process. There's more freedom, I can spend more time focusing on the actual project work than having to have a lot of superfluous issues attached to it that just drain my time unnecessarily.

Gregory's parents encouraged him to follow the traditional employee route to retirement, but after a long while, he decided against this; he wanted more control over his life. His advice to HSPs is:

I want to be able to wake up in the morning and have a lot more control over how it is I'm going to spend my time.... I'd say it would have more to do with listening to themselves, and following what it is they want for themselves, more than being concerned with what others want for them.

The HSP and Self-Employment

Is self-employment good for the HSP?

In surveys of HSPs, I've found that those who are self-employed have a higher level of satisfaction with their work than those who are employees. Generally, HSPs gave three areas—working conditions, the actual work performed, and people interactions—much higher marks (mostly As and Bs) than employees did. (Work-life balance, by the way, was still a struggle for both groups.) Throughout history the self-employed love the freedom to control their work—the tasks, the day-to-day activities, and the decisions and relationships they build with others. These needs for control, creativity, and flexibility are shared by HSPs.

Let's go back again to the story of the cane cutters and the fishermen, whom we first met in the chapter on Drudgery. The fishermen were self-employed, and they enjoyed it because of the personal growth it offered. Also, they were comfortable with the unpredictable, with being on their own and making their own decisions. This is one of the advantages and challenges of self-employment. It presents freedom along with uncertainty, and an ambiguity that calls for personal discipline and clear directions.

In my own journey in self-employment, the more I changed, the more my business changed (and I've tried almost all of these roles). Looking back, it's clear that my first business was light-years away from what I'm doing now and that personally I'm light-years from who I was then. All the changes in my working life, it seems, fit my growth as a person. You may see this in yourself, too.

What's Required of the HSP

One of the things self-employment requires of us is tremendous self-reliance and self-discipline. New habits have to be learned, new ways of thinking about work and money, new ways to motivate oneself, and so on. While HSP tendencies are very much "natural" for self-employment, that doesn't mean we can jump in right away and expect it to work out immediately. Below are traits HSPs should consider as they explore self-employment.

TRADESKILL. In the book *Honest Business*, Michael Phillips and Salli Rasberry identify what they call "tradeskill" as important if someone is to be successful on their own:

Tradeskill is a cluster of attributes that allow people to effectively start and run a business ... persistence; the ability to face the facts; knowing how to minimize risks; and being a hands-on learner. Each of these are necessary elements of tradeskill, yet none of them, individually, are sufficient for business success.[5]

Our extraverted entrepreneur, Perry, went to swap meets as a child with his father. There, Perry began his very first business of buying and selling comic books, sometimes leaving with $30 in his pocket. Perry learned some business social skills by watching his father:

[My father] loved the whole buying and selling routine because he likes to interact with people. He didn't really care so much about what he's selling, that's usually not important. So I got a very early introduction to this.

CRAFT AND CALLING. Whatever issues create Drudgery for you can follow you into self-employment. But if I were evaluating whether someone could succeed at self-employment, I would expect that person's maturity, skills, and experience to be Craftlike, or akin to being a manager in a company. The more comfortable and experienced you are in functioning at a Craft or Calling level, the more likely that you'll succeed at self-employment.

EXPAND YOURSELF. Remember the story of Josh and Dundee in Chapter 3? By trusting the HSP-like sensitivities of Dundee, Josh was able to go beyond his accepted limits and try new things. When we give ourselves permission to trust our HSP nature, we grow, and self-employment can be like a wide open prairie for stretching ourselves.

Eric, the film producer we met earlier, has grown beyond the "normal" boundaries of being an introverted HSP. He could be extraverted, outgoing, meeting people, socializing, promoting his work and helping others because he loves his work, and that love strengthens him:

It is a pretty fast-paced environment. It's very social and that's quite unlike me. I'm very much a loner to the extent that I'm not in groups or large social scenes and yet I almost plunge myself into something that is very much that. I can do anything through my work. I'll make a phone call to anyone, I'll ask any question, I'll put myself in front of any audience of any size if it's a work project and if I have my cause, a theme, or issue I'm inspired by. Maybe it takes me out of myself a bit, or gives me another role to take on that makes it a bit easier.

Living with Ambiguity

Ambiguity—a gray area—happens a lot in self-employment. Take, for example, our public image of business. It has a certain standard of professional appearance that suggests polish, stability over time, respectability, and professionalism.

Often, I see "newbies" (HSP and not) struggling to create their image, spending money on letterheads, photos, business cards, perhaps a website, and so on. The beginner worries a lot about the presentation, but others can seem less perturbed. When we're new to self-employment, seeing ourselves changing a little each day is not unusual. And being HSPs, we're more aware of our inner shifts. So the idea of establishing a fixed image of ourselves for the world to see can be disconcerting for a while.

But it should be noted that as we HSPs develop our "marketing" material, coming up perhaps with a name, a concept, an image of what the business is like, what services it provides, and what needs it fulfills, we're seemingly "freezing" ourselves, when we know that in reality we feel ourselves constantly changing. All the self-employed HSPs I've talked to have found themselves shifting, as far as how they see themselves, and thus unconsciously they butt up against these frozen images and aren't always comfortable with them.

Another positive way to look at self-employment is that the challenges allow you and your work to "morph" all the time, and at times it compels us or we compel it. While this is occurring, you'll be expected to look like a finished product that can be stamped onto a package, as slick and polished as a brand name business. This is one of the contradictions of self-employment you can expect. The important thing, though, is to be true to yourself.

The process of choosing the right businesss (the research, thought, and ruminating over choices), the start-up tasks and the public paraphernalia (business cards, brochures, name, logo, memberships, entrepreneurial classes), along with becoming emotionally and mentally committed, can be a struggle if we are not fully in tune with our inner depths. For example, read what Judi, an HSP motivational speaker, has to say about this process. This was said when Judi was still developing "version 3" of her business. In time, this will get easier.

When we work for someone else, we go into a job having a basic idea of what the job entails and what background we have for doing the work. The structure for the job is already there. The tools we need are provided to us for the most part. When we become self-employed, the tools are no longer there. We have to create them. We have to make sure we have everything we need in order to do the job. As an HSP, I've found this to be a very difficult process to go through. It's very painful emotionally and sometimes physically to create what I need. The ideas are there. There are times when I wish I was more logical and could take the ideas and just formulate them and everything would fall into place.—Judi, motivational speaker

---

Here's another example of how ambiguity can manifest itself. Geoffrey Bellman explores the personal process of how one grows through self-employment in *The Consultant's Calling*. Bellman describes how sometimes a project can be both satisfying and uncomfortable. He knows that working with certain types of organizations may generate terrific projects, but also feels that they're "laced with discomfort."[6] Consequently, he decides to reject work from these sources because the discomfort makes him aware of something he needs to attend to. Bellman encourages his readers to seek out, explore, and learn more about anything that makes them uncomfortable. These are important discriminations, and for our own boundaries and self-care, when uncomfortable emotions appear, we need to ask ourselves similar questions and to try to become aware of what is right for us.

Competition

How do you feel about competition? You almost have to have two mindsets about it. One part is practical and the other intrinsic. And the intrinsic is the part we have to work the hardest at. Eric has worked out his attitude toward competition. He sees himself as noncompetitive and focuses on the originality of his work and on being relaxed, as much as possible, with another person's freedom to choose.

> I'm not going to try and beat somebody else out for the same job. I'll do my thing in an original way, and if someone likes it, they can take it. That's how I approach my work.

Advanced Issues for the Ambitious

One day, while out for a walk, I asked myself, "If I were in a fairy tale, what would be going on?" Immediately, I saw those funny mirrors that make you look extra fat or tall, and a wild-looking face. I realized I was at a carnival. This told me that my image of myself as a self-employed person was still shifting, and that there would be surprises, that I might still be startled or spooked. I also realized that I had to have more fun with the process, that self-employment was something I should play with more than I had.

At the time I played with this imagery, I was having a hard time with one of my self-employment jobs. This exercise helped me to remember one of the big reasons why I loved being self-employed—I enjoyed the exploration, newness, and adventure. Keep that in mind, as you look at the list of experiences that can happen when you're self-employed. In the many years I've researched and talked with self-employed people, they will scratch there heads, grumble, grind their teeth, but won't give up, just because the challenges, listed

> I try hard to never stop being a kid. I have a huge imagination and am curious as hell. There needs to be a certain amount of child-like innocence in the creative process.

below, happen. The love for the work keeps them curious and encouraged. If you are doing work you *really love*, these challenges won't stop you. Sometimes it helps to let go of our expectations and just play with life.

If these challenges do stop you, ask yourself, am I being honest about how I really feel? Am I doing what I really love or what I'm curious about, or, perhaps, am I only doing it for the money? Am I in Drudgery?

So, as you look at this list of experiences one can have in business, keep in mind that these events can bring new levels of growth, self-reliance and self-confidence, creativity, and learning. They don't happen in a vacuum and alone; they cannot make or break a business unless you let them.

> ➤ The needs of a client can change very rapidly overnight.

> ➤ Sometimes work will end suddenly, without warning.

> ➤ You can't predict how well any one particular marketing tool will work.

> ➤ When a door closes, another will open, but it could be in two days or six months.

> ➤ Boundaries are important, and you have to keep working at them. Sometimes a boundary will cost you a client.

> ➤ Any internal resistance you have to the job can stifle your ability to fully grow in that business.

It also has to do with our sensitivity that we spend a lot of time on the inner states that make up being self-employed. There are so many "knees" that have to connect to various "shinbones," and the HSP is intuiting which "knee" and which "shinbone" belong together. When the link doesn't feel right or seems incomplete, we can't move forward. The inner self needs to feel full and rich in order to move into self-employment.

You can't predict where you'll be in one or two years. If there's any reassurance I can offer you, it's that HSPs change careers and jobs often. And all self-employed people do the same, frequently. Having two or five different businesses over 10 years is not unusual. Look at it positively: It's a sign of discovery, not weakness.

The Energy of Self-Employment

There are four different types of "energy" in business interactions: highly structured, free flowing and self-created, a "cake mix" that you can modify to your needs, and one that includes lots of social time. These can be seen operating, to a greater or lesser degree, in the four business formats we discuss in the following paragraphs—franchise, business opportunity, multilevel, and personal-creative—and we will need all of them at varying times. I've used these symbols in games with people to talk about self-employment and the ways we experience it. The symbols can represent something you need in you. Not necessarily the type of business it represents, but the interaction it creates. As your needs change, you may find yourself needing a different energy.

The symbols in Figure 8-1 represent the energetic quality of four types of business formats, each format being a different way of expressing ourselves in self-employment. One requires a lot of connections. Another places us inside a formal structure with rules. Another requires all creativity to come from the center (us), and a fourth is part creative and part structure. All four types are available to the self-employed and will require a different kind of relationship with others. And each has weaknesses. For example, too much structure, and creativity languishes.

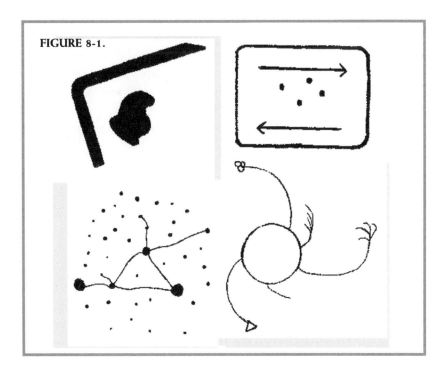

FIGURE 8-1.

Franchise

A franchise is structured, with rules, regulations, and expected behavior spelled out between the owner and the franchisee. You don't have a lot of freedom to choose the name, the way you run the business, or how you relate to the owner. In essence you're playing in someone else's sandbox, with their toys, and they tell you how to play with them. The picture of a box with an orderly give and take represents this energy.

Business Opportunity

This is where someone gives you a "starter kit" and then you run with it in your own way. You may buy a training program, or a specific product or service, and then create your own business name, market the business your way, and thus find your own niche. There are generally some guidelines you have to follow, but there's a greater level of freedom than with the franchise. Here you have someone else's toy and then you create your own sandbox.

Multilevel

This system of business is generally socially oriented and thus requires strong social skills. You spend most of your time with other people, connecting, building relationships, supporting, bolstering, being supported. It also contains someone else's toys, but typically the people relationships are far more complex and demanding than in an ordinary business opportunity.

Personal-Creative

If you take this route, you create your own business from scratch: your own toy and your own sandbox. Everything begins from within you and must move out from you into the world.

Some Observations from Paul and Sarah

Paul and Sarah Edwards have written many books on self-employment and are widely regarded as among the first to introduce the idea of working from home. Though now successful, they both recall a time when they were first starting out, when no one came to their seminars and they didn't know if they'd succeed. Their ideas were so new that it took time for people to understand, and it took patience and steadfastness on their part to continue communicating their message.

Sarah is particularly highly sensitive. She wanted to achieve something and admits that for a long time she tried to be different from her true self in order to make it professionally:

The message I got when I was going out on my own was that I had to become outgoing, extroverted in television and radio and all of this, so I've worked extremely hard to develop these aspects of myself. And I did master a good number of skills such as professional speaking, networking, being able to handle a lot of pressures and stress. I'm glad I've mastered these skills, but now I'm learning that actually being highly sensitive has many benefits. I can sense things, I can intuit things, and of course, it brings me my creativity, and so I now honor that part of myself much more instead of fighting it. Feeling confidence that I can approach the world without so much drive and push, I can be more myself.

Paul and Sarah have a number of interesting observations about self-employment, specifically for HSPs:

➤ Self-employment gives you lots of control over your environment, and that's helpful to the sensitive temperament. Sarah left her government job because it was actually making her sick, and she worked from home because she felt she could control her environment more: "I didn't realize it at the time, that it was because I could be in control of the level of stimuli and what I was interested in, and what I pursued in my own time frames. As I got into more and more self-employment, I realized I could change that even more."

➤ The self-employed person doesn't fit the mold of the entrepreneur, who is very tough, able to take risks, and has high energy. Paul and Sarah call the self-employed person a "propreneur," and they seem to attract this kind of person in their own work. They say it's all right if you don't fit the entrepreneurial mold, you can still find a niche for yourself in self-employment and tailor it to your own needs.

➤ Change is a big factor in our society today, and we have to learn more about how to manage, embrace, and create change that suits our own needs. Sometimes people need to take their time getting started in a new business venture, and it's okay to go at a slower pace if you choose. Sarah often reduced her fear of starting something new by reminding herself that she was just playing with it for a while: "I'm just going to see what happens, I'm not really doing it yet."

➤ The emotional energy we have locked up in Drudgery jobs, and the fear of not having enough energy left over to start a business is an important issue for HSPs. The worry, stress, and resulting exhaustion of being in a situation that's not right for you will change once you open yourself to doing something you enjoy. As Paul says: "If you eliminate the dampening down of your instincts, there's going to be a whole new batch of energy."

➤ Making the transition to self-employment can take time. While some people can dive in right away, others need a longer gestation period. Paul and Sarah don't recommend making snap decisions about changing from being an employee to becoming self-employed. Rather, the process of change itself needs to be done in a manner consistent with your own needs.

They've given some thought to the nature and stages of change in *Changing Direction Without Losing Your Way*.[7] Even if you don't become self-employed, they write, it's useful to approach change as a skill set. It will help you in this ever-changing work world where markets, economies of scale, downsizing, outsourcing, and self-employment fluctuate constantly.

HSPs can be resistant to change, because it is so overstimulating and brings our insecurities to the surface. Putting yourself in charge of change, instead of letting it lead you, can give you better control over your own direction.

Natural HSP Talents: Cookie

Here's a story about someone who took control of her life through her work: Cookie is a law librarian who created a business niche servicing lawyers and CPAs. She comes from a family of entrepreneurs. Her parents were opinionated and always encouraged her to be an independent thinker.

Outside the family, however, she was often lonely, with few friends who could relate to her insatiable interests (at 11 years of age she was reading Greek and Roman authors, *The Autobiography of Malcolm X*, and so on). She was sensitive, was put down for being a "know it all" by her peers, and had few friends until her teens.

In her fifties, Cookie is far more comfortable with being herself and has a career that nourishes her natural tendency to absorb information and put it into an orderly and insightful format for her clients. Because her work is unique and involves unique skill sets, it gives her confidence.

Cookie's work allows her to use her natural independent personality and her love of knowledge to her best advantage. Her job requires her to be knowledgeable about a wide range of subjects and do investigative research for her clients. "Because when you're evaluating information and melding together a story of what might or might not have happened," she says, "you can't be deterred or swayed by popular notions."

Her work nourishes her because she's respected for knowing so much and being smart. "When growing up," she notes, "those traits were not popular, especially in a girl. And this particular profession I've chosen—one, being a librarian, and two, the engineering of the job into a unique business—does nurture those traits. It's positive reinforcement."

What Cookie doesn't like are those occasions when she has to deal with people issues, when she must be in the middle and solve everyone's problems: "I have a short patience for it. I get very frustrated by it and I don't like that type of conflict." It requires mapping out the issues and seeing things from both views. "I'm very ethical and honest," she says, assessing herself, "and sometimes too righteous, and I don't always agree with what management wants, because I don't think it's best for the longterm. I think, though, that's what makes me a good consultant. Unfortunately, I do carry my angst around." To calm down, she reads, cooks, or goes to a museum.

Occasionally Cookie has a difficult client, and she doesn't take to bullies well. Boundaries are always a challenge, and she has taught herself to be very firm:

I work with difficult people all the time and I think it helps that I have a big mouth and that I set limits, though it's not 100 percent. Last week, a client bullied me into taking on an assignment that I told him I couldn't do

for the amount of money he wanted to spend, and because he is a long-term client, I put up with more of it than I would from somebody else. Then I saw myself becoming passive/aggressive about the assignment and being angry and blaming myself. I was miserable, and I decided I wasn't going to take a pay cut for a job well done.

It takes patience and determination to find one's HSP "bearings" and real balance too, especially when dealing with the inner needs and outer demands we place upon ourselves, as Cookie has done on a daily basis.

The Self-Employment Option

Before you take a fresh look at being an employee, trying self-employment, or considering any of the HSP-friendly gradations in between, it would be helpful if you would explore your own personal mythology. For example, you could write up to two pages summing up your life as if it were a fairy tale, told in the third person. This will help you learn more about the deeper meanings to the stories that make up who you are today. So, you are essentially looking down on your own life, seeing its aspects flash by and claiming its important tales and themes. In your last few lines, you can compose anew, peer into the future, and see what you might be doing from this point on.

In this era, the boundaries between employment and self-employment (and all the variations in between) are blurring, and there are many ways to be with yourself, your work, and your life. I really do believe that HSPs need to use our creativity, our imaginations; our minds, hearts, and souls, in our work. And this starts by being comfortable with ourselves: ready to assess our strengths as highly sensitive people, using them to be self-reliant as much as we can, and then finding the outer, working-world niche that is best for us.

And if you look out of the corner of your eye at that magic mirror at the carnival, you just may glimpse something special, just for you.

9

Psychic Income

*I mean I get a paycheck. I get dollars and cents too that I can
pay the mortgage with and buy food and gas with. But I think
I also get a sense of meaning and a sense of fulfillment. I guess
my job scores really high for me on the psychic income part of it.
Because I get to do some things that are really important to me,
it is not simply a matter of trying to sell something that I could
care less about but I have to sell it to make a living. Almost
everything I do has content to it that is important to me.*

—TOM, ECONOMICS PROFESSOR

Paradise and Psychic Income

In nature, in a good, healthy ecological system, everything works well
together. Paradise is the ideal image of this health, vitality, and sustainability. Whether you're a promising young dinosaur roaming the lush green
earth a million years ago or a modern human on the fast track to success
in the lush metal forest of a metropolis, that same quality of vitality, happiness, and success is suggested.

As human beings, our goal in life is to maintain optimal spiritual, mental, emotional, and physical health. When you tire, your rest should revive
you back to your optimal best. When you're challenged, you grow and
flourish, but ideally, not to the point of burnout. Healthy relationships with
work and people lead to psychological growth as well. And work, of course,
can be a setting for growth: nurturing talent, building skills, strengthening
maturity, leadership, and creativity.

To this point we've been getting inside of Drudgery, Craft, and Calling,
and experiencing what each is like. It's time to take a step back, to see the

bigger picture, just as when we look at the forest from a distance, we see things differently. Now we'll look at Drudgery, Craft, and Calling in terms of what I call "psychic income,"[1] This adds a level of complexity to these three modes of work experience. This chapter is a fun, visual way of under-standing these three dimensions of work.

Note the basic psychic income scale of Calling, Craft, and Drudgery depicted in Figure 9-1. Imagine this as your personal stoplight, similar to a regular stoplight only upside down. The top section is Calling. It is trans-parent, to remind us of the lightness of this energy, its uplifting nature, the clarity it brings to us. This is the ideal place to be and what we all want to aim for. When we do work we love, we're growing, thriving, happy, and energized. We are rejuvenated by it. This is our bliss, our Calling, and it nurtures us.

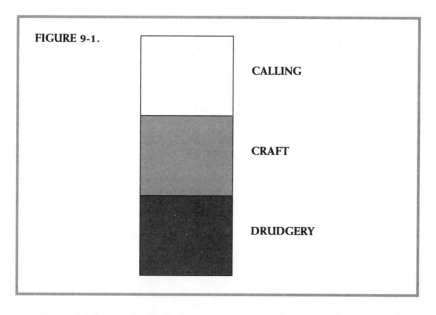

FIGURE 9-1.

CALLING

CRAFT

DRUDGERY

The middle panel, Craft, is not as clear as Calling and not as dark as Drudgery. This is a situation when work lacks the passion and joy of Call-ing. It's a little of both—not as buoyant as one, not as dense as the other.

The bottom panel is Drudgery. Perhaps a big warning sign should have been added: "Danger! Stop!" Drudgery is dark and feels dense, foggy, and murky, as befitting the emotions of that condition. This is when you are in unsatisfying, unrewarding work and in emotionally painful conditions. By now you know that highly sensitive people are especially in danger in Drudgery, and getting out is a wise course of action.

Ideally, at our healthiest and best, we begin in Calling, at the top of the illustration. But as you experience *stress and distress* at work, you will leave the ideal healthy zone and begin to move downward, out of Calling into Craft and then into Drudgery. The more unhappy you are, the farther you fall from a Calling and the closer you get to being in Drudgery.

Three Dynamic Forces

In the previous chapters, we've discussed the conditions that cause Drudgery, Craft, and Calling. But let's review them again, only now in terms of their impact on our psychic income.

There are three basic stimuli: people, job, and conditions. The three different-size balls in Figure 9-2 represent the powerful impact the largest ball makes, the lesser impact of the middle ball, and the mildest impact of the third, the smallest ball.

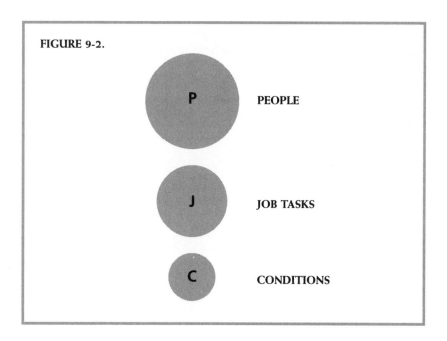

FIGURE 9-2.

P   PEOPLE

J   JOB TASKS

C   CONDITIONS

Since we work with people in a setting and on a job, these balls are not mutually exclusive from one another. But for the purposes of our examination, think of each one as representing a dominant factor in your work. For that reason, imagine them as connected with rope. That will serve to remind us that though they're separate, all three can affect each other.

Environmental Conditions

The smallest and lightest ball represents the *environmental conditions.* These conditions include the following:

> ➤ **COMMUTE:** getting to and from a place of employment

> ➤ **LIGHTS:** overhead fluorescents, desk lamps, windows, or the lack of them

> ➤ **SOUNDS:** copiers, voices, phones ringing, any harmonious or discordant sounds

> ➤ **ODORS:** construction smells, food odors, perfumes

> ➤ **SPACE:** office location, the amount of privacy, the cleanliness of the environment, the desk you have, the room and furnishings in your office or work area, the presence or absence of windows

Alone, environmental conditions affect your nervous system, but this does not necessarily last long. On a good day, with a good meal and a good night's rest, you will be refreshed from any overstimulation caused by these conditions.

Job Tasks

Are you a banker, artist, stenographer? Then the medium ball represents the *job* we do and all the tasks involved in it. You have emotions, values, ideas, and aspirations attached to your job. Therefore, its impact on you is much greater and longer lasting than those of the conditions at and attached to work. If you're bored or thrilled with a new challenge, the resulting restlessness or excitement can keep you going or weigh you down for some time.

Examples of some tasks that define the job you do:

➤ Paperwork

➤ Analyzing material

➤ Writing

➤ Negotiating

➤ Helping familiar people or strangers

➤ Working with your hands

People at Work

The largest and heaviest ball represents the *people* at your job and includes in addition to individuals, the broad, sometimes mysterious realm of office politics, company policy, and senior management. Here, we often experience the greatest impact. Both our imagination and emotions are affected, and the duration can be long-term. Trust can be built or lost, friendships forged, encouragement given and received.

Examples of those who could be in your people ball:

➤ Boss

➤ Coworkers

➤ Staff

➤ Clients

➤ Employees

➤ Anyone else you need to deal with to get the job done

Another factor for you to consider is the match between your values and the values of others at work

Being Buoyed Up or Pulled Down

Have you ever been swimming in a clean swimming pool or gone wading in murky waters? Have you ever had a nightmare of trying to run through quicksand? Do you recall how horrible it felt as that yucky substance slowed you down while you tried to escape some awful creature? This is what I'd like you to think about as you look at Figure 9-1 again. At the top, the "water" of Calling is clear, clean, and easy to move around in. The deeper you go, the more dense, murky, difficult, and slimy the substance becomes, clinging to you and impeding your progress.

Imagine yourself working happily on a productive day. You have the time to concentrate, no one is disturbing your equilibrium, your work is rewarding, you receive praise and encouragement regularly, and your office is a pleasant place to be. Under such idealistic conditions, your people, job, and conditions balls are all floating on the surface. Everything is going well. But in time things may change. The job may become ho-hum, the commute tiresome, and/or the amenable office manager might leave and be replaced by a difficult person.

Any one of the three balls will begin to sink into murkier waters, depending on whether the job, people, or conditions factors are strongly affected. You can become stressed and distressed. The balls will be coated with that horrible yucky stuff at the bottom, bringing up gunk as they slowly rise again to the surface. Each time any one of these three balls sinks so low, it will be coated with slime, get soggier, and not rise as high as it once did.

All along, I've been saying that Drudgery isn't a place where you want to stay. So, considering the image of the three balls, what do you think is the best way to keep them from sinking into Drudgery? I'll give you a clue: Remember, all the balls are connected.

While you think about that question, let's continue to observe the mechanics of the balls in this watery chart.

A stressful commute will cause the smallest ball to dip down. If your job becomes boring, the middle ball will find its way into Craft or lower. A negative performance review will certainly bring your people ball into darker waters. The law of gravity says that the heaviest object is going to sink the farthest and have an impact on the lighter objects, so if your people ball goes down, it will drag the other balls along with it. But if only the little conditions ball is affected, it won't go very deep, because the other two, more powerful balls are in higher waters and will buoy it up.

Returning to my question of how to stay out of Drudgery: The answer is to pay close attention to the people ball; that is, don't underrate the impact that people have on you. Your experiences with people—the heaviest ball—can take everything down to the bottom, into the dregs of Drudgery. Think of the people ball as either a buoy keeping you afloat above the waters or as a heavy weight dragging you down to that Davy Jones locker at the bottom of the sea.

The challenge for HSPs trying to make work *work* for them is in understanding why this happens. Some discount the significance of the people dynamics. They see a wonderful job doing work they love, but don't consider whether the people they will be working with are right for them. Or they focus on doing *only* the job and not developing connections with others, thus undermining their invisible connections to everyone in the office.

To stay out of Drudgery, your relationship with people involved in your work needs to be in Craft or Calling. Once the people ball starts to sink into Drudgery, the other two may be tainted, too. Once the people ball sinks, and stays in Drudgery, you are indeed *in* Drudgery, and you may not get out unless you leave the job completely.

Two Psychic Income Portraits

Let's see how this works with two HSPs, both of whom are introverts in a high-people-contact job and have been at their respective positions a long time.

Jillian (Figure 9-3), in her mid-thirties, works in a call center, talks to between 100 and 150 people a day, and has done this job for 10 years. Most of the time, a call center job is not good for introverted HSPs.

Henry (Figure 9-4), in his early fifties, is a technical instructor. He spends hours solving problems and teaching people how to use their complex equipment. He's been doing this for 25 years. While Henry is not dealing with quite as many people per day as Jillian, he's constantly interrupted, and he has coworkers—both on site and in the field—with whom he works by telephone and in person.

Jillian's Working Life

Conditions

Jillian spends the day in a large room with 12 to 15 others and has a desk and cubicle with her personal items and the all-important phone. All day long she can hear her coworkers answering phones, talking to people. Sometimes someone will shout out a problem he or she is having and others will respond with suggestions. It's a noisy environment, with constant interactions with people. But the commute is not too bad. And the surrounding locale is pleasant enough to go outside for lunch.

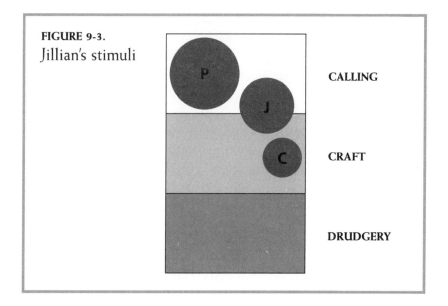

FIGURE 9-3.
Jillian's stimuli

CALLING

CRAFT

DRUDGERY

People

Jillian's boss is a supportive person, and the company has a family-first policy that lets her take herself or her child to the dentist without them subtly suggesting she make up time by giving up breaks or lunch. A third of the representatives specifically ask for her, so she's helping people she's known for quite a while. Jillian enjoys helping people solve their problems.

There's a cooperative spirit in the office. If another person, like herself, is having trouble solving a problem, they'll call out to the group in the room, and someone will usually be able to help them solve it. Her boss does not insist that she sell more products and is relaxed and unperturbed at how much she hates the idea of selling.

Job Tasks

Jillian's job is to answer phones, help the vendors track down missing shipments, and tries to get the shipments to them as quickly as possible. She enjoys the challenge of solving problems quickly and efficiently, and the problems presented by the vendors are frequently unique, so there's lots of variety in the calls. She'll also use her empathic skills to help calm them when they sound upset. While the company mildly encourages customer service reps to sell more products, Jillian does not make much effort to do so, and she doesn't participate in selling contests.

Summary

For Jillian, the two heaviest balls (people and job) are up in the Calling range and continue to float on the surface. She feels emotionally supported by the people at work, treated like a human being, respected and appreciated. The environmental conditions ball, however, is stressed by the constant stimuli of noises—phone calls, voices—that bombard this introverted HSP.

Because the heaviest balls remain in Calling, the smallest ball—representing conditions—never dips too far into Craft and returns to Calling when Jillian gets time to herself or during enjoyable weekend activities. She can endure what would be a severely taxing situation for most HSPs because the people dynamics are so enjoyable for her. So the stress from the environment, or even the tasks, is easier to manage.

Henry's Working Life

Conditions

Henry has an office, but he must move around to visit other departments throughout the day to check in on others elsewhere in the building. He doesn't mind this, since it means he's free to go here and there in the building to discuss issues with colleagues. Outside, there's lots of nature nearby, and he can take a walk if he needs a quiet break during the day. He's paid well and gets along with his colleagues, many of whom are long-timers like himself.

People

Henry is part of a fairly strong group of talented and skilled employees who have been at this company a long time, due to the values of a senior management that treated employees kindly. But Henry's new boss was chosen by a manager who's been bringing in "bottom-line thinkers and doers" for the past few years. And this new boss is rude, aggressive, micromanaging, and bullying. His brusque behavior has caused several staff members, including Henry, to go to Human Resources to complain about him.

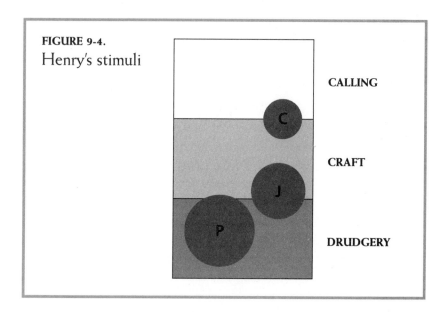

FIGURE 9-4.
Henry's stimuli

CALLING

CRAFT

DRUDGERY

Henry experiences the man's treatment of him as "emotional rape" and has battled with depression, hurt, and anger.

For a long time, the company's policies were people-oriented, giving the instructors considerable freedom in how they did their work. But conditions have changed in the past 10 years, with more cost-conscious and bottom-line thinking. Now, his new boss frequently says hurtful things, to Henry and others. Henry cannot even leave his office without his boss questioning him constantly. But Human Resources did eventually listen to the reports, and the new boss was told to change his style. By then, however, the damage was done. While he's now nicer to Henry and others, they aren't ready to trust him.

... the other day I was feeling depressed. It lasted several days. Not bad but enough to ruin a week. A little introspection has revealed deep burnout. The job may be nice, the pay is nice, the environment (office) is wonderful, the people are for the most part nice, especially my supporting friends. But the feeling is flat. It all means nothing. The workload is heavy, with intense people contact and lots of ambiguity in the workday and in the work process. It takes a toll. Now I have to rebuild. It's the cost of being stepped on.

Henry is describing Drudgery feelings. He faces a challenge many HSPs face. This is a good situation except for one boss who did a lot of damage with an unacceptable management style. Others may say, "Let it roll off your back." But that's not easy to do for an HSP.

Job Tasks

Henry's work is in a specialized area and the technology is constantly changing, so he is always learning new things and has an opportunity to help others all the time. He's interrupted a lot in order to assist other departments.

Henry's people ball is sinking rapidly due to the stress from the lack of rapport with his new superior. Using our previous metaphor, with the repeated drops into Drudgery, the people ball is getting mucky from being in the dense waters of Drudgery.

His job ball has also been dragged downward, by the pull of the people ball, and is now tainted too. Because of the presence of his boss in Henry's working conditions, that ball is also affected.

Summary

Both Jillian and Henry have (for introverted HSPs) pleasing but potentially stressful environmental conditions—with noise and interruptions. Both have enjoyed their jobs and been at them for many years. But the big difference in their situations is how the people at work affect them. Jillian is in a job where the company's people-friendly values and emotionally stable and respectful coworkers and bosses are soothing to the employees, creating trust, good morale, and a willingness to work hard. Henry is in a company that is shifting from an employee-friendly environment to one that has a more aggressive and competitive management team.

As you think about your situation, it's important to remember that HSPs are acutely aware of and impacted by other people. Too often HSPs underrate the long-term affects people have on them. In hindsight, it's easy to see, but when in the middle of it, the confusions of the moment make clarity difficult.

If you can look at your own work experiences, tease out the working conditions from the job and the people, and assess how each affects you, you can take a major step to recognizing what brings you down and what holds you up.

Money and Psychic Incomes

We're going to take a step further back and look at the original column of Drudgery, Craft, and Calling again. In Figures 9-5 through 9-10, which are presented below, there are two columns based on Figure 9-1.

Now look at Figure 9-5, below. The labels Drudgery, Craft, and Calling apply to both columns, but each column refers to either psychic or money income.

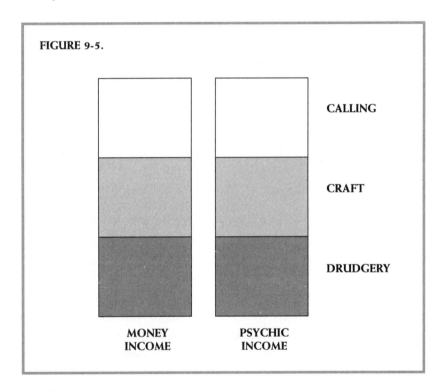

FIGURE 9-5.

CALLING

CRAFT

DRUDGERY

MONEY
INCOME

PSYCHIC
INCOME

The right column is your psychic income, or the intrinsic needs you have for your work. It includes all three of the balls we have been discussing, the people, job, and environment. Here, you have to give yourself a generalized score, based on your current emotional situation.

Do you need to get up and walk around the office and say hello to people during the day? Do you need to work outdoors instead of in an office? Do you need soft lights or fewer visual distractions in order to concentrate? Do you need a boss who trusts your judgment and lets you work at your own pace? All of these needs are your psychic income.

So the psychic income column, on the right, are all those intrinsic things we need: friendship, support, encouragement, appreciation, energizing or calming surroundings, interesting challenges, meaningful work, and a comfortable level of control over our work. The lack of these debits our psychic income.

The left vertical column is your money income, or the financial resources that sustain you. This can be a salary, savings, your lottery winnings, whatever. Money is a measurable benchmark, so we keep it separate here from the intrinsic needs, but the Drudgery, Craft, or Calling grade we give our money, is mostly subjective. You can have psychic income reactions to money, in that our feelings are buoyed or pulled down by our financial situation. For example, if you're barely making enough to live on, you're probably feeling that money is in Drudgery, whether your income is one dollar or $1000. Sometimes an individual will have a salary, but there might be another source of financial support as well. If that's the case, ask the same question about yourself, both individually and within the larger economic relationship. If one is in Drudgery and the other in Calling, well, that might have an impact on your overall psychic income.

However, because it's partially a quantifiable benchmark, money is a separate column of its own. In the business world, the practical value of money is extremely important. Yet we often assess the rightness of a career by the question: "If money was not an issue, what would you do?"

Together, these two columns are a powerful visual indicator of the impact of the circumstances you face at work, and their possible outcomes.

How Psychic Income Works

The High of Calling and the Low of Drudgery

Let's take a look at Joey, who found her dream job working for a cruise line, through the lens of psychic income. When she got the job, her psychic income was very high. Everything she said indicated she was in Calling:

The job was thrilling, new, exciting, the dream job of her life, and the cruises were wonderful. But her starting salary, in her estimation, was low. In Figure 9-6, you see Joey at the beginning of her career.

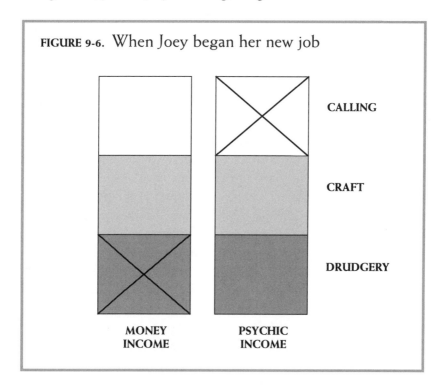

FIGURE 9-6. When Joey began her new job

This illustration is not unusual for HSPs, who often find the psychic income of their work more important than making lots of money. Many idealistic HSPs will work in low level jobs in nonprofits or start-up companies because they believe in what the organization is doing, and they love the work. Remember, Calling feeds us, and for a while we can survive, even thrive, on the high-octane-like "air" of a Calling's wonderful energy. The psychic income is very high and very rewarding under the circumstances. But still, the financial resources are in Drudgery. In a practical light, that's not good. Making ends meet on so little income is quite stressful. Drudgery, in the long run, if it's *not removed from your environment*, will pull down any Calling energy you have, no matter if the Calling was originally in money or psychic income. In the end, Drudgery will suck away or pull down the incredibly good feelings you have for your work.

In Joey's case, she was working in a big enough company, where for a long time she had the possibility of growth by moving around and learning new things. Meanwhile, her salary improved over the years. But if we're making barely survival existence for too long, with no sign of change—such as family help, a new job with better pay, winning the lottery—the happiness we feel will eventually evaporate.

Now, let's meet Joey years later, just before she quit her job.

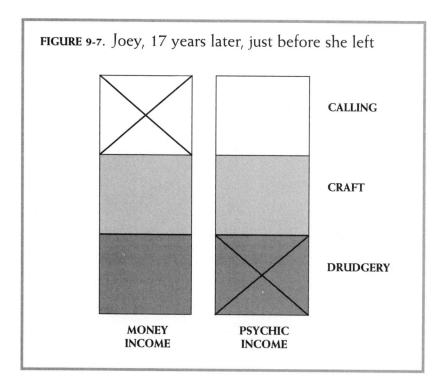

FIGURE 9-7. Joey, 17 years later, just before she left

CALLING

CRAFT

DRUDGERY

MONEY
INCOME

PSYCHIC
INCOME

Now Joey's situation is the mirror opposite of when she started her job, shown in Figure 9-6. Joey's salary here is very good—her money income is in Calling—but her psychic income is very low. Gradually, over time, the new and interesting challenges decreased as she taught herself one department after another. And the values of the company, which Joey believed in when she first came, were changing. Joey was no longer happy at this job and knew it was time to leave. Henry, whom you met earlier, is also represented by Figure 9-7.

One of the biggest challenges that we've discussed throughout this book is for HSPs to know *when* to leave Drudgery, for the longer you stay, the more chance there is that it will cause you trauma and distress. But I hope, by now, you're getting the message that getting out early on, is a good idea.

Getting Out Sooner

Now let's look at Samantha's illustration in Figure 9-8 (we met her in the Kung Fu chapter). At the time interviewed she was a marketing director who had an intellectually and creatively demanding, fascinating job that she loved, and she was making good money. While she's in a Calling/Craft job and still gets lots of thrill and enjoyment from her work, Samantha was preparing for a career change and was going to open her own holistic center. She discovered that she loved doing healing work and nurturing others, qualities she missed in her current job. This was spiritually rewarding and a career she wanted to pursue. Samantha was leaving while she was still on the border of Calling and Craft.

HSPs who leave in Craft may be doing themselves a favor. Their energy

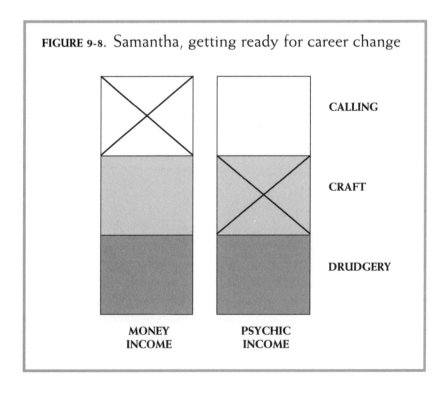

FIGURE 9-8. Samantha, getting ready for career change

CALLING

CRAFT

DRUDGERY

MONEY
INCOME

PSYCHIC
INCOME

is good, their health and emotional equilibrium is more stable, and they are not traumatized. There's no long-term Drudgery side effects, no need to sequester oneself away, to heal and lick one's wounds.

The Worst of the Worst

Let's look at another chart, in Figure 9-9. It shows where Rachel (see Chapter 4 on Stress Management) was at the time she was interviewed. Perhaps when she started this job she thought she was going into Craft or a Calling because it fed her need to help people. But the job was paid very poorly, and her psychic income from her work plunged with the problems she experienced.

As mentioned earlier in the Drudgery and Stress Management chapters, the health care field draws a lot of idealistic individuals. Unfortunately, this type of job, as you can see, is a double-dose of Drudgery! Here, it's powerful to see the combination of Drudgery money and Drudgery psychic income. The financial and emotional drain might require a time for

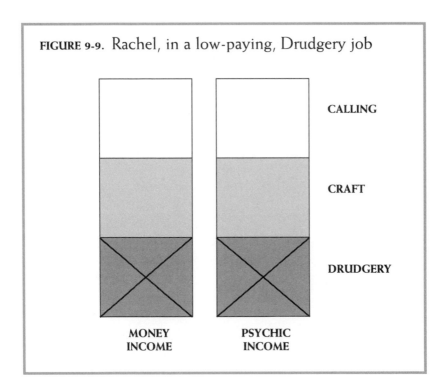

FIGURE 9-9. Rachel, in a low-paying, Drudgery job

CALLING

CRAFT

DRUDGERY

MONEY
INCOME

PSYCHIC
INCOME

recovery.

Psychic Income in Retrospect

By now you should be getting the basics of how the psychic income chart works. It's normal to have moments in the day that feel like Drudgery, Craft, and Calling. It's normal and healthy to have our money and psychic incomes bounce back and forth between these three work modes. Those are times that can challenge us and stimulate us to do more.

The ideal, probably for everyone, is to do work you love and at the same time make a good income. That would put the horizontal line in Calling for both psychic and money income scales. This is bliss.

Yourself, Today

The illustration in Figure 9-10 is a treat for you. Here again is a plain psy-

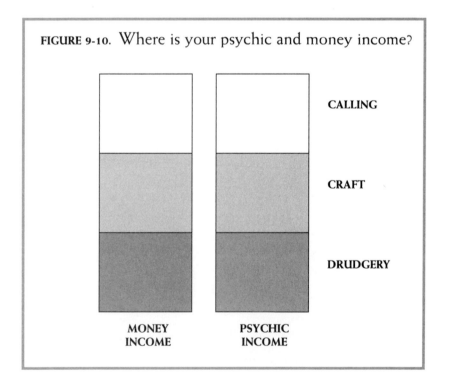

FIGURE 9-10. Where is your psychic and money income?

CALLING

CRAFT

DRUDGERY

MONEY
INCOME

PSYCHIC
INCOME

chic income chart. This is a chance for you to evaluate yourself, or if you're ambitious, to look at previous jobs you've had. What does it tell you about yourself? How often have you been in Drudgery? Did you get out at a good time or not until it was painful? Do you stay in Calling or Craft as long as you do Drudgery?

Sometimes HSPs can be very good at ignoring their own intuition, thinking that if they love the work enough, it will sustain them when people troubles arise. Now, the people factor is the biggest and most powerful element in our work history. Being treated *badly* is Drudgery. But there is a difference between being *ignored* (Drudgery) or being given "space" to work, which can stimulate Craft energy.

If you find Drudgery cropping up too much in your history, don't despair. You should know yourself a little better now. HSPs with a chronic pattern of Drudgery have some healing work to do.

Assessing Where You Are

Just like any graph, the charts in this chapter can give you an idea of where you are. The best situation is when you are in Craft or Calling for both psychic income and money. Shoot for the top two as much as you can, and don't stay in the bottom zone any more than you have to, even if your other scale is up in Calling. In the end, of course, Drudgery will always pull down Craft or Calling if you stay there too long. Drudgery drains, saps you dry; it is a toxic situation. And we may not even realize when we're there; sometimes it takes a gentle nudge from a loved one to point it out to us.

While a job can suddenly shift from Calling to Drudgery in a matter of months, moving out of Drudgery into Craft, or from Craft into Calling, can take a leap of faith, a jump into the unknown. If your confidence is weak, or your resources—both psychic and material—are drained from too long a stay in Drudgery, you may not be able to quietly extricate yourself, but you may feel compelled to take a leap off a cliff into a new world. The universe will want you to take a stand and throw yourself into divine arms. And Callings, at the other end of the work mode, will require a step into an arena larger than you imagined you could handle (but you actually can).

The slide downward from Calling to Craft and then into Drudgery can happen in one job. But transforming a job that is Craft to Calling or upgrading Drudgery to Craft is not a simple task. In fact, I have yet to meet someone who has successfully changeda long-term Drudgery job into a Craft job, or a Craft job into a Calling. Also, some healing time is needed, a transition, so that one can shake off the residual scars from Drudgery.

Many with a high level of work ethic motivation will try to change a Drudgery job into a Craft in order to make it more bearable. But if the actual tasks or the environment are not suited for you, such diligent efforts will be futile and you will still suffer in Drudgery work. Leaving and finding work that is more suitable to your temperament may be the only option.

HSPs need to evaluate their tolerance for Drudgery. If you have ever been in such a job, review your experience and see if you can identify when you began to notice a change. I can't reiterate enough the importance that HSPs should give to carefully monitoring their comfort level with their work. The more you know what Drudgery, Craft, and Calling are for you, the more effectively you can steer yourself toward the best environment.

And do not overestimate your ability to survive in a Drudgery job! HSPs cannot endure Drudgery work as long as others can, so don't let the abilities of those who tough it out for many years, living from weekend to weekend, be your model. Your timeline may be much shorter, depending on how much stress you are experiencing.

Make lists of each type of work and be as specific as possible about what bothers you and what doesn't. If possible, break tasks down into small increments and evaluate every step. The knowledge will help you avoid dead ends and pitfalls that you may encounter while doing work that appears great but has a bad core.

Psychic income is a mixture of morale, expectations, and special interests. Everyone has his or her own image of what a "normal life" is. There are certain expectations and values concerning the way we progress into careers and relationships, and HSPs are sensitive to any fluctuations in this as well as in their income. Often, HSPs with high expectations don't feel that they're making as much progress as others in life. Many don't think they fit in and see themselves as if they're from another, less stressful century.

But we are here, and we can make our work work for us.

10

Calling:
On the Edge of Paradise

I do think I have a calling, I think I was supposed to be a librarian from the time I walked in and got my first library card.

—DIANE, LIBRARIAN

In the business world, again I'm good at what I do and I know how to do things well. It's like a game to me.

—BARBARA, CFO

I swear that painting makes me healthier overall. The joy and satisfaction of doing it infuses me with a well-being.

—CHARLOTTE, ARTIST

Are You in a Calling Job?

If you find yourself experiencing most of the following items, more than likely your job is a Calling:

- ➤ Enthusiasm, laughter
- ➤ Feeling renewed, nourished by the work
- ➤ Self-confidence: an ability to relate to everyone as an equal
- ➤ Lightness in the body

➤ Sense of purpose to one's life

➤ Able to take personal time for oneself and recharge

➤ Able to adapt and change, open to change

➤ Nonthreatened

➤ A playful, childlike enjoyment of things

➤ Joyous feelings about your work

➤ Waking up with lots of ideas

➤ Eagerness to get to work

➤ This is *me*

➤ Lots of creativity, and trusting one's intuition

➤ Fearlessness

➤ Energy

➤ Can't stop talking about it and the wonder and magic of this "work"

➤ Ease with more "entrepreneurial" qualities: self-promoting, networking

➤ Overall good health and vitality

➤ A sense of rightness, of harmony in your life

➤ Greater frequency of harmonious working relationships

➤ Lots of control over what, when, and how you work

➤ Comfortable setting your boundaries

➤ Desire to do your best, and eager for challenges

➤ Dilbert attitude is gone!

➤ Philosophy: It's not that hard to get here, do what you love, have fun, all it takes is the right attitude, anything is possible. It's soul-satisfying, and the practical will take care of itself.

Conditions that Contribute to a Calling

> ➤ Never-ending variety and newness to the challenges of tasks

> ➤ Freedom to organize one's time and day

> ➤ Workplace assumes and respects one's work ethic

> ➤ Ability to set direction and pace of the work, based on your vision

> ➤ Freedom to bring one's feelings, values, and personality to the work environment, and being accepted

> ➤ Regular contacts with nature

Calling Island

Our final journey to these imaginary islands is to a place filled with breathtaking, panoramic landscapes that suggest we are entering paradise. The mountains rise to incredible heights, and the rivers and dense forests are rich with magic and deep valleys. As far as the eye can see, luxurious, cultured, aromatic, and colorful gardens span hundreds of miles. The massive waterfalls and glorious sunrises infuse this island with sound and visual delights. If you look carefully, you'll see a few cities, so blended into the landscape that it's difficult for the eye to discern when technology ends and nature beings. These cities are clean, aesthetic architectural marvels, a welcome environment for humans and nature.

The people on this island walk straight and tall, smile in a genuinely warm and friendly manner, and don't seem as hurried as those on Craft Island. Yet they are vital, alive, full of joy and energy, and seem to radiate self-assurance. They are interested in everything yet know their boundaries and can be selective. They exude confidence and peacefulness. You come across a group of them talking—a king, a chef, a professor, and a gardener—in animated discussion, at ease with each other. While they love to work, their way of working is quite different from that practiced by the denizens of Craft Island, let alone Drudgery Island. There's more conversation, more building of collaboration and cooperation, and they know what they want and aren't afraid to ask for it.

The urgency common on Craft Island doesn't seem to be here, and yet obviously this is a place where much is accomplished. And the dreams they dream! So many ideas flow around them. These people love watching their ideas evolve and are unafraid if they change or dissolve, for their thoughts are more about answering life's questions than chasing after a permanent product or a task. They see themselves as artists of their lives, constantly creating new masterpieces. They love what they do and look forward to every new day. This is a world where dreams turn into creativity.

On clear days, from the peaks, you can see Drudgery and Craft Islands. Many residents of Calling Island used to live on Drudgery and Craft, and will point out landmarks and talk about their experiences; and they can laugh about it now. From this vantage point, the exits off those islands are obvious, easy to negotiate. But they remember what it was like when they were on Drudgery Island, and how hard escape seemed to them at the time.

What Is a Calling?

Calling evokes strong emotional sentiments, so the above allegory is what a Calling *feels* like. When we're in our Calling, we do feel vast, and immersed in eternal sunshine. It requires being open to our intuition and unfolding talents. One of the things I've noticed with healthy people who listen to their intuition (or the wisest part of themselves), is that whatever their intuition guides them to do, it always leads to something positive, healing, and constructive. Even if the direction hinted at requires us to stretch ourselves, it will be for the best, and we'll experience change in a healthy, graceful, and mature way.

A lot of people wonder, "how do I find my calling?" A to-do list doesn't "find" a Calling. We are *being* our Calling. Jumps from Drudgery to Craft, from Craft to Calling, are changes in *consciousness*. You can't be in Drudgery and "get it" from a Drudgery point of view. Many in Craft will have a similar problem. Both Drudgery and Craft operate from a more practical, "realistic" point of view.

For example, a visiting reporter from Craft Island, asking how things are done here on Calling Island, will become frustrated. Craft Island folks are used to "how to" practical manuals, but Calling Island people have moved beyond being practical to merely *being*. Yes, the practical is there, but it's secondary, because all success flows from within the person, not from without. If you've ever been in Calling, you'll recognize this. If not, you may not "get it" without asking someone who is in a Calling, or taking a leap of faith. It's the leaps of faith that get us from one island to another.

It was noted in the chapter on Craft that as happiness emerged in humanity, the need for work that expressed our bliss became a possibility. It's natural that we would want happiness in every aspect of our lives, and we live in a time when we can realize that possibility.

Three Different Energies for a Calling

As we explore Calling, we'll learn of distinct conditions to tell us where we are and what's going on around us.

The most significant and noticeable sign of a Calling is the tremendous energy boost it gives our whole being. It's like tapping into an artesian well that constantly supplies us with vitality and health. Have you noticed that when you're doing something you enjoy, all your senses are engaged?

We will discuss three distinct types of energy: flow, which engages our energy in both simple and intricate activities; Phoenix, which is more complex in its relationship to our interests and how we see our work; and the most elusive and complex, a true Calling. They all have something in common: an expansive, uplifting energy that happens when we're absorbed, doing things we enjoy. This is enough to put them in the same "camp" in terms of the concept of a Calling. But while only one can be considered a true Calling, any one of the three can be a stopping point, where work can be enjoyed, and be enough of a Calling to satisfy some of your needs.

➤ Flow energy

➤ Phoenix energy

➤ True Calling

When Energy Flows

"Flow" is when an activity…

… is one of complete involvement of the actor with his activity. The activity presents constant challenges. There is no time to get bored or to worry about what may or may not happen. A person in such a situation can make full use of whatever skills are required and receives clear feedback on his actions.[1]

The above assessment is that of Mihaly Csikszentmihalyi, perhaps the leading expert on flow. Flow, he says, is that "dynamic state—the holistic sensation that people feel when they act with total involvement."[2] It's when you get lost in the experience. Your level of skill, the level of challenge just enough out of reach to captivate your interest, the freedom to choose when you're going to be challenged and use your skill—all these create moments when flow can happen. And in these moments, we become one with the experience.

It's not surprising that Csikszentmihalyi found flow more likely to occur for those working in jobs that provide greater intellectual challenges than for those engaged in repetitive blue-collar work. However, flow is also dependent on the individual's effort to find absorption within the work.

Almost everyone has experienced flow. It happens when one is absorbed in tinkering with the car, dancing to music, puttering in the garden, or spending a good evening of conversation and dinner with friends. Flow feels good, and it opens our minds and hearts, and allows our senses, intellect, and emotions to blend together.

Any kind of work can be flow so long as the work is *absorbing* (challenging), freely *chosen* by the doer (who feels properly challenged), and *intrinsically* rewarding. Flow is an energy that gives us good feelings and therefore falls within the domain of Calling.

The Phoenix Energy

Sometimes new things are like a sharp burst of enthusiasm:

If you recall, in the chapter on Drudgery we encountered the Icarus effect. This is the same as the Phoenix energy, with one crucial difference: our perception of ourselves.

Both are a pattern of high sensation; both thrilling, and each new event that consumes our attention is joyfully experienced. It can include flow, because everything feels in alignment, all juices are going and we're in charge, stretching, absorbed. Many, many people regularly experience and relish, the excitement of a new interest. Each big energy burst focused on a particular interest that lasts months or even years, and then fizzles out. For the HSP, frequently this may mean many career and job changes.[3]

In Icarus, we found each new adventure as a possible answer to our question: What is my best work, what is my passion in life, where will I be happy? Sometimes this experience can open up our awareness of new ways to apply our talents, and we feel that we've discovered a gold mine in ourselves, a new path that just might be a Calling. Has this ever happened to you? But as the exciting new interest lost its sparkle and became mundane, we catapulted down, right through Craft to the bottom of the Drudgery barrel. When this happens, we might well have felt like failures, unable to find our way to a long-term career.

In contrast, when we love new things and feel ourselves growing—with each new challenge another adventure on our life's journey—we become a Phoenix, like the mythological bird that renews itself, reborn from the flames. Just so, we feel renewed and revitalized. We are no longer ashamed to watch a new interest blossom and then wither, for each adds to our enjoyment and we are always in charge, free to grow and enjoy at our own pace. It's the same process as with Icarus, but seen from a different point of view.

While in Icarus we thought of each experience as possibly being our true work. In Phoenix, each experience is a chapter within the book of our life's experience and leads to the next exciting chapter.

Remember Jim, the director of a Humanities department? He's gone through many careers, and each one started out like a Calling and ended up in Drudgery. He now knows that he needs lots of new challenges in his life and that he'll *always* be growing into new areas and that the loss of one exciting path is not a personal loss of a "long-term career" but a phase in his evolution. In his current job, Jim is seeing, for the first time, how his past jobs help him now.

I think what's interesting for me is out of all the things I've done in the past, all serve me now, in the variety of this job that I now do. I literally can switch gears from one minute talking to an artist, to the next minute talking to a nonprofit manager, to the next minute talking to a screenwriter, to the next minute talking to a therapist, to the next minute talking to an academic dean, and so forth. I understand them, their special jargon, and what they do. I'm always on a roll.

Perry's Passion for New Things

We've met Perry in the self-employment chapter. He's a gregarious high-sensation-seeking entrepreneur in his thirties who needs to have his hands in several "pies" in order to be happy.

As a teen (and after his comic book–selling days), Perry started a new part-time business selling skateboards and had a mentor who taught him the rudiments of the retail trade. He had no fear of starting with nothing and creating something, learning as he went. In fact, Perry intensely relished hands-on learning, and never held himself back. Very sensitive to his environment, he managed to ignore his need for downtime and often pushed himself to the wall. Here he defines an entrepreneur as someone who harnesses their need for new experiences:

It's someone who follows a passion, whose passionate about what he or she does. Those two things are a parcel of each other.... I guess what I'm trying to say is that entrepreneurs are people who make things happen because they like to be a catalyst as opposed to people who are making things happen because all they want is money. Or some other gain, whether it be money, power.... I like to think of an entrepreneur as someone who's in it for the art of "doing." And passion has to be an important part of that equation.... I won't hold myself back if I think I don't know anything about it, because knowing all about it, for me, has to come from doing it.

Perry, who is now a filmmaker and creative consultant, describes how he experiences these transforming Phoenix events in his life:

[This] pattern started somewhere around a 10-year cycle, averaged out around 7 years, and it's possibly getting shorter as I get older and wiser. The stages of the cycle are jumping into something with both feet, completely immersing yourself in a certain activity or goal. Being absorbed in that, being consumed by it for a certain amount of time. Then starting to become aware of myself as separate from that process. As the awareness increases, the distance between myself and what I'm doing also increases, gets larger and larger, and what seems to happen for me is that the further I get away from what I was involved with deeply, the more aware I become both of myself and the universe at large. I really start to go through an awakening. A lot of time is spent thinking about big things outside of myself or myself relative to the world. It can get pretty experiential, and at the same time it's a spiritual journey as well. That becomes the new absorption or the new focus, to the point where I almost become incapable of doing anything because I'm so far removed from myself and my passion. And finally something new comes along, and then boom, I completely forget about everything and I jump back in again.

Phoenix is an expanding *energy*, a blending of the intense mind with the love and joy of our imagination and emotions as we discover something exciting to explore. Consider it akin to a bountiful seasonal plant that "dies" and comes back in the spring renewed. This intensity can be *inspired, uplifted* by something we're passionately concerned about. When it happens, it's as if all one's emotions, imagination, and mind can't get enough of it. And it inspires, charges, and can exhaust you. Because it is indeed, a form of stress.

There's a pattern here, as Perry and Jim eventually recognized. They are the classic Renaissance men, and they're constantly reinventing themselves because they know how to make the Phoenix energy serve them.

The Dark Side of the Phoenix/Icarus Energy

A garden, and our inner "garden" of ourselves, needs to have definite limits, or borders, in order that the plants flourish and, in our case, that we can create the kind of person we wish to be. And a Phoenix or Icarus energy can be damaging to an HSP because it has the possibility of affecting our boundaries.

Have you ever been in a situation where you and another person hit it off, with lots of great feelings and ideas flowing, and then it all fizzles? As one HSP put it, it's like the romantic love of the teenager—we don't see the flaws in our beloved. Everything is perfect and blissful. In the same way, when a new, exciting idea comes along, we're charged up, excited, soaking up everything we can about it, and everyone is rosy and bright. At such moments, *we're very vulnerable.* Our boundaries are open, expansive, as we reach out to absorb as much as we can about our new interests. We are not as attentive to subtle warning signs.

Juliana had such a problem while absorbed in a high-sensation ride with animation. She was introduced to someone who had lots of contacts that could be useful for her to get some work. But this person had his own Calling, and his work, similar to her own, was big and glamorous, and through his affiliations, was growing. In fact, he was selling his own Calling to Juliana, rather than focusing on helping her, as a mentor should. And she got caught up in helping his Calling along. He could whip up her enthusiasm and energy because of the *potential* his work had to help Juliana in her own work. But he also had all the characteristics of a bully—in pushing, and insisting on his own way—and any potential business with him would mean that he would be the only one in charge.

Juliana was lucky. She saw the signs and got out before too much damage was done:

I was blind, at first, and didn't see what a jerk he was. It wasn't until others pointed it out that I recognized the signs. Be sure to get other people's opinions, find out what others think of this grand plan.

Because of her own rising enthusiasms, Juliana had temporarily lost her critical faculties. This is the dark side of the Phoenix energy.

Watch out for people or situations that whip up your energy and draw it in with bigger plans, bigger dreams. Pay attention if you're in this situation and something doesn't feel right to you, there's more hot air than substance, or, with careful inspection, the plans and dreams lack a sound and practical foundation that can be kicked—like a tire, says Juliana.

Why Companies Love a Calling

At this juncture, I'd like to discuss an important aspect of the Calling energies. Flow, and the sensation-seeking Phoenix or Icarus, are powerful forces in the workplace and companies love these energies in us. Why? Because a person who's happy, enthusiastic, and loves what he or she does is very appealing and magnetic.

Many management theories and practices involve motivation, employee enrichment, customer satisfaction, and so on. For example, if you look at the want ads in your local paper, you can spot the language that suggests their desire for someone with a Calling energy—"enthusiastic, self-starter, motivated," and so on. While management psychology is important to sustain enthusiasm, there are some downsides to this.

The energy in a thrill, high-sensation ride cannot—and should not—be sustained over the long term. That is because, as was discussed in the Stress Management chapter, it is a form of stress; and, if not mitigated or managed so as to return the HSP to a healthy, nonhyped state on a regular basis, can be deleterious to health. It may feel good, it may be based on doing what you love, and there's an undercurrent of expectation, perhaps fueled by technology's unstoppable energy, that it can go on indefinitely. And unfortunately, it gives everyone—companies and individuals alike—the misconception that if you're doing this sensation-seeking activity, you can sustain it forever.

Try to be conscious of these situations and think through what they mean to you, what you truly value and what you can put aside, emotionally, mentally, or physically. Be sure that your boundaries and the company's are not blurred into one.

It should be noted that company mission statements that define a Calling—"calling" someone to embrace a bigger picture; something noble and good that's going to benefit society—might have certain pitfalls. For instance, the company might be interested in igniting and then capturing the energy of the sensation seeker, which can keep a staff at a constant emotional pitch of Icarus or Phoenix energy. It consumes too much adrenaline. One can love the work without the high of sensation seeking all the time. This takes us to the next topic.

The True Calling

It is this kind of Calling that is both a need and a challenge to HSPs.

A true Calling can include flow. It can include moments of Phoenix events. But a true Calling is more than either of these two. I call it "true" because it is closest to the classic meaning of a Calling, of being "called" by God to do some specific work. We are being lifted, inevitably, up toward Heaven. This is because this Calling has been one of the deepest passions in the human search for meaning from many cultures and centuries of living. It has boundless *meaning*, along with those other wonderful gifts: the choice to grow your own soul-guided way, and challenges that stimulate you. *Meaning* places this particular Calling in the center of the sublime.

If I were to put before you the top 10 books on Calling, you'd see that they all devote some time to the power of deep, meaningful things in our lives. Most will also talk of the soul, and the quest—the personal journey we all take toward self-realization. And the soul is very much a part of this Calling. Remember, I've mentioned that to find our calling, we must grow. James Hillman, in his book *The Soul's Code*, claims that our souls have a plan for us, and that "each person enters the world called."[4] But it takes time to unravel this message, because we have to be ready for the work of our soul. Gregg Levoy says:

...We do much damage by not being patient with our own evolution.... Patience is the missing link in the discernment process, in the search for clarity of calling and readiness of heart, and in the waiting for events to unfurl and talents to ripen. These things seldom burst into being all at once....Drumming our fingers won't make events move any faster.[5]

A True Calling, a purpose we love and wish for, gives meaning to what we do and is our particular key to a work that is, inexplicably, more mysterious and transforming. It doesn't have to be a paid job, but it is at the center of our purpose for living. And it feeds our soul. As long as we find this soulful enchantment in life, our spirit is constantly being renewed and, over time, evolving. If we've been hesitant about taking the plunge, yet dreaming and wishing for our Calling, our souls may test us, to see if we're really ready to draw the line and live with grace, a strong sense of self, and with the full participation of our spirit in this adventure with life.

It doesn't mean that one is always happy, always content. There may be flow or spiking enthusiasm in a true Calling, but it is more than that. There is a peacefulness, a "rightness" about the direction one is taking in life. There is a harmony, a feeling that you're doing something as natural as breathing. And true Callings *grow* you, bringing more out of you than you may realize you have.

This is the part that scares many HSPs—the possibility of change— and why we often resist. Those who know their Calling, or vocation, are ready to step onto a stage and take their work to a greater audience and be seen. The more we let ourselves grow, the more our day-to-day work seems to take on a richer element of that overarching theme. Once we shift our focus from the job we do as our Calling, and allow ourselves to grow, the stronger and deeper the theme seems to enter our lives. To those around us it may appear as if we're getting "closer" to our Calling. Perhaps what they're picking up is a deep meaning, a richer turn on the spiral.

Here's an example of what a true Calling can be like. Author Susan Chernak McElroy has loved animals and writing all her life. Animals have so much to say to her, about life, living, and being human beings. Susan combined the two to create a new career for herself that has never wavered since. Notice how she can tell the difference in her when she's tuned in to her work or not. This Calling has unfolded her true self:

That's where all my life energy comes from, I kind of have this gut feeling that if I stayed away from my work for too long, I would just kind of wind down like a top winds down—I'd spin for a while, then I'd spin slower, then I'd fall over. When I'm close to my work, I am so invigorated; it is like there is an electric current running through me.... It has been a real revelation all the time, the closer I can stick to my work, the more energy I have, the more authentic that I feel about who I really am.

One of the things noticeable about HSPs who are doing work that is deeply part of their soul is that they've expanded beyond the "norm" for HSPs. Remember Eric, in the self-employment chapter, the film producer? He is by nature an introvert, and yet he can comfortably work with and around people in an extroverted manner. He still needs his quiet time to recharge, but his comfort level with his extroverted self is stronger because he's connected to something that means a great deal to him.

You become a master, an artist, and enter the "concert hall" of a Calling. Such a state of being is roomy, big, and open. One expands in Calling not so much from thrilling energies, but from stretching and growing as a person. I often can tell by body language when someone loves what he does. He seems to sparkle and become animated. There's a confidence and joy in people who have a Calling. Often, things seem to flow together and happen seamlessly as part of work and life.

In Drudgery the imagination is stunted and hopes are dim, fear and worry dominate. When you have a Calling, the imagination soars and dreams can become reality. The dreary Dilbert-thinking is gone on Calling Island, where everyone is empowered. Of course, there are doubts and concerns, but overall, the individual is optimistic. You just have to trust yourself and go with the flow. Have you ever spoken with someone who loves what they do? Have you noticed how they say, "Do what you love," not "Do what's practical"? Sometimes, our Calling cannot support us financially. It may be our hobby or raising our children. But it still has the same qualities of this deep, resonance, of this soul-filled meaning.

Melding the Spiritual and the Professional

Consider Tom, an economics professor at a Quaker university. Tom has a true Calling because it touches deep chords in him and has been part of his psyche and quest for decades. He teaches both introductory economics and global economic issues. A practicing Quaker, Tom actively serves on the board of the Quakers' U.N. programs to bring world leaders together to discuss their concerns in a peaceful and win-win conflict-resolution environment. The overarching theme that joins his teaching and volunteer work is how people live in the world and have their basic needs met, or not. The problem of poverty is one of the deep issues at the heart of all that he teaches and the careers he helps students prepare for. In this way, Tom combines his teaching with his volunteer international work, and sees it all as part of his life's theme, the well-being of humanity: "It kind of pulls together my spiritual and professional life, as an international economist."

For Tom, his Calling connects with his sense of his mission:

There is very much a theme of service there that comes out of my religious commitment, comes out of working year after year—trying to think about what we are doing on planet earth and what we should be doing. The major theme, I keep coming back to, it keeps calling me, gives me the power to go on, keeps motivating me.

Because Tom is knowledgeable about economic systems that serve as the "engine" for businesses, I asked him questions about the workplace and the role we as individuals can play in making work work. As a professor with many students coming through his classes, Tom has something to say about finding a great career, and about the misconceptions so many of us have about finding our Calling. Notice that he believes that what's *inside of us* is the key to finding that true work:

[Students] come to school expecting that they will get a degree and that will be the magic ticket to a great career—and while the degree may be a necessary part of it, it is not sufficient, it's what is happening inside of them and what they bring to an organization as a person that is far more important in the educational process.

The Inner Captain

Those who follow the true Calling often feel as if they are embracing a vision that is bigger than they are. Yet it comes from deep within them. Their relationship with work is about creativity, vision, and flowing with the life force. Laurence Boldt, in his massive book *Zen and the Art of Making a Living*, accurately describes the journey to finding your true work:

No book can tell you how to find your way; it can at best catalyze and awaken the way within you. You can paint by numbers, but you'll never produce a masterpiece like that. A masterpiece requires the soul and inspiration of an artist. To paint the masterpiece of your life, you need more than forms and systems. You need a heroic commitment to your best self. Born in your heart, tempered by your head, shaped with your hands, and walked with your own two feet, your life's work is your special gift for mankind.[6]

David Whyte is a poet, who takes poetry into corporations to help them find meaning and purpose in their work. He uses the sea as a metaphor for work, but it can also be a metaphor for this deeper, true Calling. Work often does feel like we're "at sea" and landmarks not always useful, or present. Only our knowledge of the ocean will get us where we want to go. And we are the only captains who can take us there.

Many of us did not know early in life what we wanted to do. Most of us bumped around until we were lucky to stumble into our true work. Decades ago, I met a child of five who knew he wanted to be a paleontologist, steadfastly held to that dream, and is now a happy professor of dinosaur bones. But he's rare. The rest of us must learn through trial and error, experimenting with this interest or that talent. And sometimes, especially with a true Calling, it can take us far from the usual cookie-cutter careers. Imagine what it must be like to explain that you're a poet. Here's what David did:

I told everyone I knew that I was moving toward becoming a full-time poet. I wanted them to hear it and hold me to what they had heard. Disbelief, silence, scorn, I didn't care.... Though daunting, at the beginning, silence is good, and silence is a testing fire. There are many kinds of silence to encounter in life, but there is a particular and delicious terror to the anticipatory silence that we create from actually following our heart's desires.[7]

David Whyte, this poet who goes to work, once worked on a small tour boat. One night, he woke to find the small boat adrift from its anchor, and perilously close to crashing into a cliff. The captain was asleep, and David, half asleep himself, acted fast and secured the boat while the captain continued to sleep through it all. In that moment, he explores with his reader the difference between a formal leadership and our dependence on it, versus our own inner captaincy that we need to sail these mysterious waters:

Once we begin to engage those elemental edges through daily courageous speech, we start to build a living picture of our own nature, exactly the same way a captain gets to know her vessel and the particular way it reacts to the elements around it. As captains of our soul's journey, we feel the angle of the sails, the creak and strain of the ropes, the lean of the tiller, and learn the particular hum and song of our conversation with the elements. It is this conversation that gives us not only our powers of survival, but a music of exhilaration for our journey and our arrival.[8]

Being the captain of our lives is a tremendous challenge. For some of us, it will require courage and faith in ourselves. These true Callings require someone with the need for a deep value or passion in life. Sometimes from earliest childhood, HSPs have the capacity to see and need answers to large questions. We can see the big picture; we can feel the moral issues for which humanity cries for answers. Together, we and our Calling produce something new. That newness is first found inside of us.

The Still and Quiet Answer

If you feel a yearning for a true Calling and are willing to go into potentially unexplored territory, how do you find your way? We need our intuition as we navigate through life. But how can we get in touch with it, and use it to tease out the answer of the unexplainable things in our lives?

I'd like to introduce you to Pastor Cathy, a good-natured, funny woman who just happens to be an HSP and a minister. She was drawn to both the ministry and chemistry, and ended up choosing the former. And true to the sometimes exasperating nature of our Calling, it may test us to be sure we are steadfast. It was a challenge for Cathy, becoming a minister in an era when women pastors were still a rarity. Putting together her doctoral program meant jumping through far more hoops than normal, and certainly a test of dedication. Throughout all these permutations, she often asked herself, "What does it all mean? Where am I supposed to be going? What am I to do?" And now she helps others find their answers by working with them on these very questions. Sometimes, she says, there is a "flavor" to the questions and answers, a pattern or theme. Underneath each question there should be a *still and quiet,* yes or no, answer.

She suggests that we ask ourselves lots of questions about what's going on in our lives. Here are some of the questions she'll ask herself, or invite others to ask themselves. Also, she says listen to what others say, because they may see things you don't, but be careful about becoming too dependent on the opinions of others. Their words are to be taken as clues, not rules to be obeyed.

[You] almost have to start with what is it that really makes you passionate in life in general. What is it about that, that really makes it such a priority for you, such an overwhelming thing that you say, "I'll drop everything in order to do this." And find out, at least if you can, what's going on there because you might be finding some of the things that make you feel most alive.

HSPs yearn for authenticity, depth, honesty, having the courage of our convictions, and they have a need for meaning in their lives and work.

Being an HSP has it's challenges, but if we're willing to team up with our soul, something better will come out of us than we could have thought possible. It was Gibran, another poet, who described what the oldest and deepest Calling is like.

But I say to you that when you work you fulfil a part of earth's furthest dream, assigned to you when that dream was born.

And in keeping yourself with labour you are in truth loving life,

And to love life through labour is to be intimate with life's inmost secret....

All work is empty save when there is love;

And when you work with love you bind yourself to yourself, and to one another, and to God.

And what is it to work with love?

It is to weave the cloth with threads drawn from your heart, even as if your beloved were to wear that cloth....

It is to charge all things you fashion with a breath of your own spirit. . .

Work is love made visible.[9]

The Power of Calling

Work is one of the most profound opportunities to learn about ourselves, to find our identity. We know that Drudgery is not where our hearts belong, Craft a place where we are torn this way and that. And we know that Callings can be elusive, and a very powerful force in our lives. A Calling is not always about enthusiasm, although enthusiasm is needed. It is not always about paychecks or job security, although traditional and self-employed routes can be equally routes to one's true work.

But what is needed to follow our heart's desires, to prepare our inner self for the next step. We've cleaned up our inner garden, put up a weather vane to let us know of changing winds early on, fixed our fences, and fortified our walls. Perhaps some of us even altered the landscaping to more clearly reflect our heart's desires. But there is another step to be acknowledged: *owning our own leadership* and declaring this garden—our inner self—to be our very own, to grow, to cherish, and to define its purpose. No one can do it for you.

At the start of this book I said that to find our Calling we needed to grow as a person. We grow when we honor our boundaries and value ourselves. We grow when we know the difference between those jobs that hurt us and those that challenge us. We can stop with flow or Phoenix and go no further. Both of these energies, combined with our self-care, can make work *work* for us.

I'm certain many HSPs will need the deeper and more elusive true Calling. It is here, with the oldest and most challenging of all Callings, that we have to be ready to be self-reliant, and our own captaincy and trust that our inner voice will never let us down. We will expand beyond our normal HSPness, while taking our sensitivities with us. Sometimes the problems of the world need more than intellect or emotion—they need our soul's wisdom. And we may have to be prepared to read and trust, not our local community paper, but the soul's unique "classified section" that lies deep within each of us.

Endnotes

INTRODUCTION: THE JOURNEY BEGINS

1. Elaine Aron. *The Highly Sensitive Person*. New York: Broadway Books, 1996; Elaine Aron and Arthur Aron "Sensory Processing Sensitivity and Its Relation to Introversion and Emotionality," *Journal of Personality and Social Psychology*, 73, (1997), 352. The self-test, which appears in *The Highly Sensitive Person*, and all of Dr. Aron's other books on the Highly Sensitive, has been through a lot of rigorous clinical work. It was given to thousands of HSPs and non-HSPs. This self-test can also be found in her book and on her website at www.hsperson.com.

CHAPTER 1: WHAT IS A HIGHLY SENSITIVE PERSON?

1. Elaine Aron. *The Highly Sensitive Person*. New York: Broadway Books, 1996.
2. Jon Kabat-Zinn. *Full Catastrophe Living*. New York: Delta, 1990, 236.
3. Ibid, 238.
4. Lyle Miller, Alma Smith, and Larry Rothstein. *The Stress Solution: An Action Plan to Manage the Stress in Your Life*. New York: Pocket Books, 1993.
5. Elaine Aron. *The Highly Sensitive Person in Love*. New York: Broadway Books, 2000.
6. Martin Seligman. *Learned Optimism*. New York: Pocket Books, 1998, 83.

CHAPTER 2: THE WORST KIND OF WORK: DRUDGERY

1. Abraham Maslow. *Toward a Psychology of Being*. New York: D. Van Nostrand Company, 1968.
2. Joel Aronoff. *Psychological Needs and Cultural Systems*. Princeton, NJ: D. Van Nostrand Company, 1967.
3. Ibid, 50.
4. Scott Adams. *I'm Not Anti-Business, I'm Anti-Idiot*. Kansas City: Andrews McMeel Publishing, 1998.
5. Joanne B. Ciulla. *The Working Life: The Promise and Betrayal of Modern Work*. New York: Times Books, 2000, 75.
6. Anne Schaef and Diane Fassel. *The Addictive Organization*. San Francisco: Harper & Row, 1990.
7. Kevin Bales. "The Social Psychology of Modern Slavery," *Scientific American*, April 2002, 4. See http://sciam.com.
8. Barbara Ehrenreich. *Nickle and Dimed: On (Not) Getting By in America*. New York: Metropolitan/Owl Books, 2001, 208.

9. Christina Maslach and Michael Leiter. *The Truth About Burnout.* San Francisco: John Wiley and Sons, 1997, 17.
10. Ibid, 18.
11. Ayala Pines and Elliot Aronson. *Career Burnout: Causes and Cures.* New York: The Free Press, 1988, 3.
12. Ibid, 54.
13. Elaine Aron. *The Highly Sensitive Person.* New York: Broadway Books, 1997.
14. Barbara Kerr and Charles Claiborn. "Counseling Talented Adults," *Advanced Development,* Special Edition 3 (1995), 165.
15. Pines and Aronson, 53.
16. Claude Whitmyer. *Mindfulness and Meaningful Work: Explorations in Right Livelihood.* Berkeley: Parallax Press, 1994, 4.
17. Mihaly Csikszentmihalyi. *Flow: The Psychology of Optimal Experience.* New York: Harper & Row, 1990, 160.
18. Lee Coit. *Listening: How to Increase Your Awareness of Your Inner Guide.* South Laguna, CA: Swan Publishing, 1985.

CHAPTER 3: TIME OUT FOR HEALING

1. William Wordsworth. *Complete Poetical Works.* Thomas Hutchinson, ed. Oxford: Oxford University Press, 1936, 519.
2. Carol McClelland. *The Seasons of Change: Using Nature's Wisdom to Grow Through Life's Inevitable Ups and Downs.* Berkeley: Conari Press, 1998.
3. Thomas Moore. The Re-Enchantment of Everyday Life. New York: Harper Perennial, 1997, 102.
4. Gordon McDonald. *Ordering Your Private World.* Nashville: Nelson Publishers, 1985.
5. Linda Kohanov. *The Tao of Equus.* Novato, CA: New World Library, 2001, 93.
6. Riane Eisler. *The Chalice and the Blade.* San Francisco: Harper & Row, 1988.
7. Elaine Aron. *The Highly Sensitive Person.* New York: Broadway Books, 1996.
8. Kohanov.
9. Ibid, 202–203.
10. Stephen Bertman. *Hyperculture: The Human Cost of Speed.* Westport, CT: Praeger, 1998, 104.
11. Ibid, 46.

CHAPTER 4: STRESS MANAGEMENT THE HSP WAY

1. Alvin Toffler. *Future Shock.* New York: Bantam Books, 1971, 2.
2. Lyle Miller, Alma Smith, and Larry Rothstein. *The Stress Solution: An Action Plan to Manage the Stress in Your Life.* New York: Pocket Books, 1993, 17.
3. Judith Wyatt and Chauncey Hare. *Work Abuse: How to Recognize and Survive It.* Rochester, VT: Schenkman Books, 1997.
4. Ayala Pines and Elliot Aronson. *Career Burnout: Causes and Cures.* New York: The Free Press, 1988, 9. (Consider also reading Michael Epstein and Sue Hosking, *Falling Apart: Avoiding, Coping with and Recovering from Stress Breakdown.* Sebastopol, CA: CRCS Publications, 1992.)
5. Daniel Goleman. *Working with Emotional Intelligence.* New York: Bantam Books, 1998.

6. Pines and Aronson, 3.
7. Ibid.

CHAPTER 5: CRAFT: THE CONFIDENCE BUILDER

1. Joanne Ciulla, *The Working Life: The Promise and Betrayal of Modern Work.* New York Times Books, 2000.
2. Fernand Braudel, *The Wheels of Commerce.* New York: Harper & Row, 1982.
3. Studs Terkel. *Working.* New York: The New Press, 1974, 315.
4. Kahlil Gibran. *The Prophet.* New York: Alfred A. Knopf, 1972, 28.
5. Mihaly Csikszentmihalyi, *Flow: The Psychology of Optimal Experience.* New York: Harper & Row, 1990.
6. Peter Drucker. *The Effective Executive.* New York: Harper & Row. 1966, 4.
7. Barbara Kerr and Charles Claiborn, "Counseling Talented Adults," *Advanced Development Journal* 3 (1991): 164.
8. Carl Bridenbaugh. *The Colonial Craftsman.* New York: Dover Publications, 1990.
9. William Bridges. *Job-Shift.* Reading, MA: Addison-Wesley Publishing Co., 1994.

CHAPTER 6: BEING VISIBLE AS AN HSP

1. William Howarth. *The Book of Concord: Thoreau's Life as a Writer.* New York: Viking Press, 1982.
2. Kirk Snyder. *The Lavender Road to Success.* San Francisco: Ten Speed Press, 2003.
3. Claude Whitmyer and Salli Rasberry. *Running a One-Person Business,* 2nd ed. Berkeley: Ten Speed Press, 1989, 128.
4. Paul Woodruff. *Reverence: Renewing a Forgotten Virtue.* Oxford: Oxford University Press, 2001.
5. Ibid, 72.
6. Gregg Levoy. *Callings: Finding and Following an Authentic Life.* New York: Harmony Books, 1997, 328.
7. M. Dittman. "Open Your Mind to Mentoring." *APA Monitor* (November 2002), 50–51.

CHAPTER 7: HIGHLY SENSITIVE KUNG FU

1. Gary Namie and Ruth Namie. *The Bully at Work: What You Can Do to Stop the Hurt and Reclaim Your Dignity on the Job.* Naperville, IL: Sourcebooks, Inc., 2000; Sam Horn. *Take the Bully by the Horns.* New York: St. Martin's Press, 2002; Noa Davenport, Ruth Schwartz, and Gail Elliott. *Mobbing: Emotional Abuse in the American Workplace.* Ames, IA: Civil Society Publishing, 1999.
2. Horn, Ibid.; Susan Forward and Donna Frazier. *Emotional Blackmail.* New York: Harper Perennial, 1997.
3. Namie and Namie, 18.
4. Davenport, Schwartz, Elliott, 82.
5. Horn, Ibid.

CHAPTER 8: SELF-EMPLOYMENT, THE ALTERNATE PATH

1. Cliff Hakim. *We Are All Self-Employed: The New Social Contract for Working in a Changed World.* San Francisco: Beffett-Koehler Publishers, 1994.
2. William Bridges. *Job-Shift.* Reading, MA:: Addison-Wesley Publishing Co., 1994, 104.
3. Mahatma Ghandi. Cited in 2003 at www.Mkgandhi.OrglIndex.HTM. Available at www.mkgandhi.org/index.htm
4. Daniel Rodgers. *The Work Ethic in Industrial America 1850–1920.* Chicago: University of Chicago Press, 1978.
5. Michael Phillips and Salli Rasberry. *Honest Business.* San Francisco: Clear Glass Publishing, 1981. 14.
6. Geoffrey Bellman. *The Consultant's Calling: Bringing Who You Are to What You Do.* San Francisco: Jossey-Bass, 1990, 46.
7. Paul Edwards and Sarah Edwards. *Changing Direction Without Losing Your Way.* New York: Jeremy Tarcher/Putnam, 2001.

CHAPTER 9: PSYCHIC INCOME

1. The term "psychic income" was first introduced to me by Paul and Sarah Edwards. The development of the idea here is my own.

CHAPTER 10: CALLING: ON THE EDGE OF PARADISE

1. Mihaly Csikszentmihalyi. *Beyond Boredom and Anxiety.* San Francisco: Jossey-Bass, 1975, 36.
2. Ibid.
3. Marvin Zuckerman. *Behavioral Expressions and Biosocial Bases of Sensation Seeking.* New York: Cambridge University Press, 1994. For further information on how sensation seeking affects career satisfaction see his Chapter 6.
4. James Hillman. *The Soul's Code: In Search of Character and Calling.* New York: Warner Books, 1997, 7.
5. Gregg Levoy. *Callings: Finding and Following an Authentic Life.* New York: Harmony Books, 1997, 42.
6. Laurence Boldt. *Zen and the Art of Making a Living.* New York: Penguin/Arkana, 1999, xxvi.
7. David Whyte. *Crossing the Unknown Sea: Work as a Pilgrimage of Identity.* New York: Riverhead Books, 2001, 136.
8. Ibid, 58–59.
9. Kahlil Gibran. *The Prophet.* New York: Alfred A. Knopf, 1972, 25–28.

Additional Reading

The following are excellent supplemental reading that contributes to the material in this book:

Barzun, Jacques. *From Dawn to Decadence*. New York: HarperCollins, 2000.

Bridges, William. *Transitions: Making Sense of Life's Changes*. Boulder, CO: Da Capo Press, 2nd ed., 1980.

Campbell, Joan. *Joy in Work, Gernman Work: The National Debate, 1800–1945*. Princeton, NJ: Princeton University Press, 1989.

Christensen, Kathleen. *Women and Home-Based Work: The Unspoken Contract*. New York: Henry Holt & Co., 1988.

Edwards, Paul; Edwards, Sarah; Zooi, Walter. *Home Businesses You Can Buy*. New York: Jeremy Tarcher/Putnam, 1997.

Epstein, Michael, and Hosking, Sue. *Falling Apart: Avoiding, Coping with, and Recovering from Stress Breakdown*. Sebastapol, CA: CRCS Publications, 1992.

Handy, Charles. *The Hungry Spirit*. New York: Broadway Books, 1998.

Hoschild, Arlie. *The Managed Heart: Commercialization of Human Feeling*. Berkeley, CA: University of California Press, 1983.

Landes, David. *Revoluation in Time: Clocks and the Making of the Modern World*. Cambridge, UK: Cambridge University Press, 2000.

Morgan, Edmund. "The Puritan Ethic and the American Revolution." *William & Mary Quarterly*, 24/1 (1967).

Pence, Gregory. "Toward a Theory of Work." *The Philosophical Forum* 10:2–4 (1979).

Schor, Juliet. *The Overworked American: The Unexpected Decline of Leisure*. New York: Basic Books, 1991.

Index

About the Author

BARRIE JAEGER, PH.D., is known as The Self-Employment Doctor and Work Therapist Coach. She gives seminars and workshops on workplace issues for the HSP. Her research on self-employment has been cited in *The Secrets of Self-Employment, Finding Your Perfect Work,* and *Getting Business to Come to You.* She writes articles on work for *The Comfort Zone,* a newsletter for the Highly Sensitive published by Elaine Aron, author of the national bestseller *The Highly Sensitive Person.*